The Discovery of Things

The Discovery of Things

ARISTOTLE'S *CATEGORIES*
AND THEIR CONTEXT

Wolfgang-Rainer Mann

PRINCETON UNIVERSITY PRESS

PRINCETON, NEW JERSEY

Library of Congress Cataloging-in-Publication Data

Mann, Wolfgang-Rainer.
The discovery of things : Aristotle's Categories and their context
/ Wolfgang-Rainer Mann.
p.   cm.
Includes bibliographical references (p.   ) and indexes.
ISBN 0-691-01020-X (cl. : alk. paper)
1. Aristotle. Categoriae.   2. Categories (Philosophy)—History.
I. Title.
B438.M36   2000   160—dc21   99-37823   CIP

This book has been composed in Galliard

Printed in the United States of America

1   2   3   4   5   6   7   8   9   10

FOR MY MOTHER AND FATHER,

SIGRID AND JOSEPH MANN

Contents

Acknowledgments

I WOULD LIKE to thank David Sedley for the opportunity to discuss several of the problems I consider here, especially the textual questions addressed in Appendix 1 to Part I. I am grateful to Paul Genest and Brad Petrie for the invitation to present an 'ancestor' of Parts II and III in a talk at Union College during the fall of 1992. Don Morrison kindly made available to me a copy of his "Le statut catégoriel des différences dans l' 'Organon,' " *Revue philosophique* 183 (1993): 147–78, prior to its publication. I would also like to thank Sally Haslanger and Constance Meinwald; in years past, I have had many useful conversations about issues related to these essays with each of them. Myles Burnyeat (first in Cambridge in 1992, then in Princeton during the spring of 1994) very kindly shared his reactions to earlier versions of much of this material, thereby helping me to articulate my views more clearly. More recently, under severe constraints of time, he wrote up and sent to me several pages of challenging observations and probing questions. I have not been able to respond to all of them; in fact, I suspect that a full response would require a work at least twice as long as the present one. But it is precisely because of his disagreement with much of what I say that his thoughts have been—and will continue to be—of great value to me. I am delighted to be able to thank Steve Strange by name, after he identified himself as one of the readers for Princeton University Press. His careful written comments helped me to reformulate several points more perspicuously. My thanks also to the other, anonymous reader.

Ann Wald, now editor in chief of the press, has shown enthusiastic interest in my work, ever since we first spoke several years ago. My copy editor, Gavin Lewis, helped solve a number of difficulties I would never have noticed but for his astute comments.

Throughout the last dozen or so years, I was able to present parts of this material in graduate seminars: at Johns Hopkins, the University of Pennsylvania, Princeton, the University of Pittsburgh, and, of course, Columbia. My thanks to all the participants in those seminars.

Finally, the various notes throughout the essays are only a small indication of the special debt of gratitude I owe to Michael Frede. That debt goes back to my days as an undergraduate at Princeton, where I had the good fortune to encounter, in his teaching, a model for approaching the philosophical texts of antiquity. His lectures on Aristotle made clear that the *Categories* were far more complicated, subtle, and rich than they might appear to be at first sight. Subsequently, while I was a graduate student, he entrusted me with the task of translating two of his papers on the *Categories*. In the course of preparing those translations, I was led to a renewed sense of the difficulty of Aristotle's short treatise. But my debt to Frede is also a more general one: for throughout the years, I have benefited enormously from his work—from published and unpublished papers, as well as from lectures, seminars, and, especially, many informal conversations.

A Note on Citations

IN THE ESSAYS that make up this book, I cite the works of Plato according to John Burnet's edition (1900–1906), in the Oxford Classical Texts series. Similarly, I cite the works of Aristotle according to the OCT editions, where these exist. English translations of Plato are conveniently available in *Plato Complete Works*, ed. J. Cooper (Indianapolis, 1997). For most of the dialogues, these translations supersede those in *The Collected Dialogues of Plato*, ed. E. Hamilton and H. Cairns (Princeton, N.J., 1961). The revised Oxford translation of Aristotle is available in two volumes: *The Complete Works of Aristotle*, ed. J. Barnes (Princeton, N.J., 1984). But unless indicated otherwise, all translations are my own—though I have benefited from various existing ones.

In the case of the Presocratics, I give the fragment numbers according to sixth edition of H. Diels, *Die Fragmente der Vorsokratiker*, as revised by W. Kranz (Berlin, 1951).

In the case of Speusippus, I give the fragment numbers according to both P. Lang's collection of 1911 and L. Tarán's *Speusippus of Athens* (Leiden, 1981).

Following widespread custom, I refer to *A Greek-English Lexicon*, by H. G. Liddell, R. Scott, and H. S. Jones (Oxford, 1968) simply as LSJ.

In the notes, I abbreviate G. E. L. Owen's collected papers, *Logic, Science and Dialectic*, ed. M. Nussbaum (Ithaca, N.Y., 1986) as *LSD*; and M. Frede's *Essays in Ancient Philosophy* (Minneapolis, 1987) as Frede, *Essays*.

In the case of ancient works where specific features of the edition matter, details are given in the notes, and the works appear in the bibliography. However, those ancient works which are referred to only briefly, in one or two notes, are not featured in the bibliography; but standard editions of them are readily available in the familiar series of texts and translations, like the Budé editions, the Loeb Classical Library, the OCTs, or the Bibliotheca Teubneriana.

I have adopted the following slightly unusual convention regarding quotation marks. I use double quotes when actually quoting a work, and to enclose the titles of articles, chapters, and so on. I use single quotes (i) for quotations within quotations; (ii) for indicating, in those cases where it seems necessary to do so, that I am mentioning, as opposed to using, expressions, which however are not themselves actual quotations—whether they be words, phrases or whole sentences; and (iii) for what are sometimes called 'scare-quotes'. I do so to avoid (what seems to me) the virtually inevitable confusion wrought by using only one kind of quotation mark: are the words enclosed in quotes actually a quotation or not?

The Discovery of Things

Introduction

> Was uns als natürlich vorkommt, ist vermutlich nur das
> Gewöhnliche einer langen Gewohnheit, die das
> Ungewohnte, dem sie entsprungen [ist], vergessen hat.
> Jenes Ungewohnte hat jedoch einst als ein
> Befremdendes den Menschen angefallen und hat das
> Denken zum Erstaunen gebracht.[1]
> (*Heidegger, "Der Ursprung des Kunstwerks"*)

1. THE PROJECT

In two of his early works—in the *Categories* especially, but also in the
Topics—Aristotle presents a revolutionary metaphysical picture. This picture has had a peculiar fate. Its revolutionary theses are so far from being
recognized as such that they have often been taken to be statements of
common sense, or expressions of an everyday, pretheoretical ontology.[2]
The most striking and far-reaching of those theses is the claim that, included
among what there is, among the entities (τὰ ὄντα), there are *things*.
Aristotle, famously, goes on to maintain that these things are ontologically
fundamental. All the other entities are (whatever they are)[3] by being appropriately connected to the things, for example, either as their *features* (their
qualities, sizes, relations-to-each-other, locations, and so on), or as their

---

[1] "What seems natural to us is presumably only the customary, the result of a long-standing
custom which has forgotten the unaccustomed whence it arose. But at one time, that
unaccustomed broke in and beset mankind as something strange, and roused thinking to
wonderment." *Holzwege* (Frankfurt-am-Main, 1950), p. 14.

[2] The idea that the *Categories* presents a pretheoretical ontology may ultimately go back
to Porphyry, who is concerned to show that Aristotle is not, ultimately, disagreeing with
Plato. Thus the *Categories* can be a perfectly adequate account of our ordinary ways of talking
and thinking (about the sensible world), while Plato gives us an account of *true* reality and
how to talk and think about it. On Porphyry, see S. Strange, "Plotinus, Porphyry, and the
Neoplatonic Interpretation of the 'Categories,' " in *Aufstieg und Niedergang der Römischen
Welt*, II.36.2.

[3] This awkward formulation is meant to signal that, for Aristotle, a being (an ὄν) is always
something or other; thus for any *x*, if *x* is, there is some *y* such that *x* is *y*. Alternatively:
there is no such thing as just being a being, period.

genera and species, that is, the *kinds* under which the things fall.[4] These further claims and their proper interpretation have received considerable discussion. Yet the fundamental one has gone virtually unnoticed. To formulate it most starkly: before the *Categories* and *Topics*, there were no things. Less starkly: things did not show up *as* things, until Aristotle wrote those two works.

The essays that make up the present book seek in the first instance to situate Aristotle's thinking historically and philosophically. Here a brief word of warning is in order. The *Categories* are most frequently analyzed and discussed as a part of, or with a view towards, more extensive analyses and discussions of Aristotle's metaphysics. In any such context, it is most natural, given the present consensus about the date of the work, to see

---

[4] In the *Categories*, Aristotle posits as additional entities the genera and species *of the features*. But these items are (what they are) by being the genera and species *of* the features, while the features are (what they are) by being the features *of* the things. Thus even these further items in the ontology ultimately depend on the things for their being (what they are), albeit more indirectly. Here one might object that including the supplements, '(what they are)'—which suggest that real essences or explanations are involved—unfairly prejudges the nature of the treatise's concerns. Thus, for example, Stephen Menn, in his "Metaphysics, Dialectic and the *Categories*," *Revue de metaphysique et de morale* 100 (1995), argues that "[t]he *Categories* cannot belong to first philosophy for the same reason it cannot belong to philosophy at all: it does not consider causes" (p. 312); the work rather contains "background knowledge that the dialectician armed with the *Topics* must presuppose" (ibid., p. 315 n. 6). There surely is a close connection between the two treatises. (See I. Husik, "On the *Categories* of Aristotle," *Philosophical Review* 13 [1904], and E. Kapp, "Die Kategorienlehre in der aristotelischen *Topik*," in his *Ausgewählte Schriften* [Berlin, 1968].) Indeed, already the repeated use of ἀποδίδωμι (= render as an answer) in the opening chapters of the *Categories* shows that Aristotle assumes familiarity with dialectical question-and-answer exchanges. Now in the *Topics*, Aristotle contrasts dialectic, conceived of as relatively topic neutral (100ª18–24; cf. *Soph. El.* 183ª37–ᵇ1), with the special sciences (cf., e.g., 101ª5–17). But is that a contrast between dialectic and philosophy? Not obviously: the *Topics* is replete with metaphysical notions (see *Top.* I, 5–8), like that of essence, and the work presupposes a determinate picture of genera, species, and differentiae; a particular conception of definitions; etc. So why hold that *it* "cannot belong to philosophy?" Moreover, Menn says that by assigning the *Categories* to dialectic, he has "no intention . . . of making it constitutionally unable to contradict a metaphysical text" (Menn, "Metaphysics, Dialectic, and the *Categories*," p. 333 n. 35); but this weakens the putative contrast considerably. And while the *Categories* does not present a philosophical inquiry, my claim will be that it presents the *results* of such an inquiry; similarly, while the treatise does not present explanations, it seems to *presuppose* a great deal about what explanations must look like—for example, consider the claim that it will be more "informative" to answer the 'What is it?' question by indicating the species rather than the genus (2ᵇ7–14). Thus the phrase '(what they are)' should be taken to point to the *potential availability* of explanations, even if none are actually provided.

the treatise as standing at the *beginning* of Aristotle's philosophical development, a development that, to put matters very crudely and schematically,
leads *from* the ontological picture of the *Categories*—via the reflections
on change, and the postulation of form and matter (and their correlatives,
actuality and potentiality) in the *Physics*—*to* the ontological pictures of
the *Metaphysics* and *De Anima*. The present project is of a different kind.
My investigation of the *Categories* is guided by the conviction that the
treatise itself stands at the *end* of a long development. This is a development
that, to speak roughly and schematically once more, leads *from* Parmenides'
ontological reflections—via Anaxagoras, the Plato of the middle and late
dialogues, and the so-called Late-Learners of Plato's *Sophist*—*to* the ontological picture of the *Categories*.

While any number of commentators have recognized that the *Categories*
are as related to what came before as to what came later, Aristotle's extremely compressed formulations in the treatise and the absence of actual
references to the philosophical tradition have stood in the way of fully
appreciating both how thoroughly Aristotle is indebted to that tradition,
and how radically he is breaking with, and going beyond it. My aim thus
is to make visible what is almost wholly implicit in the *Categories*, by
showing how the characteristic concerns and claims of the work can be
seen to be the outgrowth of Aristotle's critical and reflective engagement
with earlier Greek philosophy.[5] (And it is because I have this in some ways
narrow objective that I will for the most part leave aside discussion of
those later Aristotelian treatises and the conceptual apparatus we encounter
there, which would, of course, need to figure extensively in any more
comprehensive account of Aristotle's metaphysics.) However, proceeding
in the way indicated will enable us both to see why earlier Greek thinkers,
in particular, certain Presocratics, Plato, and the Late-Learners, did not
recognize things as things, and to understand how, and why, Aristotle
was compelled to discover them as such.

But of no less importance in these essays is a second objective: achieving
greater clarity about Plato's own metaphysical project. For one of my
contentions is that crucial parts of Plato's metaphysical picture have been
misunderstood, or at least, formulated very misleadingly, by those approaching the dialogues with key elements of the ontological picture of

---

[5] In so conceiving matters I have been greatly influenced by G. Prauss's "Ding und
Eigenschaft bei Platon und Aristoteles," *Kant-Studien* 59 (1968), an article which, judging
by the bibliographies in relevant works on Plato and Aristotle, has not received the attention
it deserves.

the *Categories* (tacitly) in mind. Most notable among those elements is exactly this seemingly commonsense thought that there are things, which, in turn, leads interpreters to suppose that Plato's metaphysical theorizing, at least in part, seeks to account for these things and their features. Clearing aside those misunderstandings will allow us to make better sense of aspects of Plato's metaphysical picture that have often seemed puzzling or even seriously confused.

Thus my examination of various Platonic texts is also guided by *its* particular, circumscribed concerns. The aim is hardly to offer a complete account of Plato's metaphysics, or of his metaphysical development. Rather I am seeking to uncover and make sense of one important strand in Plato's thinking, namely, as mentioned, the at first sight startling idea that there are no things in his ontology, that Plato does not recognize things *as* things.

With a better understanding of Plato's metaphysical picture before us, we will be in a position to appreciate just how revolutionary and innovative Aristotle is being in the *Categories* and *Topics*. We will also be able to see how Aristotle set the stage for turning "the unaccustomed" into "long-standing custom" (Heidegger's phrase). The unique and central role which the *Categories* played in the philosophical curricula of late antiquity and the Latin middle ages obviously contributed enormously to this philosophical picture's successful ascendancy, to the point where it truly could appear to be nothing more than a reflection of common sense, precisely because it had become a part of common sense. And I am inclined to believe that this success, to a large extent, also explains why Plato is read in the ways he is commonly read: the mistake is neither one of simply overlooking something obvious—or not so obvious—nor one of inadvertently smuggling in Aristotelian notions. Rather, the ascent and dominance of the ontological picture of the *Categories* has so thoroughly eclipsed other pictures and interpretative possibilities that they cannot even come into view, much less be made to seem plausible, without considerable effort.

2. THE PROBLEM

In a moment, I will give a more detailed overview of the essays to come. First, though, an obvious objection must be registered, and responded to. The (seeming) utter naturalness of Aristotle's distinction between things and everything else, and the fact that the *Categories* are strikingly free of argument aimed at establishing or justifying this distinction, invite the rejoinder that introducing things into the ontology is not a distinctively philosophical move on Aristotle's part; it is rather a straightforward statement of the obvious. Indeed, what could it possibly mean to say that there were no things before Aristotle? For surely whatever there was, was there already. And to see that things were part of what there is (τὰ ὄντα), we need look no further than *Iliad* IX: things clearly are prominent among what Agamemnon promises to give to Achilles.

The absurdity of suggesting that there were no things before Aristotle is also brought out by the following contrast. When Aristotle, at the end of the *Organon*, claims to have provided a resource for reasoning about any subject whatsoever, Locke's well-known protest seems apposite:[6] "God has not been so sparing to men to make them barely two-legged creatures, and left it to Aristotle to make them rational" (*Essay Concerning Human Understanding*, iv.xvii.4). People surely were able to reason perfectly well prior to Aristotle, and continued being able to do so, in complete ignorance of him and his logical treatises. Yet if we now turn to things, matters look far worse. Consider the analogue of Locke's protest: 'God has not been so sparing to the world to make _____, and left it to Aristotle to make things.' Here we have no idea about how to fill in the blank—for what kind of item could it be that is not (yet) a thing, but can (later) be made into one?

Other considerations point in the same direction. Obvious features of Indo-European languages like English or Greek—sentences in subject-predicate form, the use of 'is' as the copula, and the singular, dual, and plural forms of nouns—suggest that a naive ontology of things is part of these languages. Ordinary sentences like 'Socrates is healthy' or 'The leaves are green' appear to be speaking of things; and the subject-expression in the first sentence appears to speak of one thing; the one in the second, of more than one. Philosophy picks up on and continues with these ordinary ways of speaking. Thus Plato had pointed out that being able to count is a minimal constituent of rationality (see *Republic* 522c–e)—but what is counting (in that context) other than being able to distinguish one thing from another, being able to tell that we are faced with, say, two things rather than only one? And in presenting their ontological theses, various

---

[6] Since the order of the books of the *Organon* is not Aristotle's own, the remark at *Soph. El.* 183ª37 ff. must be referring to the *Topics* and *Sophistici Elenchi*, but not to the *Analytics* (as Locke presumably thought it did). For present purposes this does not matter.

Presocratics had used words like πράγματα or χρήματα (note the plural), usually translated as 'things'—yet how else should we translate them?

In fact, the sentences mentioned and the metaphysical pictures alluded to seem to rely on a very natural-seeming distinction:

(i) that between *objects* and the *properties* of objects.

Now even if, as a result of our philosophical investigations, we should come to be persuaded that this is an unhelpful, misleading, or perhaps simply an untenable distinction, we are still inclined to believe that it is deeply embedded in the grammars of the languages we speak. Hence (i) does seem like a commonsense distinction, one that is available prior to philosophy, perhaps even one that is given prior to reflection.[7] After all, we do use sentences like 'The leaves are green' or 'Socrates is healthy'. And these sentences surely look as if they are attributing properties to objects. In addition, when we say things like 'The leaves are turning brown' or 'Socrates is becoming ill', it seems we are saying that (some of) their properties are changing, although the objects themselves remain. It is the same leaves, we suppose, that were green during the summer and are changing their color in the fall; it is the same Socrates who was healthy before, and is now becoming ill. (In describing these examples in the way I have described them, I do not mean to claim that this is, ultimately, the correct way of characterizing them, but simply that it is the perhaps most natural and intuitive way of speaking about them.) Furthermore, it looks as if the following sentences can be regarded similarly: 'This cat is (an) animal' or 'Socrates is (a) man'.[8] For again properties, although here perhaps necessary ones, are being attributed to objects. (And here too, this is not to say that we would or should, ultimately, so regard what is being said by these sentences.)

But a second very natural-seeming distinction seems equally relevant to all the cases mentioned:

---

[7] It is because I am concerned with an everyday conception of objects and properties that I do not even attempt to offer an account of what objects, or properties, are. That the conception adverted to, and relied on, in the text is in fact an everyday one is indirectly confirmed by works like Arda Denkel's *Object and Property* (Cambridge, 1996), which seeks to explore and refine that notion, as well as consider alternatives to it. See especially Denkel's introduction and chaps. 2 and 3. Cf. also A. Oliver, "The Metaphysics of Properties," *Mind* 105 (1996): 14–15.

[8] Greek of course lacks the indefinite article. This proves significant in certain contexts, and to prepare for them I have adopted the (no doubt artificial and inelegant) expedient of enclosing the article in parentheses.

(ii) that between what is *particular* and what is *general*.

For the cat is a particular thing (namely, this very cat), and so are Socrates and each of the leaves. Yet green, or being green, is something general, since it can be instantiated by any number of particulars. So too are being healthy, turning brown, becoming ill, and being (a) man or being (an) animal.

Thus far, I have deliberately avoided sentences where the subject-expressions are so-called *mass-terms*, that is, terms like 'water' or 'leisure' which seem not to refer to particular objects, but to something more amorphous—*stuffs* or *quasi-stuffs*. Mass-terms also (often) do not admit the formation of plurals, but even if they do, the plural forms appear to refer to kinds rather than to individuals (think of: 'waters'). We will come to see that these terms, or rather, the kinds of items to which they appear to refer, complicate matters considerably. But if we do restrict ourselves to cases like the ones mentioned, it may well seem as if we simply have two different ways of talking about one and the same distinction. Not only do distinctions (i) and (ii) coincide as a matter of fact, but being a particular just seems to be: being an object, and vice versa; and being something general just seems to be: being a property, and vice versa. Thus our single basic distinction would be:

(iii) that between *particular objects* and *general properties*.

But Aristotle, at least in the *Categories*, does not see (i) and (ii) as coinciding. Rather, (i) and (ii) cut across each other. Thus, as was already emphasized in ancient times by Porphyry and Ammonius,[9] we also have two additional kinds of items, besides particular objects and general properties.

First, there are what might be thought of as *general objects* (to use a phrase of Michael Frede's), that is, the genera and species of the particular objects.[10] Yet these genera and species are *not* to be thought of as being simply collections or aggregates of particular objects, but rather as being items having a kind of objecthood going beyond that of mere collections or aggregates; in the terminology of the *Categories*, they are *second* or

---

[9] See, for example, Porphyry *In Arist. Cat. Expos.*, 78, 22 ff., and Ammonius *In. Arist. Cat. Comm.*, 25, 5–26, 4. On the passage from Porphyry, see Porphyry, *On Aristotle's Categories*, tr. S. K. Strange (Ithaca, N.Y., 1992), p. 62 n. 102 and p. 64 n. 111; see also p. 65 n. 112 for references to relevant passages in Boethius and Simplicius.

[10] See M. Frede, "Individuen bei Aristoteles," *Antike und Abendland* 24 (1978): 16–17, 31. (Translated as "Individuals in Aristotle" in Frede's *Essays*; see pp. 49–50 and 63.)

secondary οὐσίαι. (This of course invites the question: what kind of object-hood is that?)

Secondly, there are *particular properties*. There has been considerable controversy about how to understand this notion. According to one view, these particular properties are *infimae species* of the general properties (for example, the most specific shades of colors). The salient feature of this type of interpretation is that, according to it, nothing prevents particular properties from being shared by several particular objects—for example, both this leaf and that leaf could be exactly the *same* shade of green. However, according to the traditional view (cf. Porphyry *In Arist. Cat. Expos.*, 75, 38–76, 3), the particular properties are properties that are particular to the particular objects to which they belong; these properties therefore cannot be shared. For example, Socrates' tan is Socrates', and Plato's tan is Plato's; thus they are *different*, even if they are qualitatively indistinguishable qua tan, simply because the one tan belongs to Socrates, and the other to Plato.[11] But the prima facie naturalness of (iii), and the difficulties commentators have felt with the additional items that are introduced if (i) and (ii) are seen as cutting across each other, make plausible the thought that (iii) is in fact the distinction that is actually of interest to Aristotle. Yet (iii) can equally well be understood as the (seem-ingly) commonsense or pretheoretical distinction between *things* and their *features*.

Thus what I am calling Aristotle's 'discovery of things' is the claim that bona fide things are particular objects in the sense given by his construal of distinctions (i) and (ii); and, conversely, that particular objects are the only bona fide things there are. Accordingly, the discovery of things amounts to the discovery of objects, to the discovery that all the entities need to be divided into particular objects on the one hand, and whatever

---

[11] On the controversy surrounding particular or individual properties in the *Categories*, see on the one hand, G. E. L. Owen, "Inherence," *Phronesis* 19 (1965); Frede, "Individuen bei Aristoteles"; M. Furth, *Substance, Form and Psyche* (Cambridge, 1989), pt. 1, esp. pp. 41–47, and G. Matthews, "The Enigma of *Categories* 1a20 ff. and Why It Matters," in *Nature, Knowledge and Virtue*, ed. T. Penner and R. Kraut (Edmonton, 1989) (= *Apeiron* 22, no. 4 [1989]), for a defense of the *infimae species* view. On the other hand, R. Heinaman, in his "Non-substantial Individuals in the *Categories,*" *Phronesis* 26 (1981), provides the best defense for the formerly widespread view that these properties are individuated by their bearers; cf. also T. H. Irwin, *Aristotle's First Principles* (Oxford, 1988), p. 502 n. 21. M. Wedin, in his "Nonsubstantial Individuals," *Phronesis* 38 (1993), offers a very subtle defense of this sort of view as well. I will briefly return to the question of how to understand this notion in Part III.

belongs to those objects on the other (including whatever kinds those objects fall under, in other words, their species and genera).[12] To this Aristotle adds the further claim that the objects, the bona fide things, are the most fundamental entities.

Using the terminology of the *Categories*, one could say that among the ὄντα (beings or entities), only the οὐσίαι (that is, the items so labeled in the treatise) are *deserving* of being called οὐσίαι, because only the items so labeled satisfy the criteria—whatever they might be—for being fundamental entities, for being οὐσίαι. Let us call this the Aristotelian priority claim.

An aside on the word οὐσία. To understand the Aristotelian priority claim, we of course need to know what this crucial term means. The question of how properly to translate οὐσία is vexed. Given that οὐσία is an abstract noun derived from the verb 'to be' (εἶναι), something like 'beingness' might at first sight appear to be called for.[13] Presumably, it is thinking along these lines that leads some translators to opt for 'reality', allowing them to speak both of the reality (οὐσία) of what is real (τὰ ὄντα), and

[12] It should be clear that I am using the term 'thing' in a different and more restrictive sense than A. Mourelatos does in his provocative "Heraclitus, Parmenides, and the Naive Metaphysics of Things," in *Exegesis and Argument*, ed. E. N. Lee, A. P. D. Mourelatos, and R. Rorty (New York, 1973), for his usage specifically covers the πράγματα or χρήματα of the Presocratics. Now it may seem that this is merely an arbitrary terminological difference, and that Mourelatos's employment of the term is virtually unavoidable. For we may again wonder how πράγματα or χρήματα are to be translated; isn't 'things' suitably harmless and noncommittal? It may well not be. First of all, what Mourelatos calls "the naive metaphysics of things" is itself a philosophical picture encountered in certain Presocratics, so the naiveté in question is a *philosophical* naiveté vis-à-vis above all Aristotle; it is not some sort of ordinary, prephilosophical naiveté vis-à-vis philosophy. Secondly, as we will see in connection with Anaxagoras, to think of what Anaxagoras calls χρήματα as things lands us in enormous difficulties. These difficulties suggest that *for us* the naive notion of a thing already brings with it the connotation that a thing is an object. And it is precisely for this reason that the ontological picture of the *Categories*, with its distinction between particular objects and their features, can seem like straightforward common sense. My claim is that it is, however, only because of the *Categories* and the role reflection on the treatise played in shaping traditional philosophical and grammatical thought that this distinction came to seem (and now does seem) so commonsensical. Thus while I do not dispute that the view Mourelatos finds in the Presocratics—or something similar—was theirs, that view is not naive, and while it could be called a metaphysics, it is not a metaphysics *of things*.

[13] On the formation of the abstract noun οὐσία, see Charles Kahn *The Verb 'Be' in Ancient Greek* (Dordrecht/Boston, 1973) (= *Foundations of Language*, suppl. ser., vol. 16), appendix C, "The Nominalized Forms of the Verb: τὸ ὄν and οὐσία," pp. 453–62.

of the fundamentally real items, now called 'realities' (οὐσίαι).[14] But this translation is really not very satisfying. First of all, the link with the verb 'to be' is broken by so rendering the term. Secondly, although it is possible to use the plural form 'realities'—in a way in which 'beingnesses' is simply impossible—using that plural to refer to a plurality of particular entities seems forced and contrived. The impossibility of the plural 'beingnesses' also rules out 'beingness' as a translation for οὐσία; this solecism would in any event have been an unhappy choice. The traditional rendering, 'substance', is problematic for reasons we will shortly be considering, in another aside. For now we can note that, in speaking of οὐσία, Aristotle means, at a minimum, to speak of what is really real—the most real or most fundamental entities or beings, or what is most real or fundamental in or about the entities and beings there are.[15]

To return to our story: it is a commonplace that Aristotle, in his metaphysical thinking, disagrees with Plato and rejects key elements of Plato's metaphysical picture. What exactly is Aristotle rejecting? Plato himself, at least in the middle dialogues, surely thought that (the items we think of as) ordinary things are *not* fundamental entities, whatever else there is to be said about them. He would thus explicitly reject the Aristotelian priority claim: the οὐσίαι of the *Categories* do not deserve the label.[16] Does this

---

[14] See, for example, W. C. Charlton, *Aristotle's Physics, I–II* (Oxford, 1970), pp. 56–57; cf. R. Dancy "On Some of Aristotle's First Thoughts About Substances," *Philsophical Review* 84 (1975): 338 n. 1.

[15] The cumbersome formulation is meant to register the fact that sometimes οὐσία is used as a one-place predicate: *x* is (an) οὐσία; sometimes as a two-place predicate: *x* is the οὐσία of *y*. This makes possible the thought that there could be (an) οὐσία of (an) οὐσία. We will see that in the *Categories*, Aristotle (in effect) collapses the two possibilities. But that is not built into the notion from the start.

[16] Here, however, someone might object and suggest—on the basis of *Metaphysics* VII, 2 and XII, 1—that Plato would actually *agree* with Aristotle that (certain) sensible particulars are οὐσίαι; thus Aristotle is not being at all revolutionary in calling sensibles οὐσίαι—at most his revolution consists in calling them *primary* οὐσίαι. No doubt these passages raise serious questions. But should we hold the interpretation of Plato dialogues—especially the middle ones—hostage to them? First, I have been unable to find any passage in, say, the *Phaedo, Republic*, or *Symposium*, where Plato refers to a participant as an οὐσία. Secondly, Plato uses *plural* forms of the word only very rarely (cf. L. Brandwood, *A Word Index to Plato* [Leeds, 1976], s.v. οὐσία), and then not to refer to sensible particulars, but mostly to *possessions* (a sense the word has in everyday Greek; cf. LSJ, s.v.). Thirdly, there is some tension between the *Metaphysics* passages just referred to and Aristotle's account of Plato in *Met.* I, 6; for at 987ᵇ8–10, he says that for Plato, "the sensibles are apart (παρά) from these [sc. the Forms], and are called after them; for the things having the same name as the Form

12

mean that for Plato, general properties or features do deserve to be called οὐσίαι? The following considerations suggest why the answer might seem to be: yes.

Central to the metaphysical picture Plato sketches in the middle dialogues is the division of everything into two classes—Forms and the items that participate in them, the participants. How is that division to be understood? To answer this question, we would need to be able to answer at least the following three further ones: what are the Forms; what are the participants; and how are these two kinds of items related? This may sound so obvious as not to be worth mentioning. Yet interpreters of Plato frequently proceed rather differently. They tend to neglect the participants and to focus, almost exclusively, on the Forms. Why? First of all, the being of the participants clearly depends on the Forms, and is to be explained in terms of them. But the being of the Forms is not only not to be explained by the participants, it is wholly independent of them.

We could equally well express Plato's view that the Forms are ontologically privileged as follows. Among the 'beings' or 'entities' (τὰ ὄντα),[17] only the Forms *deserve* to be called οὐσίαι, because only the Forms satisfy the criterion—ontological priority—for being fundamental entities, for being οὐσίαι. Let us call that the Platonic priority claim.

Now given this ontological priority of the Forms, it can easily seem both that we will need to understand what they are in order to understand (fully) what the participants are, and that once we do know and understand enough about the Forms, the participants will (so to speak) fall into place of their own accord, as the ontologically derivative kinds of items they are. Moreover, the very notion of a Form is one that, in and of itself,

---

exist by participation (κατὰ μέθεξιν)." But it seems to be part of the notion of οὐσία, that οὐσίαι are what they are (somehow) in their own right (see also pp. 25–26 below); yet if perceptibles are (i.e., are what they are) *by participation*, it would seem that they are *not* in their own right (i.e., are not what they are in their own right); hence perceptibles are not οὐσίαι. While these considerations by themselves may not be decisive, they are, I believe, grounds for not being as concerned as one might think we should be about the two passages mentioned. (I briefly consider a further reason for doubting that Plato is prepared to think of sensibles as οὐσίαι in n. 26 below.)

[17] The single quotes are meant to signal that the terms are being employed loosely here; for Plato holds that, strictly speaking, only the Forms deserve to be called beings. A passage like *Phaedo* 79a–b, however, shows that Plato is prepared to use 'being' (ὄν) less strictly, to apply also to the participants. The formulation in the body of the text thus is consonant with Plato's own usage. The claim that only Forms deserve to be called beings raises the obvious question of what the participants 'are', if they are not beings. Addressing that question will be one of the central tasks of Part II.

requires discussion and analysis, since it seems that we clearly do not have available anything like a pretheoretical understanding of what these Forms are—or even could be.

There are, then, sound reasons for inquiry about the Forms. But the unexpressed counterpart to the second point is that the participants are items of a completely familiar and ordinary sort. We do not need to learn *what they are*, because we already know: they are the things we ordinarily encounter in the world around us, the things we use language to talk about in our everyday lives, in short, they are things that have features. Indeed, the fact that Plato does not thematize the question, what are the participants, might appear to confirm the thought that the answer is ready to hand, all along.[18] In some sense, this is no doubt true: the participants are what we encounter in the world around us, in our everyday lives.

But does this mean that they are things which have features? Here we need to proceed cautiously. For suppose that one approaches Plato's texts with something like distinction (iii) in mind—the distinction between particular objects and general properties—as commentators frequently do. This leads them, quite naturally, to assume that the participants are to be

---

[18] Even commentators who purport to focus on Plato's picture of the participants often simply take for granted that the participants are the items labeled οὐσίαι (substances or objects) by Aristotle. Thus J. Brentlinger, after promising a discussion of Plato's "theory of particulars" ("Particulars in Plato's Middle Dialogues," *Archiv für Geschichte der Philosophie* 54 [1972]: 116), proceeds as if these particulars just were objects with features (pp. 117 ff.), without offering any argument in favor of that view. No doubt he thinks no such argument is needed. F. C. White, in a series of papers (see especially "Plato's Middle Dialogues and the Independence of Particulars," *Philosophical Quarterly* 27 [1977]: 202–4) and in his *Plato's Theory of Particulars* (New York, 1981), does argue that the participants must be so regarded. But his principal reason is that this is the only possibility which makes sense. We will see that it is not; cf. also R. Heinaman's review (*Journal of Hellenic Studies* 103 [1983]) of White's monograph. M. M. McCabe's *Plato's Individuals* (Princeton, N.J., 1994), with its insistence on the importance of the problem of individuation for Plato (pp. 1–18), looks as if it will ascribe a theory of particulars to Plato. But the contrast between "generous" and "austere" individuals or unities which she provides (e.g., p. 51), where Forms are austere, while sensible items are "generously endowed with properties," is not sufficiently fine-grained. For that contrast will not account for a difference Aristotle comes to regard as crucial: that between (mere) heaps or aggregates on the one hand, and (actual) objects, on the other; cf. my brief remarks on Aristotle, pp. 32–34 below. Thus even if Plato were to hold that the participants are individuals in McCabe's generous sense, this would not mean that they are objects, or bona fide things. Moreover, the way in which, according to McCabe, Forms are to be individuals is itself not without difficulties; cf. the reviews of her book by C. Meinwald (*Archiv für Geschichte der Philosophie* 78 [1996]) and N. White (*Ancient Philosophy* 17 [1997]).

seen as particular objects in the light of that distinction, that is, as objects *as opposed to* the features or properties these objects have. And the Forms, it would appear, are introduced to account for the general features of those particular objects. Thus in order to explain how a sentence like

(1) Socrates is just

can be true, Plato introduces a Form, *The Just Itself*, to which Socrates is appropriately related, a relation in virtue of which *inter alia* (1) is true.

This introduction is not the place to go into all the reasons why this is at best a highly misleading view of what the participants are, and hence also of what the Forms are. We can, however, already note one problem which suggests that the question, what are the participants, needs to be pursued with as much care as the seemingly more difficult and more important question, what are the Forms. The fact that the participation relation grounding (1) obtains could also be expressed thus:

(1′) The just (thing) is just.
    (I.e., τὸ δίκαιον δίκαιόν ἐστι.)

And, in general, each truth about a participant participating in some Form X can be rewritten as:

(I) The X (thing) is X.

However, notoriously, Plato insists that what has come to be called *self-predication* is possible. In the case at hand, this amounts to insisting that, in addition to (1), the following is also true:

(2) The Just Itself is just.

Hence, in general:

(II) The X (itself) is X.

Before proceeding, it is important to recall a crucial feature of the Greek language, namely, that the definite article + adjective can quite readily function as a substantive, as in (1′), (2), and (II) above. (For analogues in English, consider the following: 'The race goes to the swift' , 'The meek shall inherit the earth', or 'Only the good die young'—though it seems that, in English, this use of the definite article + adjective is largely restricted to the plural. And even when the singular can be used, as in, for example, 'The neurotic suffers because of . . .', or 'The insomniac is . . .', the subject-expressions in such sentences refer to the type, not to some particular neurotic individual or to some particular insomniac.)[19]

Moreover, in Greek, the *neuter* definite article + adjective can be ambiguous in important and interesting ways. Thus, e.g., τὸ λευκόν (the white) can refer (i) to some white thing, (ii) to white things in general, or (iii) to white (i.e., the color, white, or the quality, whiteness). This third use obviously corresponds to the abstract noun λευκότης (whiteness). Moreover, abstract nouns and the corresponding neuter article + adjective combinations are usually interchangeable.[20] Plato and Aristotle clearly rely on this feature of the Greek language, and in due course, we will see how it bears on the issue of self-predication.

To return to the issue we were considering. Given this linguistic fact, and given the understanding of Forms as something general, it must look as if Plato is simply confused about the very distinction (viz., iii) he is relying on in introducing Forms in the first place. For as commentators have again and again pointed out, Plato's acceptance of schema (II) makes it look as if he has simply failed to see the difference between being something particular and being something general, between being an object and being a feature, between having a property and being a property.[21] In fact, speaking of *The X Itself* (αὐτὸ τὸ X) might already be

---

[19] There are, perhaps, some exceptions to this. I recently heard the following announcement in an airport: "Flight 004 will depart one hour later than scheduled, because an inbound is delayed." The announcer was presumably using the adjective 'inbound' on that occasion as some sort of rebarbative shorthand for 'inbound flight' or 'inbound plane'. While usage along these lines may be becoming increasingly common, for the most part adjectives in English still cannot be used in place of substantives—and certainly not as readily as in Greek.

[20] For the grammatical point, see E. Schwyzer, *Griechische Grammatik*, 4 vols. (Munich, 1950–71), 2:175, or H. W. Smyth, *Greek Grammar*, rev. G. Messing (Cambridge, Mass., 1956) pp. 272–74.

[21] This is a commonplace of Anglo-American Plato scholarship. G. Vlastos offers an influential expression of it: "Indeed, it might be said that Plato is the first Western thinker to make the distinction between a character and the things that have that character a matter of philosophical reflection. For did not his theory of Forms call attention . . . to the 'reality' of universals as distinct from that of material existents? This is, of course, perfectly true. But what is no less true is that the Platonic ontology *inadvertently blurs the very distinction it was devised to express*" (emphasis added). See his "The Third Man Argument in the *Parmenides*" (originally in *Philosophical Review* 63 [1954]), reprinted in *Studies in Plato's Metaphysics*, ed. R. E. Allen (London and New York, 1965), p. 252. Compare Heidegger's remark at the opening of "Die Frage nach der Technik" (*Holzwege*, p. 9): "Wenn wir das Wesen des Baumes suchen, müssen wir gewahr werden, daß jenes, was jeden Baum als Baum durchwaltet, nicht selber ein Baum ist, der sich zwischen den übrigen Bäumen antreffen läßt." ("When we're seeking the essence of trees we need to recognize that that which is common to all

thought to signal this confusion, for it may well suggest that a Form is something particular, that it is something like an object.[22]

We cannot yet rule out that Plato was confused.[23] But it is important to recall two points. First, sentences conforming to schema (II) were accepted—for example, by various Presocratics—before Platonic Forms were on the scene. Secondly, in the dialogues, such sentences are accepted by speakers *other* than Socrates, speakers who cannot be supposed to have any commitment to the 'theory' of Forms. In the *Hippias Major*, Hippias readily agrees that *the beautiful* (τὸ καλόν) is beautiful (292e6–7); and in the *Protagoras*, Protagoras agrees, equally readily, that *justice* (ἡ δικαιο-σύνη) is just (330c3–7). In the *Lysis*, it seems that *the white* (τὸ λευκόν) or *whiteness* (λευκότης) are treated similarly; in particular, the sentence at 217d6–e1, which says that in old age, hair will be white through the presence of *the white* (λευκοῦ παρουσίᾳ λευκαί), implies that *the white* will itself be white.[24] But this fact suggests that accepting sentences like

---

trees qua trees is not itself a tree, to be found amongst all the other ones.") But for "Wenn wir das Wesen des Baumes suchen . . . ," Heidegger could equally well have written, "Wenn wir *den* Baum suchen . . . ," ("When we're seeking *the* tree . . . "). (This sort of formulation is quite natural in German, even though it sounds peculiar in English.) Thus Heidegger's point ends up being exactly the same as Vlastos's (even though Heidegger is not speaking of Platonic Forms but of essences [*Wesen*] more generally).

[22] It will thus turn out that we need to distinguish between being one (that is, being somehow countable) and actually being an object (that is, an object as opposed to its properties). For Forms will be countable without being objects.

[23] The train of thought and the formulations in this and the next three paragraphs are indebted to M. Frede's "Being and Becoming in Plato," *Oxford Studies in Ancient Philosophy*, suppl. vol. (1988), p. 52.

[24] John Malcolm has denied that self-predication is involved in the *Lysis*, because: "As Aristotle reminds us (*Cat.* 2ª27–34), 'white' is one of the few words that both names, or identifies, a quality (here a colour) and describes a thing qualified (here a thing coloured). The performance of these two functions is sufficient to explain the sense of 'white by the presence of white' . . . and also to account for the hair being *hoionper* or 'such as' its colour. White is the quality present in the hair and white is the colour the hair is (or has). Hence the hair is *such as* its colour (both being white). It does not follow, however, that white (i.e. whiteness) is a white thing." See his *Plato on the Self-Predication of Forms* (Oxford, 1991), p. 12. This passage from Malcolm is a striking example of importing Aristotelian notions into the analysis of Plato. I would contend that it is precisely because the term 'white' behaves in the way mentioned that it is easy *not* to draw the thing/quality distinction, and hence that the *Lysis* indeed does suggest that *the white* is white. (On this issue in the *Lysis*, cf. Prauss, "Ding und Eigenschaft," pp. 109–10; R. Dancy, *Two Studies in the Early Academy* [Albany, 1991], pp. 12–14; and G. Fine "Critical Notice" (of Dancy's monograph), *Canadian Journal of Philosophy* 22 [1992]: 396.) However, we will see that once Arisotle's analysis is in place, then something like Malcolm's account of *Lysis* 217d–e becomes possible. For

'The just is just', that is, all the so-called self-predication sentences, is *not* a *consequence* of the picture of Forms we find in the middle dialogues. Rather, these sentences are to be taken as true quite independently of, and prior to, any specific account of what being X is—both in the sense of: being an X (or an X-ish) item, and in the sense of: being X Itself. (A quick comment, to forestall a possible source of unclarity. In speaking of self-predication or self-predication sentences, I mean only to *label* senten-ces of a certain form, but not thereby to say what they mean; for their proper interpretation is something that very much needs to be established and cannot be taken for granted. Indeed, we have already seen, even if only in outline, that, on what for us would be their most natural interpreta-tion, they appear to implicate Plato in a serious confusion.)

Thus we first of all need interpretations of (I) and (II) that will allow us to see how each could seem uncontroversially acceptable, or at least relatively so. Only then should we seek accounts of what Forms are, and of what participants are, which preserve that acceptability. We should also ask ourselves: why does the most natural-seeming construal of the self-predication sentences in fact seem most natural to us?

I will argue that providing the desired sorts of interpretations of (I) and (II) requires refusing to treat the participants as particular objects, and the Forms as general features. But this in turn suggests that Plato's differ-ences with Aristotle are not exhausted by (what we might think of as) his rejection of the Aristotelian priority claim in favor of the Platonic one.[25] The issue between them thus also is not restricted to only the question of which items are deserving of the honorific label οὐσίαι. Rather, we should not approach the dialogues with the distinction between particular objects and general features (i.e., iii) in mind at all. But now we may well wonder: how then are we supposed to understand the fundamental division between Forms and participants? What is it to be a Form? And what is it to be a participant?

Here we would do well to orient ourselves by looking to how Plato actually talks about and describes the participants and the Forms—after all, he does not explicitly employ any of the distinctions we have seen, viz. (i)–(iii),

---

present purposes, what is relevant about all these texts is that agreement to the self-predication claims is easily secured and apparently involves no exotic metaphysical commitments on the part of Socrates' interlocutors.

[25] Cf. Prauss, "Ding und Eigenschaft," pp. 99–100.

in arriving at his fundamental division. But Plato, famously, does draw a distinction between *being* and *becoming*. And he associates being with the Forms, and becoming with the participants.[26] Thus this distinction looks as if it could be used to shed light on the distinction between Forms and participants. Now, when we look at the accounts commentators give of being and becoming in Plato, we find them proceeding in a manner that closely parallels their treatment of Forms and participants. Given that the Forms are privileged entities, the notion of being that Plato has in mind here must also somehow be privileged—for example, pure, real, or true being. Thus what needs to be provided is an analysis of that notion of being. (This suggestion derives clear support from the fact that Plato, quite conspicuously, does speak of pure, real, and true being in the case of the Forms.) Becoming, on the other hand, is supposed to be perfectly clear and straightforward—according to the sorts of views I am adverting to, becoming refers to change, to the fact that the participants (allegedly) are always changing. (And this suggestion would appear to derive support from the fact that Plato does think that the physical, perceptible world is somehow in flux.) But as we will see, the question, what is becoming, turns out to be just as challenging as the seemingly more weighty question, what is being. We will also see that the answers to both questions prove to be rather different from what we might have expected them to be.

The investigation of the distinction between being and becoming as it is presented in the dialogues will show, as one of its most significant

---

[26] But at *Philebus* 26b7–9, we encounter the surprising expression "the οὐσία that has come to be." This would seem to be tailor-made for referring to sensible particulars in the way mentioned before (see n. 16 above); for such generated οὐσίαι could be contrasted with ungenerated, eternal ones. But Plato seems not to be referring to sensible particulars: he rather uses this expression to speak of what comes to be as a result of the mixture of Limit and The Unlimited. Now, however the difficult metaphysical picture of the *Philebus* is to be understood, it seems that *these* mixtures are not simply to be identified with sensible particulars (as opposed to states or features of them). So the *Philebus* cannot, in any straightforward way, be used as evidence that Aristotle correctly attributes to Plato the view he attributes to him in *Met.* VII, 2 and XII, 1. (Two other seemingly relevant passages present similar problems: one is from later in the *Philebus* [53e ff.]—yet what is there spoken of as becoming, or coming to be, is *pleasure*, not any sensible particular—the other is from the *Statesman* [283d ff.]—there it seems that "measure" somehow accounts for the "necessary οὐσία of coming to be" [283d8–9]. This is no doubt difficult, but again seems not to be referring to sensible particulars as οὐσίαι.) The fact that Plato, in employing these expressions or phrases, does *not* refer to sensible particulars is a further reason for being extremely cautious about Aristotle's attribution to Plato of the view that sensible particulars are οὐσίαι.

results, that yet a further distinction (which had already been important for Anaxagoras and certain medical writers) proves crucial for properly understanding the relation between the participants and the Forms:

(iv) the distinction between *part* and *whole*.

What we will see is that while (ii)—the distinction between what is particular and what is general—is indeed at work in distinguishing Forms from participants, (ii) needs to be understood in the light of (iv) not (i). For it will turn out that, in a way, the Forms are *wholes* (to be conceived of as *stuffs* or *quasi-stuffs*) rather than properties, while the participants are not so much objects as *mixtures* or *combinations* of *parts* or *portions* of those wholes.[27] (Note that mass-terms can be seen to enter the picture here: think of the wholes as those entities that are designated by the appropriate mass-terms.) But this also means that the participants are not things, in the sense Aristotle will delineate in the *Categories*.

Equally, it turns out that the features of Indo-European languages adverted to are more metaphysically neutral (or less metaphysically determinate) than the view which sees straightforward continuity between those linguistic features and the metaphysical picture of the *Categories*. This point may emerge more clearly by way of contrast with the following claim of Alexander Mourelatos's:

> Throughout its known history, Greek, like most other natural languages known to us, has been 'in perfect logical order'—by which I mean that in its tacit transformations between surface and depth grammar *it already pre-analytically encodes* the subtle distinctions between subject-attribute, particular-universal, concrete-abstract, thing-fact which philosophers from antiquity to the present have analyzed, discovered, and formulated—or, for that matter, confused, obscured, and misstated.[28]

The problem here is that the talk of "pre-analytical encoding" can make it seem as if all the distinctions in question are already there, all along, in

---

[27] Recall also that the standard term for universal, καθόλου (i.e., καθ' ὅλου) seems to involve reference to wholes, for it literally means 'of a whole'. And Aristotle sometimes refers to the particular as τὸ κατὰ μέρος (what is in accord with, or of a part; *Rhet.* 1357ᵇ1), or to statements about particulars as οἱ ἐπὶ μέρους (those that apply to the parts; *EN* 1107ᵃ29–32). This raises the question of what sorts of wholes and parts underlie the introduction of this terminology. Cf. also Plato, *Theaetetus* 157b8 ff.

[28] Mourelatos, "Heraclitus, Parmenides," pp. 20–21 (emphasis added). The phrase in quotes is from Wittgenstein's *Tractatus*, 5.5563; the original reads: "Alle Sätze unserer Umgangssprache sind tatsächlich, so wie sie sind, logisch vollkommen geordnet."

a determinate way. But this is simply false.[29] We should rather say that ordinary language and usage do not, taken as a whole, preclude drawing these kinds of philosophical or grammatical distinctions, and that while some elements of the way we ordinarily talk may fit well with certain such distinctions, other elements of our everyday discourse may fit better with other distinctions. Of course, once a particular distinction has been clearly articulated, it may come to seem perfectly natural—it may come to seem as if had been fully present in the language, all along.

In the case at hand, it is certainly true that, once the metaphysical picture of the *Categories* is (put) in place—more accurately, a part of that picture, namely (iii)—the continuities between it and ordinary language can look impressive indeed. As Heidegger remarks in "On the Origin of the Work of Art":

> Who would undertake to challenge these simple relationships between things and sentences, between sentence structure and the structure of things? Nonetheless we must ask: is the structure of a simple assertoric sentence (the combination of the *subject* with the *predicate*) the mirror image of the structure of a thing (the unification of a *substance* with its *accidents*)? Or is this postulated structure of things rather modeled on the structure of sentences?[30] [Note that Heidegger could equally well have spoken of the unification of an *object* with its *properties*.]

Likewise, once Presocratic metaphysics and the Presocratic strands in Plato's thinking are (implicitly) criticized and (silently) replaced by Aristotle, the picture presented in the *Categories* can readily come to seem like an instance of purely descriptive metaphysics, while the pictures of Aristotle's predecessors must seem like exercises in revisionary metaphysics, and highly peculiar revisionary metaphysics at that. But after having seen

---

[29] At least Mourelatos will be committed to this claim being false. For given that the various philosophical distinctions prove, on further, careful reflection to be incompatible— better, prove to categorize nonlinguistic items in incompatible ways—it would seem that ordinary language is not "in perfect logical order" after all. On the other hand, if it is in order, then philosophical distinctions of the sort mentioned by Mourelatos turn out always to go beyond ordinary language in some way and to some extent. Thus they are not already "encoded" in everyday ways of speaking.

[30] "Wer möchte sich unterfangen, an diesen einfachen Grundverhältnissen zwischen Ding und Satz, zwischen Satzbau und Dingbau zu rütteln? Dennoch müssen wir fragen: ist der Bau des einfachen Aussagesatzes (die Verknüpfung von Subjekt und Prädikat) das Spiegelbild zum Bau des Dinges (zur Vereinigung der Substanz mit den Akzidenzien)? Oder ist gar der so vorgestellte Bau des Dinges entworfen nach dem Gerüst des Satzes?" *Holzwege*, p. 13 (all emphases added).

how Aristotle came to his metaphysical picture—namely, via criticism of his predecessors—we will be able to see that it too is *not* purely descriptive, any more than the ontological pictures of Plato and the Presocratics had been. We will also see that a simple dichotomy between descriptive and revisionary metaphysics is far too crude for characterizing the different metaphysical pictures, and their relation to each other, and to anything we might think of as an ordinary or naive ontological picture. *All* of the philosophical views in question go beyond common sense in significant ways. *All* involve commitments beyond those simply given by the 'grammar' of the languages we speak.[31] But that means that even if the extension of a term like 'thing' were (virtually) the same in ordinary usage and in Aristotle's ontology, things need not—indeed, could not—have shown up *as things* prior to the *Categories* and *Topics*.[32] No contention along these lines can so much as sound plausible until we have seen, in some detail, what the alternative, pre-Aristotelian metaphysical pictures in fact were. Only then we will be able to appreciate, against the background which they form, that even the most unremarkable, innocuous, and empty-sounding claims of the *Categories* and *Topics* are in fact distinctively philosophical.

The foregoing remarks are certainly not a full-fledged response to the obvious objection mentioned—that Aristotle's discovery of things is not a substantive philosophical move, but is rather a statement of the obvious. These remarks have aimed merely to register and allay (temporarily) the worries that gave rise to that objection, and to indicate, in outline, the strategy for addressing it head on. Let me now offer a more detailed outline of the essays that follow, before, at the end of this introduction, providing some final methodological comments and warnings.

[31] At this point, one might object: why speak of the *discovery* of things at all (especially in light of the reservations expressed about Mourelatos's remarks); would not the *invention* of things be a more felicitous formulation? It would not be. Discovery is the right notion, because the metaphysical picture of the *Categories* is *not* a purely revisionary one either. Indeed, there surely is something that is pre-analytically *available* to Aristotle for analysis, reflection, and (possibly) refinement, but to acknowledge this is not yet to say that Aristotle's distinctive conceptual framework is pre-analytically "encoded" in ordinary language.

[32] The contrary-to-fact formulation is deliberate. There is no single, neutral word used both in ordinary Greek and by Aristotle to pick out all and only (or virtually all and only) those items Aristotle ends up calling οὐσίαι in the *Categories* and *Topics*. But this is an accident of language, in the sense that speakers of ordinary Greek are hardly lacking the resources for picking out and grouping together those items Aristotle regards as primary οὐσίαι—in the first instance, individual living things and, perhaps, secondarily, artifacts as

3. The Task of Part I: The Problem of *Categories* 1 and 2

Part I is devoted to setting the stage, by examining the classificatory schemata of *Categories*, Chapters 1 and 2, and the large number of technical or semitechnical notions Aristotle employs, often without explanation, in presenting these schemata. This examination will put us in the position to ask some precisely formulated questions about the relation of the notions employed in those chapters to various projects of Plato and the Academy.

In *Categories* 2, Aristotle presents a fourfold basic ontological division that, in Michael Frede's terminology, distinguishes between: general properties, general objects, particular properties, and individual objects.[33] This division is arrived at by employing another distinction, between two ways in which something can be *predicated* of something as its *subject* (ὑποκείμενον). For if *y* is predicated of *x* as its subject, either *y* is SAID OF *x*, or *y* is IN *x*.[34] What is the difference between these two ways in which something can be predicated of something? Roughly speaking, if *y* is SAID OF *x*, then *x* is *y* in an *essential* way; while if *y* is IN *x*, *x* is *y*, but *not essentially*. What more precisely this comes to, is something we will be considering throughout the essays that follow.

An aside, to forestall yet another possible source of confusion: *predication*, as Aristotle conceives it, is in the first instance an *ontological* relation, and only secondarily and derivatively a *linguistic* matter. Thus if *y* is IN *x*, this is primarily a fact about the actual items, *y* and *x*, and about how they are related, although this fact also grounds the truth of a sentence like '*X* is *Y*' (if *X* and *Y* are appropriate subject- and predicate-expressions). In exactly the same way, if *y* is SAID OF *x*, this too is primarily a fact about the actual items, *y* and *x*; it is *not* a claim to the effect that a certain sentence

---

well. The point is that even if the language did categorize these items under a single term, so categorizing them, and so using the relevant single term, would not automatically bring with it the ontological picture Aristotle presents.

[33] Again, see Frede, "Individuen bei Aristoteles," pp. 16–17, 31 (= "Individuals in Aristotle," pp. 49–50, 63).

[34] I follow F. Lewis, *Substance and Predication in Aristotle* (Cambridge, 1991), in capitalizing the names of the relations from c. 2, in order to signal that these are technical terms, not be confused with their counterparts in more ordinary (philosophical) usage. In doing so I do not, however, mean to endorse his particular account of these relations.

is true, although here too there will be a sentence (with appropriate subject- and predicate-expressions) expressing this fact.[35] Indeed, in all cases, if *y* is ontologically predicated of *x*, there will be some sentence that expresses that *y* is predicated of *x*. Now Aristotle is notoriously lax about anything like the use/mention distinction. Thus he rather freely shifts back and forth between ontological predication and mere linguistic predication; and in particular, he sometimes uses the very locution 'said of' to refer to (mere) linguistic predication rather than to the SAID OF relation. While this is unfortunate and no doubt untidy, for the most part it does not cause any real problems.

The fourfold division looks like this: (i) Some items can both be IN something as their subject and also be SAID OF something as their subject (these turn out to be general properties). (ii) Some items can only be IN something as their subject, but not be SAID OF anything (individual properties). (iii) Some items can only be SAID OF something as their subject, but not be IN anything (genera and species of objects). And (iv) some items can neither be SAID OF anything, nor be IN anything as their subjects; rather, they are themselves *ultimate subjects* (particular objects). And these last ones are precisely the items Aristotle thinks of as primary οὐσίαι.

Reflecting on Aristotle's way of proceeding in arriving at (i)–(iv) shows that his *criterion* for something being a primary οὐσία consists exactly its being an ultimate subject, that is, something that can itself no longer be predicated of anything else as *its* subject, though it can be (and is) the subject for something else.[36]

The fact that being an ultimate subject is the criterion for being an οὐσία also goes a good way towards explaining why Tertullian and Augustine, and

---

[35] Not all readers of the *Categories* have recognized that *both* the being IN and the SAID OF relations are ontological ones. But in the wake of J. L. Ackrill's astute commentary on 1ª20 ff.—see pp. 75–76 of his *Aristotle's Categories and De Interpretatione* (Oxford, 1963)— the view presented in the text has come to be the dominant one. At this point in the history of interpretation, I see no need to argue for it.

[36] Steve Strange, in written correspondence, has suggested that being an ultimate subject is not a criterion but only a test for being a primary οὐσία; the criterion rather is ontological or natural priority. I of course agree that, for Aristotle, the primary οὐσίαι are ontologically prior to all the other entities. But in the light of the use Aristotle will make of the notion of being an ultimate subject in *Metaphysics* VII, 3 (see 1028ᵇ33–37), I think we should think of it as a genuine criterion for being a primary οὐσία. The fact that *Met.* VII, 3 reiterates the *Categories* criterion, virtually verbatim, albeit now as only *one* of the criteria for being an οὐσία, is obscured in translations that render ὑποκείμενον as 'substratum' (rather than

24

then Boethius and the medieval Latin tradition following him chose to render οὐσία with *substantia*, rather than with, say, *essentia*—which is what the morphology of Greek and Latin would lead us to expect:[37] the role of the primary οὐσίαι literally is to stand under (*substare*) everything else. If we were considering only the *Categories* and *Topics*, using 'substance' for οὐσία would do little harm, and would have the decided advantage of being in accord with long-established tradition, as well as allowing us to speak of real things (the substances), and what is really real in or about those things (their substance). But such a translation can easily obscure the facts that Plato, too, was inquiring into οὐσία, and that Aristotle will later in his career openly acknowledge that the inquiry into οὐσία that he himself is pursuing, is, in his view, continuous with the Platonic investigation—as well as with various Presocratic speculations.[38]

Note also that we can offer a formulation of the priority claim that is entirely *neutral* between the Aristotelian and the Platonic one. Among all the items that are—in an appropriately loose sense of 'are'—some deserve to be called οὐσίαι, because they satisfy the criteria—whatever they may be—for being fundamental entities.

But all of this just is to say that the metaphysical or ontological project of an inquiry into οὐσία is not an inquiry into the substances in the *Categories* sense; rather it is a general inquiry into what is really real, or what is really real in or about real things. Both for that reason and for the reasons adverted to earlier against other renditions of the term, I will, following the lead of Michael Frede and Günther Patzig, for the most part

---

'subject') in the *Metaphysics*. It seems to me that we ought to translate the term as 'subject' throughout, and then investigate whether or not Aristotle's notion of being a subject is the same in the two treatises (and in other works, e.g., the *Physics*).

[37] The Roman philosopher Plautus is reported to have used *essentia* for οὐσία, see Quintilian *Inst. Orat.* III, 6, 23–24. So too Cicero (but not in the extant work), see Seneca *Ep. Mor.* 58, 6–7. The term *substantia* is first attested in Seneca, though apparently as a rendition for ὑπόστασις (which is what the morphology would lead us to expect), not οὐσία; see *Ep. Mor.* 58, 15 (but see the whole of 58, 6–24); cf. *Quaest. Nat.* I, 6, 4 and I, 15, 6. On the history of the Latin term, see C. Arpe, "Substantia," *Philologus* 94 (1941); on ὑπόστασις, see H. Dörrie, Ὑπόστασις: *Wort- und Bedeutungsgeschichte,* Nachrichten Akad. d. Wiss., Göttingen, phil.-hist. Kl., no. 3 (1955).

[38] See *Metaphysics* VII, 1; cf. R. Dancy, "On Some of Aristotle's First Thoughts," p. 338. The thought that Plato and Aristotle are, in important respects, relying on a *common* framework for their ontological inquiries and disagreements also guides A. Code in the formulation of his elegant logic of *being* and *having*; see his "Aristotle: Essence and Accident," in *Philosophical Grounds of Rationality*, ed. R. Grandy and R. Warner (Oxford, 1986), esp. pp. 414–22.

simply use the transliterated form, *ousia*.[39] (But I will follow tradition in continuing to refer to the items in the other categories as nonsubstantial items.)

To return to Chapters 1 and 2. The overall import of the network of notions found in c. 2 would appear to be relatively clear: it provides for a way of organizing what there is (τὰ ὄντα) in a hierarchically structured way, with individual objects (primary *ousiai*), i.e., particular things, as the basis of, or foundation for that organization. And the famous remark at 2^{b}5–6—"So if the primary *ousiai* did not exist it would be impossible for any of the others to exist"—seems to confirm this ontological primacy of the primary *ousiai*.[40] Thus when Aristotle speaks of the others here, these must be *all* the items which are *not* ultimate subjects; that is to say, these others must be the general properties, particular properties, and general objects, i.e., *all* the items mentioned under (i)–(iii), in the fourfold division of c. 2.

But in *Categories* 1, Aristotle had introduced another set of distinctions, those between *synonymy, homonymy,* and *paronymy.* Let us, following Jonathan Barnes, call these the '-onymies'.[41] Now unlike the SAID OF and being IN relations, these notions do depend, crucially, on features of the language. More specifically, they rely on the *names* that are used to introduce items into discourse (in sentences of certain sorts), and on the *accounts* or *definitions* that can be given of the items so named. What is of central importance for Aristotle—or so I shall argue—are two distinctions that Plato had either failed to notice, or whose significance he had failed fully to appreciate. First, there is the distinction between abstract nouns, which name qualities, and the predicate adjectives derived from those abstract nouns, which name what is qualified (viz., qualified things). Consider for example the noun, 'justice', which names the quality, justice, and the predicate adjective, 'just', which names Socrates in the sentence, 'Socrates is just'.[42] (As we will see, Aristotle's notion of paronymy is meant to capture

---

[39] See M. Frede and G. Patzig *Aristoteles 'Metaphysik Z': Text, Übersetzung und Kommentar,* vol. 2: *Kommentar* (Munich, 1988), pp. 16–17 (ad 1028^{a}15).

[40] All line numbers refer to the Oxford Classical Text: *Aristotelis Categoriae,* ed. L. Minio-Paluello (Oxford, 1956).

[41] Barnes employs this succinct and amusing term in his "Homonymy in Aristotle and Speusippus," *Classical Quarterly,* n.s. 21 (1971).

[42] The idea that the predicate adjective names Socrates in that sentence, and hence can be thought of as *a* name of him, may seem less strange if we consider that we can go on to say things like 'The just (sc. one) is . . . ', i.e., that we can form subject-expressions for new

these kinds of cases.) Secondly, there is the distinction between terms naming natural kinds (the names of secondary *ousiai*, the genera and species of primary *ousiai*) and the predicate nouns derived from those natural kind names, which name things belonging to the kind. Consider for example the term, 'man', which names the kind or species, man, and the predicate noun, 'man', which names Socrates in the sentence, 'Socrates is (a) man'. (Aristotle's notion of synonymy is meant to capture these kinds of cases.) And again, recall that in Greek there is no indefinite article; hence the distinction between predicate adjectives and natural kind terms (as well as sortal nouns quite generally) does not show up in the way in which it does in English. We will see how Plato and Aristotle come to terms with this fact about the Greek language in order to draw various distinctions that are of interest to them, distinctions which we might seek to capture precisely by exploiting the differences in the linguistic behavior of predicate adjectives versus that of sortal nouns. In fact, Aristotle draws far-reaching ontological conclusions on the basis of differences in the linguistic behavior between predicate-expressions derived from abstract nouns, on the one hand, and those derived from natural kind terms, on the other. Though there are various complications here—only some of which Aristotle addresses—by the end of Part I we will see that it is relatively clear how the distinctions are meant to work, at least as far as these '-onymies' from *Categories* 1 on their own are concerned.

While coming to understand how the distinctions from the first two chapters are meant to work is a central objective of Part I, it is not the only task. One striking feature of the text of the treatise as we have it is that Aristotle nowhere explains how the classifcatory schemata of the two chapters are related—they are simply juxtaposed, with no attempt at establishing a connection. (Nor does he explain how these two classificatory schemata are related to the list of the ten kinds of entities that we encounter in c. 4.)

Thus the main task of Part I will be getting clear about how, despite appearances, the distinctions of the first two chapters are in fact *systematically* related. For to my mind, the real philosophical difficulty with which the *Categories* confront us, is that nowhere in these first two chapters (nor anywhere else in the treatise) does Aristotle motivate his plethora of distinctions, much less justify them. Which issues is he seeking to address? What problems is he seeking to solve? Without answers to these questions,

---

sentences based on the predicate-expression in the old one. In that new sentence, 'the just (sc. one)' obviously refers to Socrates. See also below, Part II, Section 15.

the treatise can easily seem (and has seemed) as if it is drawing attention in an arid and arbitrary way to certain linguistic facts on the one hand, and to a dogmatically asserted ontological picture on the other. But I believe that Aristotle—at least implicitly—does have answers to these pressing questions. By the end of Part I, we will see how the notions of Chapters 1 and 2 are related. And it will also be clear that when Aristotle says what he says, he is (implicitly) continuing, replying to, or modifying Platonic/ Academic notions and arguments. Thus it is in order to see the point of, or the motivation for, the conceptual apparatus introduced, that I turn to Plato in Part II. Examining the relevant Platonic texts will put us in a position to realize that Aristotle develops his contrast between synonymy, homonymy, and paronymy in response to (what he perceives as) difficulties in Plato and in Plato's curious alter egos, the Late-Learners of the *Sophist*. It will prove illuminating to regard these difficulties as centered around the following question: what is involved in a thing being a thing—what is it for a thing to be a thing?

In Appendix 1 to Part I, I argue that the received text of *Categories* 1–5 may be in rather worse shape than we might have thought. In particular, there might be some gaps in the text, and there is at least one passage (2^{a}19–34) that has been dislocated from its proper place. And I suggest that two others (1^{a}16–19 and 1^{b}16–24) might also have been displaced. I am inclined to believe that if we take note of these difficulties with the text, some of the interpretative issues that arise with respect to cc. 1–3 become less difficult, while others become more clearly focused; however, the argument about the *Categories* in the body of the book, in Parts I and III, does not depend on accepting these suggestions, though I proceed with them in place. Appendix 2 involves a brief look at Speusippus and a question that arises about his use of the '-onymies'. We will, however, see that, sadly, the reports about Speusippus's use of the '-onymies' prove of no real help in understanding Aristotle.

4. The Task of Part II: Plato's Metaphysics and the Status of Things

Part II, then, is concerned both with the views characteristic of the middle and late dialogues—and certain Presocratic theories to which Plato is replying—as well as with the rather strange-sounding claims of the Late-Learners of the *Sophist*. As already mentioned, the contrast between being and becoming is of great importance for Plato in his characterization of the difference between Forms and participants. Thus after a brief initial formulation of the contrast between Forms and participants, I begin the investigation of Part II by considering Plato's *introduction* of the distinction between being and becoming. We will want to see what Plato means by these notions, and how they provide him a means for distinguishing between Forms and participants. By looking at certain pre-Platonic uses of γίγνεσθαι (to become)—in particular, at what I call its 'funerary use', as encountered in inscriptions and other commemorative contexts—we will be able to establish that Plato's metaphysical contrast is not one between *unchanging* things and *changing* ones, but between *unchangeable* and *changeable* ones, between stable and unstable items. Recognizing this at first glance rather subtle point puts us in a position to realize how, precisely, Plato is continuing with the projects and preoccupations of certain Presocratics.

These Presocratics had developed their theories in response to Parmenides, who had denied that change of any sort is possible, and had maintained that being must be wholly stable and unchangeable. However, the world around us obviously contains change and changing things. This fact leads these post-Parmenidean thinkers to posit a distinction between what is stable, and what is not, agreeing with Parmenides that (real) being is stable (and thus not changing), but disagreeing with him in allowing for change. But these changing items thus can no longer be (real) beings—although they are somehow related to what is really real, to what has real being. (To have a sense of the sort of two-tiered picture this way of thinking leads to, consider Democritus's distinction between atoms and the void on the one hand—these are what is really real—and the items constituted from the atoms on the other—these are the perceptible things in the world around us.)

Most relevant for our purposes is the view of another Presocratic thinker, namely Anaxagoras. Anaxagoras posits certain *elements* as what is stable and therefore really real, whereas *mixtures* of *portions* of those elements—corresponding to ordinary things—are not really real. Moreover, these mixtures are as they are, because portions of the elements are *present in* them; or conversely, the mixtures are as they are, because the mixtures *have a share* of those elements. In addition, the mixtures are *called* what they are called *from* or *after* the elements present in them, while the elements are *called* what they are called *in their own right*. Thus to take a characteristic kind of example, a given item will be gold, because gold is an element in it; and it will accordingly be called 'gold', while gold itself, the element, is called 'gold', because that is what it is. In the *same* way, something will be hot, because (some of) the hot is mixed in; and it will accordingly be called 'hot', while the hot itself, the element, is called 'hot', because that is what it is. (To us, the two kinds of examples might well seem to be quite *different*; the question of why they should really be seen as similar is one I will address in Section 7 of Part II.)

Anaxagoras proves to be directly of relevance to Plato, because the conception of Forms and participants, and their relation to each other, shows close affinities to Anaxagoras's conception of elements and mixtures, and their relation to each other. This is especially clear in the *Phaedo*—as was noted long ago by Ludwig Heindorf (1810) and Immanuel Bekker (1825). Taking seriously the idea that Plato is in some ways a quasi-Anaxagorean will allow us to view the participants in a rather different light: they are best regarded as (what we might initially think of as) bundles or clusters of Form-Instances, rather than as bona fide objects, or things. This view also has a long ancestry: a version of it was adopted by no less distinguished an interpreter of Plato's than John Burnet (1914). Taking this idea seriously (and seeing how it is properly to be taken) will also allow us to recognize that certain problems for Platonism are not as problematic as they have often appeared to be—especially the question of how the self-predication sentences are to be understood.

However, before continuing, yet again a cautionary note: as just mentioned, I am focusing on one very important strand in Plato's treatment of the Forms and participants, namely, the prima facie astonishing idea that the participants should not be regarded as particular objects, as bona fide things in the *Categories* sense. That deliberately narrow focus is motivated by the thought that Aristotle, in the *Categories*, is just as concerned with criticizing and replacing precisely this element in Plato's thinking about the participants as he is committed to rejecting the idea that something general, namely, Platonic Forms, could be what is ontologically most basic.[43] By approaching Plato with these concerns in mind, I do not mean to claim that Plato conceives of the participants in this way in all contexts. He might not. My claim rather is that the importance of the quasi-Anaxagorean picture of the participants in Plato has not yet been recognized as clearly as it should be. And the failure to recognize its importance is, in part, no doubt due to the fact that it is difficult wholly to see this strand in Plato's thinking and to keep its implications fully in view. There

---

[43] On this point, Prauss's "Ding und Eigenschaft" is once again instructive.

is something of a paradox in the further fact that this difficulty—or so I am maintaining—is itself a prominent result of the *Categories'* success.

One further comment on Plato. I have deliberately refrained from speaking of Plato's Theory of Forms *in propria persona*, and will continue doing so. This is because I believe that, in the dialogues, we do not find anything that is, strictly speaking, a *theory* of Forms.[44] Rather, what we find in the dialogues are various theoretical arguments, claims, and proposals. A central one of these—perhaps the preeminent one—is that we cannot account for how the ordinary, perceptible world is, purely in terms of the ordinary, perceptible items that constitute this world. Thus we need to postulate certain other items; these items, however, are *not* apprehensible by perception; nonetheless, on the basis of reason, we can infer that there must be such items. Postulating Forms thus is a distinctively theoretical move on Plato's part. But what the dialogues give us is a *picture* of Forms. They also leave us with the task of articulating that picture and furnishing an adequate account of what the claim that there must be Forms comes to. We might equally well say that the dialogues leave us with the task of formulating a theory of Forms. But the picture of Forms, and of their relation to the sensible world, which Plato actually does present—by way of what are, after all, relatively few remarks, scattered throughout various dialogues—is not yet the theory. This picture rather presents some crucial constraints on any fully worked-out theory that we might be able to provide. Such a theory will need to answer to, or incorporate, or perhaps, in some respects, even go beyond that picture. (I will return to the question of what it means to say that Plato does not have a theory of Forms in Part II, Section 11.)

Now in my discussion of Plato, I will in fact be ascribing a number of very specific claims and arguments about the Forms to him, which at times will seem to go beyond the texts themselves. Is this approach not directly in tension with the remarks about the absence of a theory of Forms in the dialogues? It is not. Offering such claims and arguments is rather part of

---

[44] The perhaps most thoughtful and reflective set of considerations for why we should hesitate to ascribe a theory of Forms to Plato is provided by W. Wieland, in his *Platon und die Formen des Wissens* (Göttingen, 1982). See chap. 2, § 8: "*Ideen ohne Ideenlehre*," pp. 125–50, esp. pp. 148–50. (It is unfortunate that this brilliant, nuanced, and provocative work has not yet received the careful attention it decidedly deserves.) The question of whether Plato has a theory of Forms is briefly discussed by J. Annas in her *An Introduction to Plato's Republic* (Oxford, 1981), pp. 217, 235–36. Cf. also K. Sayre, "Why Plato Never Had a Theory of Forms," and C. Griswold, "Commentary on Sayre," both in *Proceedings of the Boston Area Colloquium in Ancient Philosophy* 9 (1993).

the task indicated in the previous paragraph—steps to be taken towards formulating a version of the theory only hinted at in the dialogues. Indeed, these steps will not provide a full-fledged theory either, but will bring into sharper focus what such a theory would need to account for, and what shape it would need to take.

To return to our story. Despite the fact that attributing the quasi-Anaxagorean picture to Plato brings with it genuine interpretative gains, we will also see new problems arising, especially once Plato extends this picture in the direction that is of greatest interest to him. For he wants to consider entities like justice, virtue, and beauty, not just items like gold or silver, or the hot and the cold, and the wet and the dry. But these entities that are of primary interest to Plato are far less readily construable as literally being *ingredients* in the participants that are just, virtuous, or beautiful than were the more straightforwardly physical stuffs and quasi-stuffs Anaxagoras had relied on. Moreover, if Plato's picture is extended to cover natural kinds—and Aristotle apparently thought that Plato did so extend it—problems of this sort become especially telling: for how is Man to be thought of as an *ingredient* in human beings, or Animal in animals?

However, most troubling, from an Aristotelian perspective, is something else: this picture seems not to allow for a genuine contrast between what a thing essentially is, and what it merely happens to be.

Aristotle criticizes certain Presocratics, including Anaxagoras, for treating things—especially living organisms—as if they were in effect mere *heaps* of *stuff* (see *De Caelo* III, 4, 302[b]10–26; cf. *Physics* I, 6, 189[a]32–34).[45] Suppose we are confronted with such a heap. Does the heap remain the *same* heap, if we add or subtract some of the stuff or stuffs already present in it? Does the heap remain the *same* heap, if we add some different stuff? Is there even such a thing as being *this* heap, independently of its being constituted out of the stuff that actually does constitute it? According to Aristotle, the answers to all such questions are in effect arbitrary. But if we ask the analogous questions about things (Aristotle thinks) the answers

---

[45] In this passage from *Phys.* I, 6, Aristotle is criticizing Empedocles, not Anaxagoras. But the objection applies equally to both: "We say that *ousia* cannot be contrary to *ousia*. So how could (an) *ousia* come from what are not *ousiai*? How can non-*ousia* be prior to (an) *ousia*?" With the *De Caelo* passage, compare Alexander of Aphrodisias *In Met.*, 98, 8–9, which may derive from Aristotle's now lost *On Ideas*; the criticism is directed against Eudoxus, but Aristotle sees Eudoxus as relevantly similar to Anaxagoras (cf. *Met.* 991[a]9–19).

are not arbitrary. There is a clear-cut distinction between a *change* that a (living) thing can undergo, whilst remaining the same thing, and its *replacement*—the initial generation of the thing, which results in a new thing, or the destruction of the thing, which results in the absence of the old one (and perhaps in the presence of another, new one, or other new ones). Thus according to Aristotle, it is wrong to assimilate things to heaps. In particular, while a heap *can* be identified with the stuff that constitutes it, a thing *cannot* likewise be identified with what constitutes it. In the parlance of contemporary metaphysics, we can say that while Aristotle holds that *mereological essentialism* is possible, perhaps even mandatory, in the case of heaps, in the case of bona fide things, mereological essentialism must be rejected. (At least it must be rejected, if we think of the parts of a thing as being parts in the most straightforward sense of part.) This is because whatever it is that makes a thing be the very thing it is, cannot be a further constituent of the thing, on a par with all the other constituents. Thus whatever it is that makes a thing be the very thing it is will either not be a part of the thing at all, or if it is (somehow) a part of the thing, it will be a part in a wholly different way than its other constituents are. (For this line of argumentation, see *Metaphysics* VII, 17 and VIII, 3. In the *Metaphysics* and *De Anima*, this whatever-it-is, is the form—as distinguished from the matter—in a form-matter compound. We might gloss the Aristotelian notion of form as: the internal structure of a thing, in contrast to what gets structured. Thus, to take a typical example, the way in which the architect's or the house-builder's plan of the house is 'in' the finished house is completely different from the way in which the various physical constituents are in the house, say, the timber and the nails.)[46]

Alternatively, we could say, as Aristotle sometimes does, that while both a heap and a thing are *one*—for each is unified such as to be one heap, or

[46] One factor that complicates properly understanding Aristotle's account of form and matter is that while he frequently *illustrates* these notions by means of examples drawn from the realm of artifacts, he holds that speaking most strictly, only natural things, e.g., plants and animals, have matter and form, and that the artifact examples are ultimately misleading. For the matter of an artifact, or its material constituents, can have an existence of their own, e.g., in the case of a house, as building materials that exist as such whether or not the house is built. Thus these examples may suggest that the matter quite generally has a certain sort of priority vis-à-vis the form: it could exist without the form, yet no form could exist without the matter. But in the case of natural things, Aristotle insists that the form rather has priority vis-à-vis the matter, and that the matter thus *cannot* exist independently of the form. This

one thing—the kind of unity characteristic of things is (so to speak) much stronger than that of heaps. One way that greater strength manifests itself is precisely in the fact that the kinds of questions adverted to in the previous paragraph have determinate, nonarbitrary answers in the case of things (according to Aristotle), but only arbitrary ones in the case of heaps. This shows (Aristotle holds) that things are *genuine* unities, whose cause of being one is (as we might say) *intrinsic* to them, while heaps are merely accidental unities, whose cause of being one is wholly *extrinsic* to them.

From Aristotle's perspective, Plato's quasi-Anaxagoreanism leaves him vulnerable to a similar line of criticism (again see *Metaphysics* VII, 17 and VIII, 3). For according to Aristotle, Plato too has no good way of distinguishing between a participant *changing* (while remaining the same participant) and a participant being *replaced* (by some new participant), because he ultimately has no clear way of regarding the participant as anything other than a 'mixture', that is, as anything other than a mere heap, rather than a thing. Thus, as a first approximation, what is wrong with the Platonic view is that it treats all predication in the sensible world as, in effect, accidental predication. (The restriction to the sensible world is important, because, as already adumbrated in connection with the self-predication sentences, different questions arise regarding predication in the realm of Forms.)

The Late-Learners of the *Sophist* have a view that in one important respect sounds like a promising alternative to Plato's. For they seemingly do allow for things; indeed, they seemingly allow that ordinary things can count as bona fide objects. But their concern that one thing should not be made into two, nor two into one (see *Sophist* 251b6–7), leads them to place very stringent restrictions on what can be predicated of what. Thus while we can, for example, say of a man that he is a man, or of a good (thing) that it is good, we are forbidden to say of the man that he is good, or of the good (thing) that it is a man. According to the Late-Learners, each item has only a single λόγος, where this seems to mean, that *only* (something like) self-predication is possible. This view sounds strange, not to say outlandish. (Examining the relevant passages of the *Sophist* will confirm its strangeness, but show it not to be as outlandish as it at first sounds.) The strangeness results from what I will argue is wrong

---

point alone should suffice for showing that we must exercise considerable caution in moving from the artifact examples to the items for whose sake Aristotle introduces form and matter. Still, for present purposes, these examples may help us to grasp, in a preliminary and rough way, what Aristotle means when he speaks of the form and the matter of a thing.

(from Aristotle's perspective) with the Late-Learners: namely that, at the level of a first approximation, they treat all predication as if it were, in effect, essential predication.

But what the problems with the views of Plato and the Late-Learners really reveal, in Aristotelian terms, is that we need both essential and accidental predication. From the perspective underlying and underwriting the *Categories*, we could say the following: at least some items must both be something or other (in and of themselves), and have certain features. Aristotle discovers that these items, in order to play the role of mediating between the alternatives of Platonism and Late-Learnerism—alternatives which have shown themselves to be extremely unattractive—must be *things*.

5. THE TASK OF PART III: THE *CATEGORIES* ONCE MORE— THE ROLE OF THE '-ONYMIES'

Thus I return to Aristotle in Part III. We will see the crucial importance of the '-onymies' for his program; he uses them precisely to make room for things in a way that does mediate between the Scylla of Platonism and the Charybdis of Late-Learnerism. But we will also see that some of the notions which Aristotle relies on in the *Categories* (and *Topics*) in presenting his ontological picture lead to difficulties—difficulties that threaten to undermine that whole picture. Most problematic is Aristotle's notion of the *differentia*. On the one hand, it is crucial for articulating Aristotle's notions of species and genus—indeed, the differentiae in part serve to constitute the species and genera. (Recall that for Aristotle, and for Plato and the Academy, species are arrived at by dividing genera via the differentiae; think of arranging living things on Linnaean trees.) On the other hand, the ontological status of the differentiae proves ambiguous and unstable— for some of what Aristotle says, assimilates them to things (*ousiai*), but some of what he says, to features.[47] Yet a central goal of his project had been sharply to demarcate things from features. So finding items that (appear to) fall on both sides of this divide is problematic, to say the least.

However, we will find a way of interpreting Aristotle's unclarity or inconsistency about the differentiae that not only defuses this threat, at

---

[47] This difficulty with the differentiae was already recognized by the ancient commentators; see for example Porphyry *In Arist. Cat. Expos.*, 94, 27–96, 3, or Ammonius *In Arist. Cat. Comm.*, 45, 5–46, 19.

least to some extent, but sheds further light on his overall project. We will see that the linguistic tests which Aristotle proposes and relies on in arriving at his distinctions—and which lead to the problems about differentiae—are best treated as heuristic devices, not as ultimate standards. These tests and the linguistic data (according to Aristotle) can and do reveal deep facts about the structure of the ontology. However, once that structure is properly understood and systematically articulated, further linguistic data which might seem to undermine the ontological claims can be set aside; more precisely, at this stage, language can be refined, regimented, or even reformed to conform with the ontological picture. (Thus, if you will, what starts out sounding like a descriptive project ends up being, in large part, a revisionary one.) It is a testimony to the remarkable success of Aristotle in the *Categories* that the theoretically motivated picture he presents there could have come to seem to be a simple reflection of ordinary language and its grammar. This makes it all the more striking that Aristotle himself calls it into question later in his career. That further story, however, will remain untold in the present work.

6. FINAL METHODOLOGICAL PRELIMINARIES

The use made of secondary literature in the essays that follow is deliberately selective: as anyone familiar with the texts and issues to be discussed knows all too well, the body of relevant literature is extensive indeed. In no way do the references in the essays aim at completeness. I have sought primarily to refer to books and articles which have proved especially illuminating, and to which I am heavily indebted. Secondly, I have included references to certain works that readers may find interesting and valuable, especially ones that lie somewhat further afield than those familiar exegetical and critical writings which, for the last fifty years or so, have formed the center of interpretative efforts seeking to make philosophical sense of these Aristotelian and Platonic texts. Thirdly, I mention and cite works which offer particularly clear formulations of points with which I disagree. I tend not to discuss such works at length, nor in a fully nuanced way. This may well make the criticisms of them sound more polemical than they might have, if formulated more extensively and more judiciously. Here I have been guided by the thought that some sacrifice of nuance (and the epicycles and digressions it would necessarily entail) for the sake of providing greater *Übersichtlichkeit*—of maintaining sharper focus on the central line of argument—is a worthwhile trade-off.

Finally, it may occasion surprise that I have mentioned Martin Heidegger several times in this introduction. Heidegger's interpretations (if that is the right word) of ancient Greek philosophy have not won widespread acceptance—and certainly not among analytic philosophers, analytically inclined historians of philosophy, or traditionally oriented classical philologists. On the whole, this rejection of Heidegger, or rather, the refusal to engage with him, is probably justified—especially on points of detail. Yet what comes to be overlooked in that rejection and refusal is the importance of the kind of inquiry Heidegger is urging on us. Heidegger seeks to remind us of the need to uncover paths of thinking that have been covered over, and thereby to recover what he often calls *ursprüngliches Denken*, or, *das ungedachte Denkwürdige*.[48] He rightly reminds us that "the unspoken standard for the interpretation and evaluation of the early thinkers is the philosophy of Plato and Aristotle."[49] This should not be understood as a familiar-sounding and rather banal historicist claim to the effect that we should seek to understand those thinkers only 'in their own terms' or only as situated 'within their own time and place'.[50] Much less is it the claim that the vocabulary Plato and Aristotle employ in reporting and discussing earlier views inevitably falsifies those views.[51] Heidegger's point is deeper and more subtle. The task is to re-think what has come to be *unthought*, because it is no longer reflected on, and so no longer straightforwardly *available* for reflection.

---

[48] The former phrase is usually (and not especially felicitously) rendered as 'primordial' or 'originary thinking'; the latter might be rendered as 'the unthought-but-worthy-of-thought'; see, for example, Heidegger, "Moira (Parmenides, Fragment VIII, 34–41)," in *Vorträge und Aufsätze* (Stuttgart, 1954), p. 237.

[49] "Das unausgesprochene Richtmaß für die Deutung und Beurteilung der frühen Denker is die Philosophie von Platon und Aristoteles." "Der Spruch des Anaximander," *Holzwege*, p. 297.

[50] Sceptically inclined historicists will of course hold that we are similarly situated within our time and place, and caught up in our own terms of thinking to such an extent that we cannot genuinely understand philosophers of other times, if that is to be a matter of understanding them in their own terms rather than ours. I discuss this kind of historicism briefly in my "The Origins of the Modern Historiography of Ancient Philosophy," *History and Theory* 35 (1986).

[51] This seems to be the view of H. Cherniss: "We know that certain concepts and theories were introduced by Aristotle and others by Plato. If a Presocratic theory is presented in a way which involves such a notion, there is clearly something wrong with the statement." See his *Aristotle's Criticism of Presocratic Philosophy* (Baltimore, 1935), p. xi. This is far too crude. There need be *nothing* wrong with such a presentation. (Think of Aristotle's use of ὁμοιομερής—usually rendered just in the transliterated form, as 'homoiomerous'—in characterizing Anaxagoras's views; this a word Anaxagoras did not use, but is Aristotle wrong

My aim in the following essays is not to offer a comprehensive interpretation of the *Categories*. My aim rather is to locate and to retrace the path of thinking—a path I am calling the discovery of things—which led Aristotle to arrive at and embrace the ontological picture that finds its expression in the early chapters of that work. It will therefore be important to analyze carefully not only what the relevant texts explicitly say, but to recover *das Denkwürdige* that underlies those texts; for on this point, I share Heidegger's conviction, expressed in the passage from "Der Ursprung des Kunstwerks" which serves as the epigraph to this introduction, that we have often "forgotten" what was once "unaccustomed," precisely because it has come to be part of "long-standing custom." Thus the goal of the present investigation is in line with the objectives Heidegger sets, even if both the method of investigation and the style of exposition that I adopt are very different from those associated with Heidegger's name.[52] With these various introductory concerns now addressed, let us turn to Aristotle's *Categories*.

---

to do so? See also Part II, Section 7 below.) Equally, having, say, a Presocratic philosopher's *ipsissima verba* offers absolutely *no* guarantee that we will be in a position to interpret them correctly. In "Der Spruch des Anaximander," Heidegger insists that we must distinguish between what we might describe as merely *literal* translations and genuinely *faithful* ones (p. 297; cf. p. 326 where he asks, about a given translation, "Aber ist dieses Wörtliche schon wortgetreu?"—"But does the fact that this translation is literal make it faithful?"). The counterpart of Heidegger's point could equally well have been made about interpretation. Cherniss's position seems to be a curious mixture of exaggerated scepticism and naive optimism. Neither the scepticism nor the optimism is warranted.

[52] A quick glance at an essay like "Der Spruch des Anaximander" suffices for seeing clearly those features of Heidegger's thinking and writing that make readily understandable why his work on ancient philosophy has not enjoyed the kind of reception one might have expected it would have had except for those features—after all, Heidegger is arguably the twentieth century's major philosopher, and he is certainly the one who has engaged with ancient Greek thought most extensively. Indeed, a quick glance at that essay (or at any other of his works on Greek philosophy) also makes readily understandable why readers of Heidegger often recoil from his writings with outright revulsion. Consider only the bloated and pretentious phraseology; the attempts at elevated or even poetic language, attempts that simply seem embarrassing; the self-important grandiosity; the bizarre speculations about the fate of thought; and so on.

Setting the Stage:
The "Antepraedicamenta" and the
"Praedicamenta"

> . . . let us ask why on earth the philosopher is
> contented with obscure teaching. We reply that it is
> just as in the temples, where curtains are used for the
> purpose of preventing everyone, and especially the
> impure, from encountering things they are not worthy
> of meeting. So too Aristotle uses the obscurity of his
> philosophy as a veil, so that good people may for that
> reason stretch their minds even more, whereas empty
> minds that are lost through carelessness will be put to
> flight when they encounter sentences like these.[1]
> (*Ammonius,* On Aristotle's Categories)

1. Preliminary Remarks: The Role of the First Two Chapters of the Treatise

It has long been noticed that Aristotle's *Categories*, in the form in which we have this work, does not form a unified treatise.[2] In the first century B.C., Andronicus of Rhodes began the tradition of focusing on the first part (cc. 1–9) and neglecting the obviously fragmentary and incomplete second part (cc. 10–15).[3] Andronicus was also the first person we know to have had doubts about the authenticity of the second part; he argued

---

[1] Ammonius, *On Aristotle's Categories*, tr. S. M. Cohen and G. B. Matthews (Ithaca, N.Y., 1991), p. 15 (= Ammonius *In Cat.*, 7, 7–14 Busse).

[2] See M. Frede, "Titel, Einheit und Echtheit der aristotelischen Kategorienschrift," in *Zweifelhaftes im Corpus Aristotelicum*, ed. P. Moraux and J. Wiesner (Berlin, 1983). (Translated as "The Title, Unity and Authenticity of the Aristotelian *Categories*" in Frede, *Essays.*)

[3] On Andronicus, see P. Moraux, *Der Aristotelismus bei den Griechen*, 2 vols. (Berlin, 1973–84), 1:45–136, and J. Barnes, "Roman Aristotle," in *Philosophia Togata*, vol. 2, ed. J. Barnes and M. Griffin (Oxford, 1997), esp. pp. 21–44.

that it had been attached to the main work by those who wanted to call it "Before the Topics" or "Pre-Topics" (Πρὸ τῶν τόπων or Πρὸ τῶν τοπικῶν).[4] Discussions of the unity of the treatise have, quite naturally, concentrated on the connection between the first part of the work and the so-called "Postpraedicamenta."[5] However, it is hardly the case that this first part, on its own, forms an independent, unified work. Indeed, the traditional division of the *Categories* into the "Antepraedicamenta" (cc. 1–3), the "Praedicamenta" (cc. 4–9), and the "Postpraedicamenta" (cc. 10–15) shows that already in antiquity, the first part of the treatise was thought itself to consist of two natural groupings. Yet while commentators maintain that Chapters 1–3 are introductory, the relationship between these chapters and Chapters 4–9 has never been made sufficiently clear. The aporia, apparently first raised by Nicostratus, of why Aristotle begins with a discussion of homonymy in a work about categories is symptomatic of this perceived lack of connection or transition.[6] The fact that later commentators went to some lengths to address this question shows that it was perceived to be a real problem. (See, for example, Porphyry *In Arist. Cat. Exp.* 59, 34 ff.) And Nicostratus's aporia seems apposite even if we give up the thought that the treatise is a treatise about categories: we still would like to know how the "Antepraedicamenta" are related to the body of the work. Addressing this issue is one of our central tasks.

Each of the first two chapters of the treatise provides us with a classification of things. But, as mentioned in the introduction, it is far from clear how the two classificatory schemata are related. The juxtaposition of Chapters 1 and 2 in fact calls into question the unity of the "Antepraedicamenta" themselves, for there seems to be no motivating transition between these chapters. Indeed, at first glance it looks as if the distinctions from Chapter 1—that is, the '-onymies'—are quite irrelevant not just to Chapter 2, but to the rest of the work as well. (Of course $3^a33–34$, $3^b8–9$, $6^b11–14$, and, especially, $10^a27–^b11$ show that Aristotle does make use of them.) Moreover, while the distinctions from Chapter 2 look fairly systematic,

---

[4] See Simplicius *In Cat.*, 379, 8–12; compare both Boethius *In Cat.* IV, 263 B3 ff. (Migne, *PL* 64), as revised by J. Shiel in his "Boethius and Andronicus of Rhodes," *Vigiliae Christianae* 11 (1957): 183, and also Ammonius *In Cat.*, 14, 18–20. See also Frede, 'Titel, Einheit und Echtheit," pp. 11–16.

[5] See Frede, "Titel, Einheit und Echtheit," p. 3.

[6] Simplicius *In Cat.*, 21, 2–4. On Nicostratus, K. Praechter's "Nikostratos der Platoniker," *Hermes* 57 (1922), reprinted in his *Kleine Schriften* (Hildesheim, 1973), remains fundamental; on his dates (middle of the second century A.D.), see Moraux, *Der Aristotelismus bei den Griechen*, 2:528–29.

those of Chapter 1 do not. Symptomatic of this seeming lack of systematicity is the fact that commentators have often thought that the notion of paronymy is not on a par with those of synonymy and homonymy.[7] Thus it will be useful to begin with the first chapter. But let us remind ourselves of how the text reads:[8]

CHAPTER 1

1ª1. Items that have only a name in common, but where the account of being[9] corresponding to the name is different, are called *homonyms*. For

---

[7] See J. Ackrill, *Aristotle's Categories and De Interpretatione* (Oxford, 1963), p. 72. G. E. L. Owen believes the notion of paronymy is "merely grammatical" (see "Logic and Metaphysics in Some Earlier Works of Aristotle," p. 188), and he proceeds on the assumption that the philosophically important distinction Aristotle is working with in his early works is only "the simple dichotomy of synonymy and homonymy" (ibid., p. 192); cf. also "Aristotle on the Snares of Ontology," pp. 261–64; and "The Platonism of Aristotle," pp. 208–11; all in *LSD*. Barnes says, in connection with Speusippus, "paronymy has no place with the other *onymies*" ("Homonymy in Aristotle and Speusippus," *Classical Quarterly*, n.s. 21 [1971]: 75); and since he cites Ackrill, Ammonius, and Olympiodorus, he presumably believes the same is true for Aristotle. Unlike Owen, J. L. Austin recognizes the significance of paronymy (see "ἀγαθόν and εὐδαιμονία in the *Ethics* of Aristotle," in his *Philosophical Papers*, 2d. ed., ed. J. O. Urmson and G. J. Warnock [Oxford, 1970], pp. 26–27), but he assimilates paronymy to things being spoken of πρὸς ἕν (this is what Owen called "focal meaning").

[8] The translation is my own, though I am much indebted to Ackrill's exemplary version, and at times follow him closely. I use angled brackets around words to supplement or paraphrase the extremely compressed formulations Aristotle employs; they do *not* indicate actual supplements to the Greek text! For the convenience of readers wishing to compare the present version with Ackrill's, I have followed his paragraph divisions.

[9] Ackrill uses 'definition of being' for λόγος τῆς οὐσίας. (On how to understand *ousia* here, see p. 43 and n. 15 below.) As Steve Strange reminds me, there is a question about the text worth noting briefly. In the *Categories*, the phrase λόγος τῆς οὐσίας first occurs at 1ª2 and 1ª4, in connection with the definition of homonyms, then at 1ª7 and 10, in connection with synonyms. But according to Simplicius (*In Cat.*, 29, 28–30, 5), Porphyry, in his longer, now lost commentary, said that Andronicus of Rhodes and Boethus of Sidon had not taken up the words τῆς οὐσίας in their texts of the *Categories* at 1ª2, because they had not found them in all the manuscripts; but, again according to Simplicius (30, 5 ff.), Porphyry himself did include them, following Herminus. (Cf. Porph. *In Arist. Cat. Expos.*, 64, 22–65, 11.) It would appear that there was even greater disagreement about reading the words τῆς οὐσίας in 1ª7 (cf. Minio-Paluello's ap. crit. ad loc.). But when Porphyry comes to discuss the issue at 68, 15 ff., he indicates clearly that even if the text were only to read λόγος that that would need to be understood as λόγος τῆς οὐσίας, i.e., as something like an account or definition. Cf. also S. Strange's comment, in his translation of Porphyry, *On Aristotle's Categories* (Ithaca, N.Y. 1992), p. 49 n. 75. In the *Topics*, Aristotle uses the shorter forms (i.e., without τῆς οὐσίας). For homonymy, see *Top.* I, 15: ἕτερος γὰρ ὁ κατὰ τοὔνομα λόγος αὐτῶν (107ª20); for synonymy, see VI, 10: συνώνυμα γὰρ ὄν εἷς ὁ κατὰ τοὔνομα λόγος (148ª24–25).

example, both a man and a picture are animals.[10] They have only the name in common, but the account of being corresponding to the name is different; for if someone were to render <the answer to the question>, what is it, for each of them, to be an animal, he will render a distinct account for each one.

1ᵃ6. Items that have a name in common, and where the account of being corresponding to the name is the same, are called *synonyms*. For example, both a man and an ox are animals. Each of these is called (an) animal by a common name, and the account of being is also the same; for if someone were to render the account of each—what it is to be an animal for each of them—he will render the same account.

1ᵃ12. Items that receive their name from something, with a difference in grammatical ending, are called *paronyms*. For example, the grammarian receives his name from grammar, the courageous receive theirs from courage.

In examining Chapter 1, we will want especially to see if the '-onymies' might not be systematically related after all. We will also want to see why Aristotle introduces this classification in the first place. Given the fact that Speusippus produced a rather similar schema, we would also like to see how such divisions fit in with projects with which the Academy was concerned.[11]

First, though, a note about the notation. Throughout, lowercase letters are used for nonlinguistic items; and uppercase letters are used for expressions quite generally, while *S* and *P* are used to signal that the expressions are being used as the subject- and predicate-expressions in a sentence of the form, '*S* is *P*'.[12] Given the availability of participles in Greek, even sentences that are not in this form initially, e.g., 'Cassandra runs' or 'Motion moves' can be rewritten into the canonical form, i.e., 'Cassandra is running' and 'Motion is moving'.[13] (Note that this rewriting should not be construed as importing a contrast in *verbal aspect* or *Aktionsart* analogous to the contrast between the English present progressive and simple

---

[10] See LSJ, s.v. ζῷον; when the term is used in the sense of 'picture' it need *not* refer to a picture of an animal, but can be used for picture or figure quite generally. However, it seems that Aristotle is here thinking of the depiction (τὸ γεγραμμένον) of a human being.

[11] See Boethus apud Simplicius *In Cat.*, 38, 19 ff.; cf. also *In Cat.*, 29, 5 and 36, 25–31 [= Fragments 32a–c L / 68a–c T]. I will briefly consider Speusippus in Appendix 2.

[12] I wish to leave aside the delicate and complicated question of whether we should think of only ' . . . *P*' as the predicate, or perhaps rather ' . . . is *P*'.

[13] The converse is also true, i.e., 'Cassandra is running' can be rewritten as 'Cassandra runs'. The remarks about Lycophron at *Physics* I, 2, 185ᵇ26 ff. suggest that some philosophers went so far as to coin new verbs, so as to be able to rewrite a sentence like 'Cassandra is white' as 'Cassandra 'whites'.'

present tenses. If there is a contrast here at all, it rather is something like 'Cassandra runs'—*meaning* Cassandra is running—versus 'Cassandra is [a] running [one]'. However, given that the paraphrase is supposed to leave the meaning unaffected, it seems we ought to regard the two formulations as simply equivalent.)

2. THE DEFINITION OF THE '-ONYMIES'

In Chapter 1 we find the following three definitions:[14]

(1) *x* and *y* are *synonyms* iff

(a) there is a name *P* such that both *x* and *y* are called *P* (i.e., if *X* is an expression for *x*, and *Y* for y, then both '*X* is *P*' and '*Y* is *P*' express truths);

and

(b) the account of what it is to be[15] *P* is the *same* for *x* and *y*. (See also *Topics* VI, 10, 148ª24–25.)

---

[14] I recall Michael Frede presenting a very similar account of the definitions from c. 1 in lectures at Princeton in 1977.

[15] That is, the λόγος τῆς οὐσίας (the account of their *ousia*; see also n. 9 above). Here in c. 1, *ousia* should presumably not be understood as *ousia* in the sense Aristotle will go on to discuss in cc. 4 and 5. Note that at the start of the later discussion of *ousia* in the *Categories* sense, at 1ᵇ27–28, he is quite careful to say: "In rough outline, *ousia* is . . . " In other words, Aristotle is precisely *not* presupposing that we already know how the term is to be taken; this of course makes perfect sense, if the term had been used differently at the beginning of the treatise. Moreover, *Laws* X (895b1 ff.) shows that several of the key terms of *Cat.* 1 were used in the Academy. There we find οὐσία and λόγος τῆς οὐσίας used in the same way as in c. 1: i.e., for something like 'essence' and 'definition', respectively. Note also Plato's use of προσαγορεύω and ὄνομα. The whole passage from the *Laws* strongly suggests that Aristotle is presupposing familiarity with the Academy's discussions of the issues he goes on to treat in (the early chapters of) the *Categories*, and that the treatise should accordingly be seen as his contribution to those discussions.

This suggestion is reinforced by some observations of Philip Merlan's, in his "Beiträge zur Geschichte des antiken Platonismus: I. Zur Erklärung der dem Aristoteles zugeschriebenen Kategorienschrift," *Philologus* 89 (1934). Merlan notes the conspicuous role that *the-more-and-the-less* and the question of *opposites* play in Aristotle's detailed discussions of *ousia*, quantity, relatives, and qualities (in *Cat.* 5–8); and Merlan reminds us of the role these concepts play in the so-called Platonic *Prinzipienlehre* and the ontological speculations of the Old Academy more generally (see pp. 35–45). He is surely right also to conclude that the *Categories* must thus be directed towards an audience thoroughly familiar with the relevant debates and discussions in the Academy (p. 45).

(2) *x* and *y* are *homonyms* iff   (a) there is a name *P* such that both *x* and *y* are called *P*;

and

    (b) the account of what it is to be *P* is *not* the same for *x* and *y*. (See also *Topics* I, 15, 107[a]20; cf. VI, 2, 139[b]19–31.)

(3) *x* is a *paronym* of *y* iff   (a) *x* is called *P* after *y*;

and

    (b) the name *P* is linguistically derived from,[16] yet different from *the* name of *y*.

Before we can evaluate the import of these definitions there are various questions that we need to answer, or at least consider. There is, first of all, the general question, what is it for a thing to be *called* something? (N.B.—In the preceding sentence and throughout the present discussion, I am employing the term 'thing' in a completely general way, not restricted to things in the sense of primary *ousiai*.) More importantly, what is the relevant notion of a thing being called something *from* or *after* something? For, as Ackrill has noted, "The whole idea of *X*'s being called *X from something* is of importance in the *Categories*."[17] (Consider the uses of ἀπό in 1[a]12, 1[a]14, and in 10[a]27–10[b]11.)

Secondly, what is meant by a *name* in this context? More specifically, what is the significance of saying of some name that it is *the name* of something? (Notice the use of τοὔνομα in 1[a]2, 4, 7 and 13; cf. also 3[b]7.) Jonathan Barnes maintains that the '-onymies' are not mutually exclusive, because "things in general have more than one predicate true of them— more than one 'name.' " However he goes on to note that "if it were supposed that *each thing had only one name* [emphasis added], then Aristot-

---

[16] Aristotle's own locution is ἀπό τινος διαφέροντα τῇ πτώσει; but since the examples he gives are not ones involving a difference of grammatical case, strictly speaking, we should rely on a less technical notion. (See Porphyry *In Arist. Cat. Expos.*, 69, 20–29.) The point surely is that the name for the one item is somehow derived from the name of the other item, in such a way that it is manifest that the name is a derived form. (One further observation: in speaking this way, Aristotle is obviously not making a claim about the actual history of the language, that is, the paronymous forms need not have been introduced into Greek at a later time than the words from which they are 'derived'. Aristotle's point rather concerns something like the conceptual priority of the one form versus the others.)

[17] See Ackrill, *Aristotle's Categories*, pp. 72–73.

le's *onymies* would be exclusive." According to Barnes, "it is hard to avoid the impression that the commentators come near to adopting this supposition," but, he concludes, "it is an absurd supposition."[18] Yet in a footnote to this very sentence, he observes that "Aristotle speaks of *the* name"—in other words, Aristotle in fact does proceed as if each thing did have only one name—Barnes, however, finds himself unable to say whether "there is any significance in this."[19] My suggestion is that, in fact, we very much do need to ask: What, precisely, is the significance of this?

And of course, there is the question of what the relevant notion of an *account* is. (This is a question I will not take up directly, but we will get a fairly clear sense of what Aristotle has in mind in Section 4; cf. also Part III, Sections 1–2.)

Let us suppose that if we can apply a term T to x, x can be called T; and let us suppose that if x can be called T, T is a *name* of x.[20] Now Aristotle also explicitly speaks of *common names* in Chapter 1 (at 1ᵃ3, 7, and 9). While there is no reason to think that he is employing this as a worked-out technical notion, it is characteristic of the expressions Aristotle calls common names that several things can legitimately be named by them; indeed this is exactly what seems to make them be common names. (Thus all predicate-expressions, occurring in sentences where the subject-expressions refer to primary *ousiai*, turn out to be common names.) It is also characteristic of things—perhaps of all things—that more than one common name can be applied to each of them.

Yet not all names are common names: in the case that, say, N is a name of x such that only x can properly be called N (i.e., N is what we might call a *proper name* of x), let us say that N is *the name* of x.[21] (And let us stipulate that every x has only a single, genuine proper name.) It is reasonable to suppose that some names are used as proper names (e.g., 'Socrates', 'Aspasia'), while some (other?) names are used as common names (e.g., 'courageous', 'grammatical').[22]

[18] "Homonymy in Aristotle and Speusippus", p. 74.
[19] Ibid., p. 74 n. 3.
[20] Notice that this does not yet distinguish between nouns and adjectives; 6ᵇ11–14 suggests that perhaps even some verbs could count as names.
[21] I owe the suggestion that we should think of what Aristotle calls *the name* as the *proper name* to Michael Frede.
[22] The objection that more than one person can have the same proper name can easily be met, by supposing that the proper names (implicitly) come with the appropriate subscripts, or some similar device.

Is every name then (exclusively) either a proper or a common name?
No. Or rather, at least Plato and the Academy cannot answer: Yes. For
they are committed to the possibility that some expressions can function
both as common names and as proper ones.[23] Examples like the following
reveal why they are so committed. 'Man' (ἄνθρωπος) is a common name
of Socrates, Plato, Xanthippe, Aspasia and all the particular human beings;
however it is also the proper name of the Form or species (i.e., the εἶδος),
Man. Similarly, 'white' (λευκός) is a common name of all the things that
can correctly be called white; but it is also the proper name of the color,
white. (Some commentators go further and hold that in a sentence like,
'Socrates is white', the term 'white' is being used as both a common and
a proper name simultaneously.)[24] Moreover, Plato and the Academy rely
on the following quadripartite assumption:

> At least in some cases, if P is a common name of a group of items x,
> w, v, . . . (i.e., given X, W, V, . . . as suitable subject-expressions, and
> thus given all of 'X is P', 'W is P', 'V is P', etc. as true sentences), then
> (i) there is some item y, which
> (ii) has Y as its *proper name*,
> (iii) such that each of x, w, v, . . . are *called P after y*,
> (iv) because each of x, w, v, . . . are *appropriately related to y*.

Part (ii) of this assumption needs some comment. Certain cases prove to
be trivial. Consider, for example, the term 'white' and the color, white.
If 'white' is a common name of v and w (i.e., if 'V is white' and 'W is
white' are true), then (i') there is some y, namely, the color itself, which
(ii') has 'white' as its proper name, such that (iii') v and w are called white
after the color, because (iv') they are appropriately related to the color
(viz., they are colored white). But now consider the term 'just' and the
virtue, justice. Again, if 'just' is a common name of Socrates and Coriscus
(i.e., if 'Socrates is just' and 'Coriscus is just' are true), then (i") there is
some y, namely, justice, which (ii") has 'justice' as its proper name, such
that (iii") Socrates and Coriscus are called just, because (iv") they are
appropriately related to justice (viz., they are just individuals).

---

[23] A passage like *Phaedo* 103e2–104b4 shows that Plato has the relevant notion of a proper
name—in 103e3 and 104a2, he uses the locution 'its *own* name' in a way that is virtually
the same as Aristotle's use of '*the* name' in the *Categories*.

[24] See, for example, K. W. Mills, "Some Aspects of Plato's Theory of Forms: *Timaeus*
49c ff" *Phronesis* 13 (1968): 145–46. But cf. the critical remarks of J. Malcolm, "Semantics
and Self-Predication in Plato," ibid., 26 (1981): 289, who rightly notes that, in a sentence

Yet as we know from the dialogues, Plato is prepared to use *both* the abstract noun 'justice' and expressions like 'the just' or 'the just itself', as proper names for justice (i.e., the Form). The notation is meant, at this stage, to leave open which is *the name*; that is because Plato, at least in the middle dialogues, regards these various formulations as, in effect, the same name.[25] In other words, before the *Theaetetus* (see 182a–b), he seems to ascribe no ontological import to the sort of linguistic phenomena Aristotle tries to capture under the heading of paronymy. Or, equivalently, we could say that expressions like 'the Υ' and 'Υ-ness' or 'Υ-ity' (i.e., both the neuter definite article + adjective *and* the appropriate abstract nouns) are all *treated* as if they were one and the same name.[26]

This Platonic-Academic assumption, of course, is simply a formulation (perhaps generalized beyond what we find in Plato's dialogues), at the level of language, of (i) a version of the so-called One-Over-Many principle; (ii) the claim that this one (singled out by whatever means are appropriate) has a proper name; plus (iii) the claim that the many are called—or named—as they are from or after this one, because (iv) they stand in an appropriate relation to this one. It is endorsed by Plato in various places. And he uses the term *eponymy* to capture this way of being named after something, that is, the way ordinary things are called (what they are called) from or after the Forms in which they participate.[27]

Thus a participant is an eponym of a Form, if it has as (one of) its common name(s) the proper name of the Form. And in that case, a participant is called (what it is called) eponymously from or after the Form.

Morever, given that I am not distinguishing between the neuter definite article + adjective formulation of the proper name of a Form and the abstract noun formulation, I also do not distinguish between a participant being named *homonymously* after the Form in which it participates—in

---

like 'Socrates is white', the term 'white' in the first instance just is *a* common name of Socrates.

[25] J. Malcolm holds that " 'Justice' and 'just,' to take a particular instance, cannot by any stretch of the imagination be looked upon as being the *same name*" ("Semantics and Self-Predication," p. 287). This seems to me to be a mistake, at least to this extent: given that, in the relevant contexts, Plato freely moves between the abstract noun formulation and the neuter definite article + adjective formulation, it is clear that he attaches absolutely no significance to the (merely lexical) differences between the two sorts of formulation. Neither should we.

[26] For more on the neuter definite article + adjective construction, see pp. 15–16 above and p. 120 below.

[27] See, for example, *Phaedo* 102b2 and c10; 103b7–8; *Parmenides* 130e5–131a2; and *Timaeus* 65b5; 83c1–3.

47

Plato's sense of homonymy—and a participant being named *eponymously* after the Form in which it participates.[28] Calling the relation one of eponymy rather than homonymy, however, highlights the fact that the eponym, i.e., the participant, is not merely called by the same name as the Form, but is so called *from* or *after* the Form—and this surely is the force of, for example, *Phaedo* 100b–e; cf. 102b2.[29]

The fourth part of the assumption is needed to rule out cases of something being named from or after something, where the items named, however, stand in some merely accidental relation to one another.[30]

3. THE FOUR KINDS OF EPONYMY

However, given the account of the '-onymies' presented in the *Categories*, when x is called *P* after y (and this can always be expressed in a sentence of the form '*S* is *P*'), there turn out to be several possibilities, depending on how the predicate-expression, *P*, and the proper name of y, *Y*, are related, and on how the definitions of the items x and y are related. From the perspective of the *Categories*, Plato's single way of being named eponymously from or after something seems to break apart into four rather different ones, as shown in the following diagram.[31]

Now it may be objected that even if Speusippus and perhaps the Academy more generally take an interest in heteronymy (i.e., iv), Aristotle does not.[32] In fact, he does not discuss heteronymy by that name in *Cat.* 1, or

---

[28] J. Malcolm seems to think there is an important difference here; see "Semantics and Self-Predication," pp. 286–88.

[29] For more on eponymy, see T. W. Bestor, "Common Properties and Eponymy in Plato," *Philosophical Quarterly* 28 (1978), and "Plato's Semantics and Plato's *Parmenides,*" *Phronesis* 25 (1980).

[30] Bestor provides a useful overview of cases where the relation of eponymy is not metaphysically significant; see "Common Properties and Eponymy," pp. 194–96.

[31] I recall Michael Frede presenting a schema essentially the same as this in lectures at Princeton in 1977. Klaus Oehler offers a very similar division in his commentary on the treatise: Aristotle, *Kategorien,* tr. K. Oehler (Berlin, 1984), p. 162. Compare also M. Wedin, "The Strategy of Aristotle's *Categories,*" *Archiv für Geschichte der Philosophie* 79 (1997): 2 and n. 7

[32] The way I am using the term here does not exactly correspond to Speusippus's usage; see Fr. 32a L / 68a. However, Porphyry calls heteronyms "those of which both the name and the account is different," *In Arist. Cat. Expositio,* 69, 12–13. The terms 'synonym', 'paronym', and 'heteronym' are all explicitly reported as having been used by Speusippus (Fr. 32a L / F 68a T); and the context of Fr. 32b L / 68b T strongly suggests that Speusippus also used the term 'homonym'; cf. L. Tarán, *Speusippus of Athens* (Leiden, 1981), pp. 412–13.

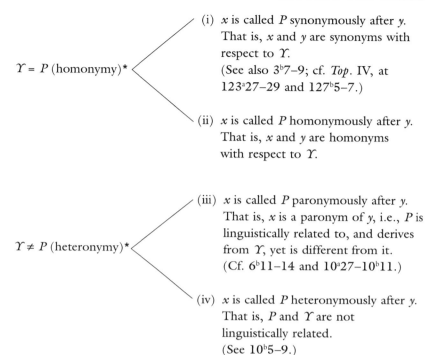

$\Upsilon = P$ (homonymy)*

(i) *x* is called *P* synonymously after *y*.
That is, *x* and *y* are synonyms with
respect to Υ.
(See also 3^{b}7–9; cf. *Top.* IV, at
123^{a}27–29 and 127^{b}5–7.)

(ii) *x* is called *P* homonymously after *y*.
That is, *x* and *y* are homonyms
with respect to Υ.

$\Upsilon \neq P$ (heteronymy)*

(iii) *x* is called *P* paronymously after *y*.
That is, *x* is a paronym of *y*, i.e., *P* is
linguistically related to, and derives
from Υ, yet is different from it.
(Cf. 6^{b}11–14 and 10^{a}27–10^{b}11.)

(iv) *x* is called *P* heteronymously after *y*.
That is, *P* and Υ are not
linguistically related.
(See 10^{b}5–9.)

*Obviously, 'homonymy' and 'heteronymy', as they occur in the left part of the diagram, must be regarded as generic or nontechnical notions, while in (ii) and (iv) they are specific, technical ones. Speusippus seems to have used the term 'tautonymy' for what I am calling 'generic homonymy'; see Fr. 32a L/68a T.

anywhere else.[33] However, the discussion of paronymy in Chapter 8 makes clear that Aristotle is perfectly familiar with cases of this sort: " . . . the good man is so called [sc. good] from virtue . . . ; but he is not called paronymously from virtue" (10^{b}7–9).[34] Thus although heteronymy (iv) is not expressly mentioned in Chapter 1, the schema given above reflects

[33] E. Heitsch says the term 'heteronym' was first introduced by Speusippus; see *Die Entdeckung der Homonymie*, Abhandlungen Akad. Mainz (1972), p. 50. It is certainly not attested for either Plato or Aristotle.

[34] David Sedley (in conversation) has suggested that the word 'from' (ἀπό) in 10^{b}7 seems as if it might refer only to the fact that the good man is called good on account of the virtue he has, rather than that the term 'good' is derived, nonparonymously, from the term 'virtue'. We cannot rule this out, but in the light of both 10^{a}27–29, "These, then, that we have mentioned are *qualities* (ποιότητες), while things called paronymously because of these, or called in some other way from them, are *qualified* (ποιά)," and 10^{b}9–11, "Qualified things

49

Aristotle's view of these different '-onymies' in the *Categories*—and in the *Topics*.[35] (Near the very end of Part I, we will see why it was natural for Aristotle to ignore heteronymy.)

4. THE DISTINCTIONS OF CHAPTERS 2 AND 3

Let us now turn briefly to the classificatory scheme of the second chapter (elaborated further in the beginning of c. 3 and in lines 2ª27–34 from c. 5). Again, let us first remind ourselves of the relevant part of the text:[36]

CHAPTER 2

[1ª16–19; for the excision of these lines from c. 2, see below, Appendix 1.]

1ª20. Of beings: (i) some are said of a subject but are not in any subject. For example, man is said of a subject, the individual man, but is not in any subject. (ii) Some are in a subject but are not said of any subject. (By 'in a subject' I mean what is in something, <but> not belonging as a part, and incapable of existing separately from what it is in.) For example, the individual knowledge-of-grammar is in a subject, the soul, but is not said of any subject; and the individual white is in a subject, the body[37] (for all color is in body), but is not said of any subject. (iii) Some are both said of a subject and in a subject. For example, knowledge is in a subject, the soul, and is also said of a subject, knowledge-of-grammar. (iv) Some are neither in a subject nor said of a subject, for example, the individual man or the individual horse—for nothing of this sort is either in a subject or said of a subject. Items that are individual and one in number are, without exception,[38] not said of any subject, but there is nothing preventing some of them from

---

(ποιά) are called <what they are called> paronymously from (ἀπό) the qualities (ποιοτήτων) we mentioned, or are called from (ἀπό) them in some other way," I find the second alternative somewhat more attractive. In any event, Aristotle says nothing to rule out one thing being called something after another heteronymously.

[35] The point about the *Topics* may seem controversial. But see Appendix 2.

[36] Once more, the translation is my own; though in the lines from c. 2, I follow Ackrill very closely. I have indicated additions (i.e., lines transposed from their traditional place) by vertical lines in the left margin.

[37] Despite the fact that Aristotle speaks of *the body* (τὸ σῶμα), he may well mean to be saying that all color is in body in general, i.e., that bodies (or surfaces) are the sorts of things that have colors, rather than that each color is in some particular body or other. See also my remarks in Part III, Section 1, p. 189.

[38] Ackrill's rendition of ἁπλῶς as 'without exception' seems correct, even if something like 'without qualification' or 'simpliciter' would be more literal.

being in a subject—for the individual knowledge-of-grammar is among the things that are in a subject.

Chapter 3

1ᵇ10. In case something is predicated of something else as of a subject, then, whatever items are said of what is predicated, all of them will also be said of the subject. For example, man is predicated of the individual man, and animal of man; so animal will also be predicated of the individual man—for the individual man is both a man and an animal.

[1ᵇ16–24; for the excision of these lines from c. 3, and for the transposition of the following lines from c. 5 to c. 3, see below, Appendix 1]

2ᵃ19. It is clear from what has been said that when something is said of a subject, necessarily, both the *name* and the *account* are predicated of the subject. For example, man is said of a subject, the individual man—<here> the name is obviously (γε) predicated (since you will be predicating man of the individual man), but equally, the account of man will be predicated of the individual man (since the individual man also *is* a man). Thus both the name and the account will be predicated of the subject.

2ᵃ27. But when something is in a subject, in most cases neither the name nor the account is predicated of the subject. Yet in some cases, nothing prevents the name from being predicated of the subject, but <nonetheless> it is impossible for the account to be predicated: for example, white, which is in a subject, the body, is predicated of the subject (since a body is said <to be> white). But the account of white will never be predicated of the body.

In Chapter 2, Aristotle draws the distinction between the two ways items can be *predicated of other items as their subjects*: something either (i) is SAID OF something as its subject, or (ii) is IN something as its subject.[39] Before proceeding any further, it is important once more to recall that, in the *Categories*, predication is a relation between things, not linguistic items. However, whenever we apply a common name to a thing, this will be a matter of (linguistically) predicating an expression of a (name of a) thing. And, in all cases, if *y* is (ontologically) predicated of *x*, there will be some sentence that expresses that *y* is predicated of *x*. (Note, however, that the surface grammar of a sentence may be misleading; we thus cannot

---

[39] As mentioned in the introduction, I follow F. Lewis in capitalizing the names of the relations from c. 2, in order to signal that these are technical terms, not be confused with their counterparts in more ordinary (philosophical) usage. Once more, however, let me add that in doing so, I do not mean to endorse his particular account of these relations.

directly infer what is being ontologically predicated of what, simply by looking at the subject- and predicate-expressions of simple subject-predicate sentences, of the form 'S is P'. Let us call a sentence of the form 'X is Y' *revelatory*, if it in fact expresses, and thus reveals, that y is predicated of x. We can, for our present purposes, restrict ourselves to sentences that are revelatory in this sense, and ignore the complications posed by the nonrevelatory ones.) We should also recall that, as noted in the introduction, Aristotle pays virtually no attention to anything like the use/mention distinction; thus he moves rather freely between mere linguistic predication and real predication; for the most part this does not cause any serious problems.[40] Now, as Chapter 2 makes clear, these two ways of predicating something of something cut across each other as shown in the chart.

	IN	Not IN
SAID OF	Genera and species of non-substantial items.	Genera and species of primary *ousiai*, i.e., the secondary *ousiai*.
Not SAID OF	Individual nonsubstantial items, like *this* white, or *this* knowledge-of-grammar.	Individual, i.e., primary *ousiai*, like *this* man, or *this* horse.

I would like, for the moment, to leave aside the fourfold division of items and consider rather some further things Aristotle says about these two basic ontological predication *relations*. In Chapter 3, at 1^{b}10–15, he goes on to point out that the SAID OF relation is transitive; that is to say, if z is SAID OF y, and y is SAID OF x, then z is also SAID OF x.[41]

---

[40] On this whole matter, see the very helpful discussion by A. Code in "Aristotle: Essence and Accident," in *Philosophical Grounds of Rationality*, ed. R. Grandy and R. Warner (Oxford, 1986), especially § 4, "Linguistic Predicability," pp. 422–23.

[41] Steve Strange has suggested that someone might object that, in 1^{b}10–15, Aristotle is talking about predication in general, not about something being SAID OF something as a subject. (In other words, the objection would have it that λέγεται at 1^{b}11 and ῥηθήσεται at 1^{b}12 are not being used in the sense of SAID OF.) Three considerations tell against this less restrictive reading. First, it leaves us with a false principle: for if z is predicated of y and y is predicated of x, it does not follow that z is predicated of x. The examples the ancient commentators give have the following form: genus is predicated of animal, animal is predicated of man, but genus is not predicated of man (see Ammonius *In Cat.*, 31, 2–12); or species

However, in the *textus receptus* of Chapter 3 there is nothing about the being IN relation. Perhaps Aristotle thinks it is quite obvious that this relation is not transitive; nonetheless some remark about it would have been helpful at this juncture. And we know, from Chapter 5, that Aristotle has things to say on the point. For 2^a27–34 precisely calls attention to a feature that distinguishes being IN a subject from being SAID OF a subject. Thus these lines (actually, the whole of 2^a19–34) should in any event be considered together with c. 2 + 1^b10–15, quite independently of whether they should be transposed in the way I have transposed them.

Now one crucial fact about the two relations defined in Chapter 2 (and characterized further in 1^b10–15 + 2^a19–34) is that while things (ὄντα) are being talked about and classified, they are classified on the basis of the expressions (λεγόμενα) used to refer to them or to introduce them into discourse. This is obviously true of the '-onymies' in Chapter 1: as we have seen, the relevant items come to be classified as homonyms, synonyms, or paronyms with respect to names. But it proves to be equally true of the SAID OF and being IN relations: if *y* is SAID OF *x*, both the *name* of *y* and the *definition* of *y*—for in effect, that is what the correct and relevant account of *y* is—can be predicated of *x*; yet if *y* is IN *x*, the *name* of *y* can in general *not* be predicated of *x*, but even in case it can be, the *definition* of *y* still *cannot* be predicated of *x*.

---

is predicated of man, man is predicated of Socrates, but species is not predicated of Socrates—for Socrates is not a species (see Porphyry *In Arist. Cat. Expos.* 80, 29–81, 22). The interpretations Porphyry and Ammonius offer of 1^b10–15 show that they construe the passage in the more restrictive sense, that is, as saying that the SAID OF relation is transitive. Secondly, the formulation in 1^b10–11 seems like a mere variant on the formulations of c. 2— with κατηγορῆται taking the place of λέγεται. But in that case, it seems entirely plausible to suppose that the further occurrences of κατηγορῆται are shorthand for κατηγορῆται ὡς καθ' ὑποκειμένου. (And perhaps we should even emend ῥηθήσεται at 1^b12 to κατηγορηθήσεται, although this would violate the principle of *lectio difficilior*.) Finally, the examples Aristotle gives suggest the more restrictive transitivity claim: if man is SAID OF the individual man, and animal is SAID OF man, then animal is SAID OF the individual man. See also Wedin, "The Strategy of Aristotle's *Categories*," pp. 14–17. The issue is complicated for him, since he holds that the very highest genera are the categories themselves; in other words, in the case of *ousia*, this means that *ousia* is SAID OF animal, which is SAID OF vertebrate, and so on (cf. Porphyry *Isagoge* 4, 21 ff.). But there are serious doubts about whether the *Categories* actually give us Porphyrian Trees, i.e., genus-species trees with the categories at the top level. Recall that Aristotle begins *Cat.* 6 by saying that there are four (irreducibly) *different* kinds of quantity (4^b20–22); and in *Cat.* 8, he says that "quality is one of the things spoken of in *many* ways" (8^b25–26; tr. Ackrill). There is, then, no *single* account of what a quantity is, or of what a quality is. This means that, at best, quantity and quality are predicated homonymously of whatever they are predicated. Thus at least quantity and

Thus a *test* (presented in 2ª19–34) of whether some *z* that actually is predicated of *x* is SAID OF *x*, or is IN *x*, will be to see whether the *name* of *z* can be applied to *x*, and to see, in case it can be applied, if this name can be replaced by the *definition* of *z*. We will have occasion to consider this test in greater detail in Part III. But we are able, already at this stage, to see how the classificatory notions of Chapters 1 and 2 + 3 (treating c. 3 as: [1ᵇ10–15 + 2ª19–34] minus [1ᵇ16–24]) are straightforwardly related.

(I) If *x* is called *N* synonymously after *y*, then *y* is SAID OF *x*.[42]
And if *y* is SAID OF *x*, *x* is synonymously called (what it is called) after *y*.

Socrates, for example, is called 'man' synonymously after the second substance or species, man; and man, the species, is SAID OF Socrates. (Note that this implies that the correct and relevant account of man, or what it is to be a man, will be the *same* for the individual and the species, as Aristotle expressly notes in *Topics* VI, 1, at 139ª26–27.[43] We will obviously need to investigate further why Aristotle is committed to this and, indeed, what it even means to make that claim.)

(II) On the other hand, if *y* is IN *x*, there are three possibilities:

(A) If the relevant names are the same, that is, if there is only one name here, then *x* is called homonymously (what it is called) after *y*.[44]

To use Aristotle's own example: Socrates is called 'white' homonymously after the color, white. (This implies that the correct and relevant account of what it is to be white will be *different* for Socrates and the color. As commentators sometimes say, Socrates *has* the color, white, while the color itself *is* white. Here again we will need to see what this amounts to.)

---

quality cannot be *genera* (and so, a fortiori, cannot be *highest genera*), because a genus is always predicated synomously of what it is predicated (*Cat.* 3ª33 ff.; cf. *Top.* 109ª34–109ᵇ12; 123ª27–29; and 127ᵇ5–7).

[42] Notice that *x* and *y* can be synonyms with respect to some name *M*, without either *x* being called *M* synonymously after *y*, or vice versa; e.g., Socrates (or man) and Fido (or dog) are synonyms with respect to 'animal'. In such a case, of course, *y* is neither SAID OF *x*, nor is *x* SAID OF *y*.

[43] *Topics* VI is concerned with definitions; and it is in that context that Aristotle says, "For the definition (ὁρισμός) of man ought to be true of every man" (139ª26–27); cf. also *Top.* IV, 3, 123ª27–29 and IV, 6, 127ᵇ5–7.

[44] On homonymous versus synonymous predication, see also the extensive discusion in *Topics* VI, 10, at 148ª23–148ᵇ22.

(B) But if these names are different, yet related, then *x* is called paronymously (what it is called) after *y* (e.g., Socrates is called 'just' paronymously after the virtue, justice).[45]

Moreover, if *x* is called *N* homonymously after *y*, then *y* is IN *x* (e.g., white is IN Socrates); and if *x* is called *N* paronymously after *y*, then again *y* is IN *x* (justice is IN Socrates).

(C) But if these names are different and *unrelated*, then *x* could be said to be called heteronymously (what it is called) after *y*.

Nothing in the text exactly corresponds to (C). But Chapter 8 makes clear that Aristotle has in mind two kinds of examples that can easily be subsumed under (C). (i) Suppose Crison is called '(a) runner' after a certain natural capacity, which, however, has no particular name—we might say, which has no *proper name*, but only admits of various descriptions (cf. 10ᵃ32–ᵇ5). Here we could say that Crison is called '(a) runner' after that capacity, not paronymously but in *some other way* (ἄλλως; cf. 10ᵃ28 and 10ᵇ11). Yet we could equally well say Crison is called '(a) runner' heteronymously after the relevant natural capacity. (ii) Suppose Pericles is called 'good' (σπουδαῖος) after the virtue (ἀρετή) he has (cf. 10ᵇ5–11). Here too he is called nonparonymously after the quality, virtue. And here too we could equally well say that Pericles is called 'good' heteronymously after virtue. Of course, in both (i) and (ii), Aristotle thinks of the quality as being IN the relevant individuals.

Why, though, does Aristotle neglect (C) and proceed as if (A) and (B) were sufficient? He has, I believe, three reasons for doing so. First, as he notes in the discussion of qualities in c. 8, "in most cases, indeed in practically all, things are called paronymously <after the qualities they have>, as the pale man <is called pale> from paleness, the grammatical <is called grammatical> from grammar, the just <is called just> from justice, and so on" (10ᵃ29–32). In other words, Aristotle holds that there are in fact very few actual instances of heteronymy. Secondly, it seems that we could easily enough coin a new term (i.e., an appropriate abstract noun) *based on* the adjectival form, in case the quality does not have a name; or we could substitute a new term (again, an appropriate abstract noun) *based on* the adjectival form, for the established name, in case the quality does

---

[45] Cf. *Topics* II, 2, 109ᵃ34–109ᵇ12.

have a name (e.g., substitute 'goodity' for 'virtue').[46] But if we were to do so, we would have changed what was initially an instance of something being named heteronymously after a quality into a matter of that thing now being named paronymously after that same quality (which has been given a new name). Finally, as we will see more clearly in Part III, Aristotle is especially concerned with cases where the surface grammar of the language can be misleading in a very particular way, namely, those cases where one might be led to confuse homonymy with synonymy. He introduces paronymy to shed light on homonymy, and, in effect, to reveal homonymy to be akin to paronymy rather than to synonymy. But when there either simply is no name at all for the quality, or when there is no linguistic relation between the name of the quality and the name of the qualified item, then there is no possibility of being misled in the ways about which Aristotle is concerned. So it is safe to ignore such cases. And thus there again is no need to be concerned about heteronymy as an actual, linguistic phenomenon. For all these reasons, we too can ignore (IIC) and proceed as if (I) and (IIA) and (IIB) were the only cases that mattered.

We are now in a position to see what is of greatest importance in all of this: contrary to our initial impression, there turns out to be a most intimate connection between the '-onymies' of Chapter 1 and the being SAID OF and being IN relations of Chapters 2 and 3. We have also seen that the various notions in Chapter 1 are themselves far from haphazardly related. We are not faced with homonymy and synonymy on the one hand, and paronymy on the other, as completely different sorts of ideas, not coordinate with one another. On the contrary, all of these '-onymies' are systematically related through the concept of a thing being named something after something. And the interest in things being named after something is, of course, taken over from Plato.

However, it is still not at all clear why Aristotle (and Speusippus too) should seek to divide Plato's relation of eponymy into these four kinds of eponymy. Unless we suppose, quite implausibly, that they are pursuing taxonomical complexity for its own sake, we will need an account or explanation of that division. In addition, as we have just noted, some

---

[46] I am using the made-up word 'goodity' (rather than 'goodness', which of course is unproblematic) to show how one might coin a new abstract noun for the kind of example Aristotle considers. LSJ, s.v. σπουδαῖος, in fact give the abstract noun σπουδαιότης as attested in the Pseudo-Platonic *Definitions*, in Diodorus Siculus, and in the Septuagint. What Aristotle says in the *Categories* suggests that he would have regarded this as an unacceptable solecism.

seemingly important and rather difficult questions arise about what, exactly, is implied by (I) and (IIA). All these issues can, I believe, be put in sharper focus by turning first to Plato, to get a sense of the broader philosophical context within which these Aristotelian schemata are developed and presented. That will be one of the central tasks of Part II. Appendix 1 to this part examines the text—and the proposed changes to it—more closely; but it is not needed for the main argument. In Appendix 2, I briefly consider a question that arises in connection with Speusippus's use of the '-onymies'; it, too, is not needed for the main argument.

Appendix 1

DIFFICULTIES WITH THE RECEIVED TEXT AND
A ROLE FOR CHAPTER 4

I AM INCLINED to think that the text of the first several pages of the *Categories* is in worse shape than it appears to be. In this appendix, I would like to consider several difficulties and offer *three* suggestions for their amelioration. The discussion will also serve to elucidate the role of c. 4. One way in which the raggedness of the text perhaps manifests itself is its very beginning. The first sentence of the treatise is hardly satisfactory: ὁμώνυμα λέγεται κτλ. There is no indication of what the treatise will be about.[1] This lack of an appropriate opening was evidently felt very early on. In Ammonius we read that "in the ancient libraries" there was another version of the *Categories*, also attributed to Aristotle, which began τῶν ὄντων τὰ μὲν ὁμώνυμα λέγεται, τὰ δὲ συνώνυμα, i.e., "*Of beings*, some are called homonyms, some synonyms" (*In Cat.* 13, 20–23).[2]

And, as Paul Moraux has suggested, Andronicus's paraphrase of the *Categories* may well have begun:[3]

---

[1] As M. Wedin, in his "The Strategy of Aristotle's *Categories*," *Archiv für Geschichte der Philosophie* 79 (1997), observes: "The *Categories* begins without fanfare. Missing is the promotional pitch customary in Aristotle's works, and even the obligatory announcement of the subject matter is absent" (p. 1). It seems to me that this actually understates the abruptness of the opening of the treatise.

[2] Olympiodorus (*Prolegomena* 24, 14–18) has ἔστι for λέγεται, and continues: . . . συνώνυμα τὰ δὲ πολυώνυμα. Simplicius (*In Cat.* 18, 16–20) reports that Adrastus, in his work, "On the Order of Aristotle's Writings," mentions another "brief and concise" version of our text, differing little from it, which had as its beginning: τῶν ὄντων τὸ μὲν ἔστιν . . . I am rather suspicious of the τό. One might think that the τό points to something like: τὸ μὲν γένος . . . , especially in light of the fact that Περὶ τῶν γένων τοῦ ὄντος and Περὶ τῶν δέκα γένων are also reported as titles. However, given the enormous interest in the question about the true subject matter of the treatise and the related question about its correct title, we would expect to learn of such an opening to the work, had anyone, e.g., Adrastus, known of it. This makes it extremely unlikely that any version, thought to have any kind of authoritative status, actually did contain the words τὸ μὲν γένος in the opening sentence. But in that case, τά seems better than τό, since we must assume that the version known to Adrastus continued more or less the way our familiar text does. Indeed, perhaps the version Ammonius reports as having been in the ancient libraries just is the version known to Adrastus.

[3] Moraux's reconstruction is based on Simplicius *In Cat.*, 21, 22–4; 26, 17–20; and 30, 3–5; see his *Der Aristotelismus bei den Griechen*, 2 vols. (Berlin, 1973–84), 1:101.

58

<u>τῶν λεγομένων</u> τὰ μὲν ἄνευ συμπλοκῆς λέγεται, τὰ δὲ μετὰ συμπλοκῆς· καὶ τῶν μὲν ἄνευ συμπλοκῆς ὁμώνυμα μὲν λέγεται, ὧν ὄνομα μόνον ταὐτόν, ὁ δὲ κατὰ τοὔνομα λόγος ἕτερος.

Of expressions, some are said without combination, others are said in combination; and of those said without combination, those are called homonyms which have only the same name, but where the account which corresponds to the name is different.[4]

Andronicus is clearly committed to the view that the treatise is about linguistic items, while the now lost second version (referred to by Ammonius) is committed to the view that it is about nonlinguistic entities. Yet even though both versions go some way towards making clear the intended subject matter of the treatise, both fail to provide a connection between Chapters 1 and 2.

On Andronicus's version, we would expect an explanation of ἄνευ συμπλοκῆς and μετὰ συμπλοκῆς, i.e., uncombined expressions and expressions used in combination (with other expressions).[5] This is of course provided at 1ᵃ17–19. Yet given the order of exposition Andronicus adopts, it surely would have been better to have provided that explanation *before* presenting the distinction between homonyms, synonyms, and paronyms. Moreover, Andronicus's opening makes the transition to ὄντα in 1ᵃ20 ff. even more abrupt than it already is. Why, in a treatise about λεγόμενα (expressions), does Aristotle suddenly start speaking about ὄντα (entities)? (To reiterate: I take λεγόμενα here to be a very general term for expressions; it will not necessarily cover the items that are *said of something as their subject,* a notion Aristotle introduces only in c. 2. As we have seen, that relation is an ontological one; though as we have also seen, given the way in which this relation is characterized, if *y* is SAID OF *x* as its subject, we can conclude certain facts about the expressions used to name the items *x* and *y*.)

The lost second version does not fare much better. For now supposing that the announced subject matter of the treatise is (at least primarily) ὄντα, 1ᵃ16–19 appears intrusive and quite unmotivated. Why should Aris-

---

[4] A peculiarity of this formulation is that it suggests that, for Andronicus, homonyms are names of expressions; but we would surely have expected them simply to be the expressions having differing accounts themselves. I do not know what to make of this.

[5] While there has been considerable discussion of which distinction, precisely, Aristotle has in mind, it seems that he means to distinguish *terms* or *expressions* standing in isolation from those used in *sentences.* In other words, the combination (συμπλοκή) of which he speaks is not just any concatenation of words, but one which yields sentences.

totle, after having classified entities into homonyms, synonyms, and paronyms, briefly speak about λεγόμενα κατὰ συμπλοκήν and ἄνευ συμπλοκῆς only to turn back to entities in 1ª20? What we know about possible alternate first sentences for the work does not seem to help much, either in ameliorating the abruptness of the opening of the treatise, or in compensating for the absence of any announcement about its subject matter.

But the difficulties we have just been considering point to a way in which the second chapter is in fact problematic by itself. It divides naturally into two parts, the first (1ª16–19) a division of expressions, the second (1ª20–1ᵇ9) of entities. While either of the divisions is perhaps sufficiently clear on its own, the connection between the two parts of the chapter is not. Nothing in the discussion of ὄντα seems to presuppose or to make use of the distinction between uncombined expressions and expressions used in combination. One can see this by simply reading 1ª20 ff. on its own: the difficulties this passage raises cannot be solved by relying on 1ª16–19. Furthermore, 1ª16–19 is peculiarly incomplete. A distinction—perhaps an important one—is introduced only to be dropped. Unlike the treatment of ὄντα that follows, this treatment of the λεγόμενα seems truncated and quite inadequate. On the other hand, c. 4, which also begins without any connecting particle, seems precisely to pick up the discussion of c. 2, 1ª16–19. So two questions to consider are: do these lines from c. 2 belong with c. 4; and if so, where does the whole, combined passage belong?

The third chapter also presents difficulties. While it has been argued that it follows quite naturally on c. 2, this is only true of the first part, 1ᵇ10–15. The discussion of differentiae does not belong here, at least not obviously. And it too is not linked to what precedes it by a connecting particle. However 1ᵇ10-15, even on its own, is incomplete. In c. 2, Aristotle had drawn the distinction between the two ways items can be predicated of other items as their subjects: as we have seen, something either (i) is SAID OF something as its subject, or (ii) is IN something as its subject. And as we have already noted in Part I, while Aristotle goes on, in 1ᵇ10–15, to point out that the SAID OF relation is transitive, he says absolutely nothing about the being IN relation. But we know, from c. 5, that Aristotle does have things to say about being IN: at 2ª27–34 he calls attention to an important feature that distinguishes being IN a subject from being SAID OF a subject. In Part I, I proceeded on the (to my mind) uncontroversial assumption that, as far as their *contents* were concerned, these lines, indeed the whole of 2ª19–34, belonged with the earlier passage. I would now like to consider whether we should actually *transpose* the lines from Chapter 5 to Chapter 3. In short, the question is: what exactly is the relation between 2^{a}19–34 and Chapter 2 and the first part of Chapter 3?

To begin with, we should note that 2^{a}19–27, indeed, the whole of 2^{a}19–34, in fact fits much more naturally and smoothly with c. 2, or even better, immediately after 1^{b}15. The opening comment of this passage, "It is clear from what has been said . . .," makes far better sense if it refers to 1^{b}10–15 (rather, to the whole of 1^{a}20–1^{b}15) than to what immediately precedes it in c. 5. Commentators have certainly noticed this. Ackrill, for example, suggests that we should take these lines as referring back to that earlier discussion.[6] He is surely right to do so. But it is difficult to see how, given the present location of the passage, a reader could be expected to understand the words, "from what has been said," as in fact pointing back to that earlier discussion.

Secondly, 2^{a}19–34 interrupts Chapter 5. For 2^{a}34 ff. seems to belong with 2^{a}11–19; and in 2^{a}34 ff. no reference is made to the points mentioned in 2^{a}19–34. Minio-Paluello, in his punctuation, does signal that these lines have a certain independence; he marks them off with dashes. Yet marking off these lines with dashes does not go far enough towards making them seem nonintrusive, much less does it make them seem properly to belong, even if only as a parenthetical remark.

Moreover, the central point of 2^{a}19–34 is briefly reiterated later in c. 5, at 3^{a}15–21. Yet in the later short summary, *ousiai* are explicitly mentioned (3^{a}17, 21) to point out that no *ousia* is IN a subject. 2^{a}19–34, however, makes no reference to *ousiai*, but simply contrasts the SAID OF and being IN relationships. Such a general characterization, it seems to me, again fits much better after 1^{b}15, while the briefer, more restricted comment at 3^{a}15–21 seems entirely apposite in a chapter on *ousia* (which c. 5 obviously is). Also, if 2^{a}19–34 does belong with the earlier discussion from cc. 2 and 3, then the summary at 3^{a}15–21 will not be an otiose repetition of a point that had been made only a page before, but will be a useful reminder of the relevance of the earlier discussion to the characterization of *ousiai*.

For all these reasons, it seems clear to me that 2^{a}19–34 really does belong immediately after 1^{b}15; and this is the *first* suggestion I offer for changing the text.[7] With this transposition, the discussion of the two

---

[6] Ackrill, *Aristotle's Categories and De Interpretatione* (Oxford, 1903), p. 82.

[7] It is also the suggestion in which I have the most confidence; this is the only one of the proposed transpositions I would actually take up in the text, if I were preparing a new edition

relations becomes much more complete, and the argument in Chapter 5 is easier to follow, because it is no longer interrupted.

Transposing 2^a19–34, however, does nothing to make 1^b16–24, the second half of Chapter 3, seem fitting or relevant in any way. Given that the *Topics* (107^b19 ff.) contains a parallel passage, we will be reluctant simply to bracket these lines as spurious. So we should ask if there is anywhere else in the treatise where they would fit better, where a discussion of the differentiae of different, nonsubordinate genera would make sense. Though I am much less confident of this, let me offer the following *second* suggestion.

One striking fact about the offending lines from Chapter 3 is that they do not seem to have a proper beginning; that is, they seem to presuppose that the topic of differentiae has already been broached, and they then go on to discuss differentiae of a certain type.[8] Given the lack of a connecting particle, it is possible that we are simply faced with a gap in c. 3; and it is possible that if we had the missing material, we would see how 1^b16–24 fits with 1^b10–15 or rather, as suggested, with the whole of 1^b10–15 + 2^a19–34. This possibility cannot be ruled out. Another possibility that cannot be ruled out is that these early chapters of the *Categories* are an epitome (of a longer and fuller work), and that the various troubling features they exhibit—frequent asyndeton at the syntactic level, abrupt transitions from subject to subject, truncated treatments, and so on—are to be explained as the result of the epitomizer's activity.[9]

However, it is worth noting that Aristotle introduces the topic of differentiae in a very natural way in c. 5, at 3^a21. There he points out that differentiae are like *ousiai* in crucial respects. Thus I wonder whether these lines from c. 3, 1^b16–24, might not belong with the later explicit treatment of differentiae, perhaps after 3^a28. No use seems to be made of the notion of differentiae before 3^a21, and 3^a21 ff. in fact seems like a nice transition to a discussion of differentiae from the discussion of primary and secondary

---

of the *Categories*. The remaining two are much more speculative, and are meant (principally) to draw attention to moments where the text is quite awkward.

[8] These lines also seem to presuppose familiarity with the notions of genus, species, and sameness and difference in species or genus. Of course, given that this treatise was written while Aristotle was in the Academy, or at any rate was influenced by and responding to Academic discussions, it might seem that he could perfectly well presuppose such familiarity. However, he does not in fact seem to do so, but rather introduces species and genera in c. 5, in connection with the notion of secondary *ousiai*.

[9] I owe this suggestion to David Sedley.

ousiai. Of course, this is not to claim that if we insert 1ᵇ16–24 after 3ᵃ28, we have anything like a seamless text or argument. Most likely, something has been lost.

There remain the questions initially raised about 1ᵃ16–19 and c. 4—do these texts belong together, and if so, where do they belong? In examining both the '-onymies' of Chapter 1 and the two relations defined in Chapter 2 (and characterized further in 1ᵇ10–15 + 2ᵃ19–34), we noted the crucial role that *expressions*, i.e., linguistic items, played in defining these notions. On the other hand, 1ᵃ16–19 referred to nonlinguistic *entities*, as does Chapter 4.

In the light of this, consider a *third* suggestion: suppose 1ᵃ16–19 were to be transposed to the beginning of c. 4. First of all, this would give us, a single, unified discussion of expressions within the "Antepraedicamenta." Secondly, if the whole of 1ᵃ16–19 + c. 4 were placed after cc. 1–3 (with c. 3 changed as suggested, i.e., [1ᵇ10–15 + 2ᵃ19–34] minus [1ᵇ16–24]), we would also be given a fairly reasonable transition between cc. 1–3 and their discussion of expressions, on the one hand, and cc. 5–9—chapters clearly devoted to the different kinds of entities—on the other:[10]

CHAPTER 3

1ᵇ10. In case something is predicated of something else as of a subject, then, whatever items are said of what is predicated, all of them will also be said of the subject. For example, man is predicated of the individual man, and animal of man; so animal will also be predicated of the individual man— for the individual man is both a man and an animal.

[1ᵇ16–24]
2ᵃ19. It is clear from what has been said that when something is said of a subject, necessarily, both the *name* and the *account* are predicated of the subject. For example, man is said of a subject, the individual man—<here> the name is obviously (γε) predicated (since you will be predicating man of the individual man), but equally, the account of man will be predicated of the individual man (since the individual man also *is* a man). Thus both the name and the account will be predicated of the subject.

---

[10] Again, the translation is my own, though once more heavily indebted to Ackrill's. And I have again indicated additions (i.e., transposed lines) by vertical marks in the margin, and have placed square brackets around the line numbers of the lines moved from their traditional place. Angled brackets enclose words that supplement the compressed formulations; they do *not* signify supplements to the Greek text.

2ᵃ27. But when something is in a subject, in most cases neither the name nor the account is predicated of the subject. Yet in some cases, nothing prevents the name from being predicated of the subject, but <nonetheless> it is impossible for the account to be predicated: for example, white, which is in a subject, the body, is predicated of the subject (since a body is said <to be> white). But the account of white will never be predicated of the body.

CHAPTER 4

1ᵃ16. Of expressions, some are said <viz., used> in combination, while others are said without combination. Those <said> in combination <include>, for example: 'man runs', 'man wins'. And those <said> without combination <include>, for example: 'man', 'ox', 'runs', 'wins'.

1ᵇ25. Of the things said without any combination, each one signifies either (an) *ousia* or (a) quantity or (a) qualification or (a) relative-to-something, or (a) where or (a) when or (a) being-in-a-position, or (a) having or (a) doing or (a) being-affected. To speak, as it were, in outline, examples of *ousia* are: man, or horse; of quantity: two-foot, or three-foot; of qualification: white, or grammatical; of a relative-to-something: double, half, or larger; of where: in the Lyceum, or in the agora; of when: yesterday, or last year; of being-in-a-position: lying down, or sitting down; of having: has-shoes-on, has-armor-on; of doing: cutting, or cauterizing; of being-affected: being-cut, or being-cauterized.[11]

2ᵃ4. No affirmative sentence consists of any of the ones mentioned, just said by itself; rather, an affirmative sentence is produced by the combination of these with one another. For every affirmative sentence, it seems, is either true or false; but of those said without any combination, none is either true or false (e.g., 'man', 'white', 'runs', 'wins').

CHAPTER 5

2ᵃ11. An *ousia*—that which is called *ousia* most strictly, primarily and most of all—is that which is neither said of any subject nor is in any subject, e.g., the individual man or the individual horse. Secondary *ousiai* are what

---

[11] I use 'cauterizing' and 'being-cauterized' to bring out the medical provenance of these otherwise perhaps baffling examples; in that case, 'cutting' and being-cut' should presumably be thought of as referring to surgical procedures. Cf. G. Patzig, "Bemerkungen zu den Kategorien des Aristoteles," in *Einheit und Vielheit*, ed. E. Scheibe and E. Süßmann (Göttingen, 1973), p. 61 n. 1, where he refers us also to Plato *Gorgias* 456b; *Republic* 406d2; and *Statesman* 293b3.

the species are called, in which the things primarily called *ousiai* belong; likewise, the genera of these species <are also called secondary *ousiai*>. For example, the individual man belongs in a species, man, and animal is a genus of the species; so these—i.e., man and animal—are called secondary *ousiai*.

[2ᵃ19–34]

2ᵃ34. All the others either are said of the primary *ousiai* as subjects, or are in them as subjects. This is evident from examining them one by one. For example, animal is predicated of man and therefore also of the individual man; for if it were predicated of none of the individual men it would not be predicated of man at all. Again, color is in body and therefore also in an individual body; for if it were not in some individual body it would not be in body at all. Thus all the others are either said of the primary *ousiai* as subjects, or are in them as subjects. So if the primary *ousiai* did not exist it would be impossible for any of the others to exist.

[The rest of c. 5 is to follow in the usual order, though possibly with 3ᵃ21 ff. changed as suggested, i.e., adding 1ᵇ16–24 and marking one lacuna, or possibly more.]

Now this third suggestion—transposing 1ᵃ16–19 to the opening of Chapter 4—is obviously the most speculative one. But it would give us the following structure for the treatise. Chapters 1–3 present us with ways of *classifying things by means of expressions*, and show that there are certain important relations among the things and among the expressions. Chapter 4 in its new form focuses on the most *basic expressions* (those occurring "without combination"—in effect, terms) and indicates that ten rather different kinds of *items* can be introduced by them. The remaining chapters then are meant to take up the *ten kinds of items*, beginning with *ousiai* in Chapter 5. But as we have seen in Part I, the principles of classification used in Chapters 1–3 prove to be crucial for understanding, in greater detail, how these ten kinds of items are related amongst themselves. Thus those chapters really do belong at the beginning of the treatise.

Obviously, each of these suggestions would become more plausible, if a specific explanation for how and why the text came to be rearranged improperly were available. Commentators have not hesitated to suppose that the text—or rather, the papyrus manuscript—was physically damaged at a fairly early state. That is why, for example, the transition between the "Praedicamenta" and the "Postpraedicamenta" is missing, and why 11ᵇ10 ff. were interpolated, to provide at least *some* transition between the obviously fragmentary and incomplete c. 9 and the discussion of opposites in c. 10.¹² And perhaps the beginning of the papyrus roll was also damaged. While I am prepared to make that assumption, and while it does, in a general way, provide a means for explaining what happened, it is not sufficiently specific for settling the questions of how and why the passages discussed came to be displaced.

Finally, as a less intrusive alternative, supose that we think of the *Catgeories* as being like the *De Interpretatione* in the following important respect: the work opens by *setting out* (but *not* immediately explaining) certain useful notions, whose use and significance, however, does become clear in the course of the work, where we find these notions being applied in various ways. (Recall the first sentence of the *De Interpretatione*: "First we must set out [θέσθαι] what a name [ὄνομα] is, and what a verb is, and then what a negation, an affirmation, a statement [ἀπόφασις] and a sentence [λόγος] are" 16ᵃ1–2.) Now it could be argued that this fact suffices for explaining the abrupt opening of the *Categories*, as well as the abrupt transitions from topic to topic: thus there is no need to posit problems with the text.

In principle, this is an attractive suggestion. But turning to the details of the opening chapters of the two works shows that there are significant differences between them. In the *De Interpretatione*, after briefly discussing how language signifies thoughts and things (16ᵃ3–18), Aristotle proceeds systematically to discuss the various notions mentioned in the first sentence. As C. W. A. Whitaker correctly observes: "Chapter 2 is devoted to the name, [C]hapter 3 to the verb; each chapter begins with a definition, which is then elucidated, point by point. The two chapters have closely

---

¹² The matter of the transition between the "Praedicamenta" and the "Postpraedicamenta" is further complicated by the question of whether the "Postpraedicamenta" originally belonged with what came before (see Frede, "Titel, Einheit und Echtheit"), or whether they were added by a later editor (see Ackrill, *Aristotle's Categories*, pp. 70–71)—though recall that already in the first century B.C., Andronicus knew the text in its familiar form. Fortunately, the correct answer to this difficult question makes no difference to the present point. For regardless of whether the "Postpraedicamenta" actually belongs with cc. 1–9 or not, it is clear that c. 9 is woefully incomplete—and thus it is quite possible that something is missing even from the end of the "Praedicamenta." In addition, virtually all modern commentators agree that *at least* lines 11ᵇ10–16 are not by Aristotle. Thus there is clear evidence of early editorial tampering, evidently in response to a felt sense of the treatise's disrupted state.

parallel structures . . . [and] the elucidations are *systematically* arranged."[13]
Moreover, in the *De Interpretatione*, Aristotle avoids asyndeton (except
in the first sentence, where it is not objectionable). This is not merely a
stylistic matter, for in the opening chapters of that work, the discussion
does move from "point to point" in a coherent and highly organized way.
So while this new suggestion may well take care of the transition, within
Categories 2, from the division of expressions (into those ocurring without
combination versus those used in combination [1^a16–19]) to the fourfold
division of beings (arrived at through the SAID OF and being IN relations
[1^a20–1^b9]), the suggestion does not, it seems to me, help with the transition, viz., the lack of one, within *Categories* 3, to the discussion of differentiae (1^b16 ff.). Similarly, one may wonder how any of this helps with the
question about 2^a19–34, the lines that I have argued should be transposed
from c. 5 to come immediately after 1^b15.

There is another point worth noting. In the *De Interpretatione*, the
progression from topic to topic seems eminently reasonable: after discussing names (c. 2) and verbs (c. 3), Aristotle offers a characterization of
sentences (c. 4), then one of affirmative and negative sentences (cc. 5-6),
and then a characterization of ones involving quantifying expressions
(c. 7). (This is not to say that everything is perfectly smooth and seamless—
there are, no doubt, questions to be asked about some of the explanatory
remarks Aristotle provides along the way—but it is fairly easy for the reader
to see why the text proceeds as it does.) By contrast, in the case of the
Categories, commentators have felt enormous difficulty both in seeing the
relevance of the first chapter to the rest of the work, and in finding *any*
connection between cc. 1 and 2, between the statement of the '-onymies'
and the presentation of the SAID OF and being IN relations. So if Aristotle
is setting out some notions that will be used later on, and whose relevance
and usefulness will emerge in the course of that later discussion, he is
doing so in a far less transparent way than in the *De Interpretatione*.

In the light of this difference between the two works, I am inclined to
see the new suggestion as a supplement, rather than an alternative, to my
approach. The *Categories* may well have originally aimed first to set out
some concepts and then to apply them systematically; but for one reason
or another, some material was lost, other material (viz., 2^a19–34) came
to be dislocated. This makes for the difficulties in the opening chapters
of the *Categories*.

---

[13] See his *Aristotle's De Interpretatione: Contradiction and Dialectic* (Oxford, 1996), pp.
35–36; emphasis added.

In any event, as mentioned before, what is of greatest importance for our present investigation is that 2^a19–34 should be *read* with Chapters 2 and 3, and that the whole of 1^a20–1^b15 + 2^a19–34 should be *interpreted* as forming a unified discussion. No doubt the proposals for emending the text make this easier, but adopting them is by no means required for doing so.

Appendix 2

SPEUSIPPUS, THE SPEUSIPPEAN '-ONYMIES', AND *TOPICS* I, 15

SPEUSIPPUS also discussed and classified the '-onymies'. (See: Simplicius *In Cat.*, 38, 19 ff. [= Speusippus Fr. 32a L / 68a T]; *In Cat.* 29, 5 and 36, 25–31 [= Fr. 32b L / 68b T and Fr. 32c / 68c T].) There are difficult questions about the transmission—Simplicius is using Porphyry's lost commentary on the *Categories*, Porphyry is likewise using a lost commentary of Boethus's, and Boethus is using a lost text of Speusippus's—which are discussed at some length by Jonathan Barnes and Leonardo Tarán.[1] With one exception, to which I will come shortly, I would like simply to set those questions aside and ask rather, what, if anything, do these reports of Speusippus's views contribute to our understanding of Aristotle's classification and use of the '-onymies'? Sadly, the answer proves to be: very little. (Some readers may thus want immediately to move on to Part II.)

The starting point for recent discussions of this and related issues was provided by Ernst Hambruch, who argued for two claims.[2] (i) Aristotle and Speusippus differ in their account of the '-onymies', in that (ia) the Aristotelian '-onymies' classify *things*, while (ib) the Speusippean ones classify *words*. (ii) Despite his 'official' position, Aristotle himself, at times, but conspicuously in *Topics* I, 15, drifts into using the '-onymies' in the Speusippean way. Following Barnes, let us call (i) and (ii) the "Hambruch thesis."

In 1934, Philip Merlan argued against Hambruch, claiming that even if (i), in particular (ib), were true, this does not make for a *philosophically significant* difference between Aristotle and Speusippus.[3] Indeed, as Barnes

---

[1] See Barnes, "Homonymy in Aristotle and Speusippus," *Classical Quarterly*, n.s. 21 (1971); and Tarán, "Speusippus and Aristotle on Homonymy and Synonymy," *Hermes* 106 (1978), and *Speusippus of Athens* (Leiden, 1981), especially pp. 406–14.

[2] Ernst Hambruch, *Logische Regeln der platonischen Schule in der aristotelischen Topik*, Wissenschaftliche Beilage zum Jahresbericht des Askanischen Gymnasiums zu Berlin (Berlin, 1904).

[3] P. Merlan, "Beiträge zur Geschichte des antiken Platonismus: I. Zur Erklärung der dem Aristoteles zugeschriebenen Kategorienschrift," *Philologus* 89 (1934). Consider especially the following: "Thus when Hambruch maintains that 'a noteworthy difference shows itself in how the term συνώνυμον is used by Speusippus and Aristotle' (sc. in the *Categories*), in

notes, Merlan's position is that the Hambruch thesis is "trivial."[4] Barnes
and Tarán—who disagree about a great deal—both agree that Merlan is
wrong. They follow Hambruch in holding that there is an important
difference in whether the '-onymies' are taken in a Speusippean or an
Aristotelian way—though Barnes, unlike Tarán, also holds that Speusippus
himself did not construe the '-onymies' in the Speusippean way.

However, it seems to me that Merlan was fundamentally right. More
precisely, given (a) the absence of more information about the role the
'-onymies' played for Speusippus, or about the philosophical problems he
was seeking to address with them; and given (b) the familiar fact that
Aristotle quite generally switches (all too readily, we might think) from
talking about things or entities to talking about linguistic expressions,
there is no reason for rejecting Merlan's claim. Thus I will argue that while
Aristotle does sound Speusippean in *Topics* I, 15, he is not there using
the '-onymies' in a way that differs importantly from the way he uses them
in the *Categories*.

First (ia). All parties to the present dispute agree that in the *Categories*,
Aristotle uses the '-onymies' to classify things on the basis of expressions.
Thus we need consider this part of the Hambruch thesis no further.

Next (ib). Here a question of transmission becomes important. I am
inclined to agree with Tarán against Barnes that, in *In Cat.* 38, 20–24,
"Simplicius is quoting Boethus verbatim and . . . the latter is giving Speusippus' classification of names, if not verbatim, at least in a paraphrase

---

that the former uses it to mean 'one and the same ὄνομα . . . with the same conceptual
content (ein und dasselbe ὄνομα . . . mit stets gleichem begrifflichen Inhalt), the latter
however, [uses it to mean] several things or descriptions which can be subsumed under the
same name and the same concept (mehrere Dinge oder Bezeichnungen, die unter demselben
Namen mit gleichem Begriff zusammengefaßt werden können),' I must confess that I am
unable to see any difference here, except, possibly, for one in the *direction* in which matters
are viewed (so gestehe ich, hier keinen anderen Unterschied erblicken zu können, als höchstens
den der *Richtung* der Betrachtung): going from names to things in the case of Speusippus,
but from things to names in the *Categories*. 'In an exactly analogous way, a ὁμώνυμον, for
Speusippus, is one and the same name with different meanings . . . , rather than [ὁμώνυμα]
being different things with the same name, yet differing in their essential concepts.' Here I
find that the [alleged] distinction becomes completely imcomprehensible. [Merlan then gives
the following example, which does not work in English, so I have left it untranslated:] Rose
ist ein homonymer Name, denn ein und derselbe Name (Rose) hat in Anwendung auf die
Blume und auf die Krankheit verschiedene Bedeutung—oder, *ganz gleichbedeutend damit*, die
Blume und die Krankheit sind homonym, denn sie haben denselben Namen in verschiedener
Bedeutung [emphasis added]" (pp. 48–49).

[4] "Homonymy," pp. 65 n. 6, 70 n. 2.

which reproduces Speusippus' own terminology."[5] More specifically, there is every reason for thinking that the words with which the important sentence in Fr. 32a L / 68a T begins go back, in all essentials, to Speusippus himself; those words are: "*Of names*, some are tautonyms, some are heteronyms (τῶν γὰρ ὀνομάτων, τὰ μὲν ταὐτώνυμά ἐστιν, τὰ δὲ ἑτερώνυμα)." In short, Speusippus does begin his account by saying that the classification is to be a classification of *names* (and not things). Does this not settle matters in favor of Hambruch and against Merlan? It does not. For Merlan's claim is not that Speusippus is not classifying names, but that his doing so is not *by itself* sufficient to establish that he is pursuing a project fundamentally different from Aristotle's.

More interesting for our purposes is (ii). Here Hambruch has been followed by Tarán, who maintains that in *Topics* I, 15, Aristotle "twice uses *synonymon* in the Speusippean sense," and that "such a use is at variance with . . . Aristotle's definition of *synonyma* in *Categories* 1ᵃ6–7"; the two passages to which Tarán refers us are *Topics* 107ᵇ4 and 17.[6] In fact, however, nothing Aristotle says in *Topics* I, 15 about synonyms and homonyms is actually *inconsistent* with his account of them in the *Categories*.

Let us consider homonyms first. The term 'homonym' occurs ten times in our chapter. The uses at 106ᵃ21, 106ᵇ4 and 8 (and at 107ᵇ6, 17, 25, and 31) fit, or can easily be made to fit with the *Categories* definition. (We will consider the occurrence at 107ᵃ39 in connection with synonymy.) And while it may seem as if, at 107ᵃ5, 'homonym' were being used to refer *only* to words, the explanation Aristotle provides, at 107ᵃ3–12, of how *the good* is a homonym shows that he has the *Categories* definition of homonymy in mind:[7]

> Consider also the genera of the predicates that correspond to the name (τὰ γένη τῶν κατὰ τοὔνομα κατηγοριῶν), and whether they are the same in all cases. For if they are not the same, it is clear that the expression is a homonym (δῆλον ὅτι ὁμώνυμον τὸ λεγόμενον). For example, the good in the case of food is what is productive of pleasure; in the case of medicine, what is productive of health, but applied to the soul, what is qualified a

---

[5] "Speusippus and Aristotle," p. 81; see also Tarán's discussion in his *Speusippus of Athens*, pp. 406–14 (= commentary on Fragments 32a–c L/68a–c T).

[6] *Speusippus of Athens*, p. 76 and n. 361.

[7] In speaking this way, I do not mean to suggest that the *Categories* were written before *Topics* I, 15.

71

certain way, e.g., temperate or courageous or just. Likewise when applied to a person. . . . Thus the good is a homonym. (107ᵃ3–12)

Here Aristotle does say that an expression (rather than a nonlinguistic item) is the homonym. But notice his reason for saying so. Aristotle holds that if the account of what it is to be good is different for the items *x* and for *y*, then the term 'good' is a homonym. In the *Categories*, he says that in such a case the items *x* and *y* are homonyms with respect to the term 'good'. However, if we now think of the sentences 'X is good' and 'Υ is good', it is easy to see how what Aristotle says here in the *Topics* fits with the *Categories* account; for it turns out that the term 'good' is a homonym in this new sense *because* the items *x* and *y* are homonyms in the *Categories* sense, not the other way around. Thus a term can be a homonym (or, we might say, can be a homonymous term) in a derivative and secondary way. Saying that 'good' is a homonym seems like a readily understandable, albeit imprecise, shorthand formulation for the fuller claim.[8]

That Aristotle has the *Categories* account of homonymy in mind is, I believe, confirmed by another passage in the chapter:

Consider also the genera of the items falling under the same name, and see if they are different without the one falling under the other. For example, donkey is both the animal and the engine.[9] *For the account of them that corresponds to the name is different* (ἕτερος γὰρ ὁ κατὰ τοὔνομα λόγος αὐτῶν). The one will be said to be an animal of a certain kind, the other an engine of a certain kind. (107ᵃ18–21)

Note the verbal echo of *Categories* 1ᵃ1–2—the definition of homonyms[10]— and note that the account corresponding to the name to which Aristotle refers must be an account of the actual items, the animal donkey and the

---

[8] See also Barnes's comments in § 18 of "Homonymy," pp. 76–77; he usefully reminds us of the fact that 'the *X*' is often ambiguous between the item *x* and the word *X*; cf. p. 77 n. 1. Thus from the fact that Aristotle speaks of the good, the sharp, and so on, we cannot directly conclude that he is speaking of the terms *rather than* the items denoted by them. And even when he is speaking of the terms rather than the items, he can readily switch back to speak of the items.

[9] S.v. ὄνος LSJ give "*ass*," and then under VII, "from *ass as a beast of burden* the name passed to: 1. *windlass* . . . 2. *the upper millstone* which turned round."

[10] Recall that the *Categories* definition also included the words 'of being', viz. ". . . if the account of being which corresponds to the name . . ." The absence of those words here in *Top.* I, 15 makes no difference for the point at issue; see also p. 41 and n. 9 above. Later in the *Topics*, Aristotle will give a similarly abbreviated version of his definition of synonyms; see *Top.* VI, 10, 148ᵃ24–5.

engine. Thus even though he does not here say that the animal and the engine, the actual items, are homonyms with respect to the term 'donkey', 107ª18–21 is equivalent to precisely that statement.

The corresponding point is true of Aristotle's uses of the term 'synonym' at 107ᵇ17 and 4. Thus at 107ᵇ4, Aristotle's contention is that if being λευκός (light) were a synonym, then, in the sentences 'This sound is light' and 'This color is light', the sound and the color would be synonyms with respect to the expression 'light', because the account of what it is to be light would be the *same* in both cases.[11] But since we can see that the accounts of what it is to be light are in fact *different* for sounds and for colors, we can also see that a sound and a color are actually homonyms (107ª39) with respect to the expression 'light'. Aristotle expresses this point in an overly compressed way, saying that 'light' would be a synonym, if the accounts of being light were the same for a light sound and a light color (this is the force of 107ᵇ2–5). Similarly, when Aristotle says that synonyms must "always be comparable" (107ᵇ17), he is saying that the items that are synonyms must always have the *same account*, or the account of the one must be part of the account of the other.[12] I thus see no reason for thinking that Aristotle is using these notions in a way that is seriously at variance with his accounts of them in the *Categories*. Moreover, his use of 'synonym' and 'synonymously' in *Topics* IV, 6 corresponds exactly to the *Categories* account (see 127ᵇ5–7).

Thus I am inclined to think that Merlan is fundamentally correct. (One oddity of Barnes's account is that while he chastises Merlan for dismissing the Hambruch thesis as trivial, he agrees with Merlan on *Topics* I, 15, holding that Aristotle is *not* using the '-onymies' in a 'Speusippean' way there, and that any indications to the contrary are merely superficial features of Aristotle's exposition.[13] But that, I would have thought, is exactly what Merlan is claiming.)

There are far more interesting questions to ask about Speusippus. Consider even only: why did he produce his classification? Or: were there any *philosophically* interesting differences between him and Aristotle that led to the different emphases in their respective accounts of the '-onymies'? These questions are ones we are unfortunately not in a position to answer. (And

---

[11] Normally λευκός is of course rendered as 'white', but in the present context, we need a word that can apply to both colors and sounds; 'light' seems to fit the bill.

[12] See Barnes, "Homonymy," p. 78; on being comparable, cf. *Phys.* VII, 4, 248ª10–249ª29 to which Barnes refers.

[13] Barnes, "Homonymy," pp. 77–79.

unless Barnes and, especially, Tarán offer us answers to them, it remains unclear what, if anything, is actually at stake in rejecting Merlan's account.)

However, if the suggestions offered in the body of the essays about Aristotle's motivation for distinguishing the '-onymies' are at all along the right lines—he is seeking to address problems he sees arising for Platonism, in particular, for Plato's claim that all participants are named eponymously after the Forms in which they participate—then we might speculate that related concerns also motivated Speusippus. But that would make it even more unlikely that his classification of names should proceed with no regard for how the names in question apply to the nonlinguistic items they name.

If we can suppose that there were in fact debates within the Academy about how to come to terms with the various matters Plato considered under the heading of eponymy, that *might* help in explaining the extremely compressed formulations in *Categories* 1. Aristotle would be writing for an audience that was thoroughly familiar with those debates, so that the briefest and most condensed formulations would suffice for reminding his readers of his views. We could thus also suppose that Aristotle in fact did have available arguments for his position, but that they formed part of the discussion and debate of which the text we have is only a partial, almost summary record. With this brief look at Speusippus behind us, we can now turn to Plato.

Plato's Metaphysics and the Status of Things

> Suppose you were molding gold into every shape there is, going on non-stop remolding one shape into the next. If someone then were to point at one of them and ask you, 'What *is* it?', your safest answer by far, with respect to the truth, would be to say, 'gold,' but never 'triangle' or any of the other shapes that come to be in the gold, as though it *is* these, because they change even while you're making the statement.[1]
>
> (*Plato*, Timaeus 50a–b)
>
> And next the Forms will be homoiomerous, if all the things having some part of one of them are like each other. But how can the Forms be homoiomerous? For a part of Man cannot be a man, as a part of gold *is* gold.[2]
>
> (*Alexander of Aphrodisias*, On Aristotle's Metaphysics)

1. PRELIMINARY REMARKS

Part I ended with the suggestion that Aristotle's interest in something being named from or after something was taken over from Plato. Yet the fact that Plato had spoken of eponymy to cover all the cases of something being named from or after something in which he was interested gave rise to the question of why Aristotle sought to break apart Plato's notion of eponymy into the four '-onymies'. Plato's position can be formulated slightly differently, in a way which links it more closely to Aristotle's terminology. Plato's notion of *x* being called *P* after *y* (in effect) has all of (i)–(iii)—on p. 49 above—count as instances of *x* having the same name

---

[1] Translated by D. J. Zeyl in *Plato Complete Works*, ed. J. M. Cooper (Indianapolis, 1997).

[2] Translating *In Met.* 98, 6–9: ἔπειτα ἔσται μὲν ὁμοιομερῆ, εἴ γε πάντα τὰ ἔχοντά τι μέρος ἐξ αὐτοῦ ὅμοιά ἐστιν ἀλλήλοις· πῶς δὲ οἷόν τε τὰ εἴδη ὁμοιομερῆ εἶναι; οὐ γὰρ οἷόν τε τὸ μέρος τοῦ ἀνθρώπου ἄνθρωπον εἶναι, ὡς τὸ τοῦ χρυσοῦ μέρος χρυσόν. The text is D. Harlfinger's, in W. Leszl, *Il 'De Ideis' di Aristotele e la teoria platonica delle Idee* (Florence, 1975), pp. 21–39; see pp. 36–37.

as *y*, in other words, all of (i)–(iii) will count as cases of *homonymy*, but in a *less restrictive sense* of homonymy than Aristotle employs. Thus our question can be recast. Why did Aristotle seek out a more restrictive notion of homonymy, distinguished from synonymy on the one hand, and from paronymy on the other?

To make progress with this question we should first (Sections 2–14) turn to Plato, in order to get some sense of the issues he is trying to address, and then (in Section 15) turn to the so-called Late-Learners of the *Sophist*, whose view, at least as regards ordinary, sensible things, is a radical alternative to Plato's. In Section 16, I will briefly consider whether, and to what extent, the modifications in Plato's picture of the Forms in the late dialogues affects the status of sensible particulars. Only in Part III will we return to Aristotle's *Categories*. The reason for proceeding this way is that I believe it is instructive to see Aristotle's position as an attempt to find some middle ground between what he regards as the unacceptable alternatives presented by Platonism and Late-Learnerism.

To give some more intuitive sense of what is at issue, and to counter the impression that all this concerns only arid terminological distinctions, let me offer the following remark. Recall Bishop Butler's famous saying: "Everything is what it is, and not another thing." Now, what does Butler's essentialist dictum mean?[3] I do not propose to answer this question straight off. What I would like to suggest is that the disagreements among Plato (and various Presocratics), the Late-Learners, and Aristotle can be seen as revolving around interpretations of the essentialist dictum. These interpretations will in turn depend on how we are to understand the notion of a **thing**, on the one hand, and the notion of a thing **being what it is**, on the other. My claim is that, from the perspective of the *Categories*, only Aristotle seems to provide an acceptable interpretation of Butler's claim, at least as regards ordinary, everyday things.

2. Forms and Participants in Plato's Middle Dialogues

With these brief observations behind us, let us turn to Plato (and some Presocratics). Suppose that a sentence of the form '*X* is *Y*' is true (where *X* introduces an item, *x*, into discourse, and *Y* introduces *y* into discourse).

---

[3] In calling Butler's dictum essentialist, I mean to take no stand as regards the interpretation of Butler himself. I call it essentialist on account of its prominent place in recent, influential discussions about essentialism and identity, and more importantly, because I think it can play a useful heuristic role in interpreting the texts with which I am concerned.

According to Plato, there are two very different ways in which this could be so:

(I) '*X* is *Y*' is true, because being *y* is (part of) what being *x* is;[4] or alternatively, because *x* is *y* in virtue of its own *nature*.

(II) '*X* is *Y*' is true, because *x* is *y*, even though being *y* is *not* (part of) what being *x* is; or alternatively, because *x* is *y*, but *not* in virtue of its own nature.

We can see that there must be a difference between what schemata (I) and (II) are saying, but it is far from clear what that difference amounts to. As an initial but admittedly only partial attempt at giving content to the distinction, consider the following. In the first case, *x* is *y* in virtue of itself (καθ' αὑτό). Thus *x* is called *Y*, because being *y* is (part of) what *x* is, i.e., *x* is called *Y* in its own right, in a nonderivative way. The force of this emerges in contrast with the second case. Here *x* again is *y*, but now not in virtue of itself. So *x* cannot be called *Y* because being *y* is (part of) what *x* is, for being *y* is not (part of) what being *x* is; rather *x* is called *Y* because *x* is appropriately related to *y*. Let us use *participation* as the name for the appropriate relation.[5] Then we can say that *x* is *y*, because

---

[4] Here and throughout I am using 'being *y* is (part of) what being *x* is' as shorthand for: either being *y* is part of what being *x* is, **or** being *y* is what being *x* is. The perhaps clearest kind of case where being *y* is part of what being *x* is, is if *x* is a species of a genus *y*. Thus being an animal is part of what being a cat is. Note that this involves being a part in a nonextensional sense of part. Given that the set of cats is a proper subset of the set of animals, there will be another, extensional, sense of part in which the cats can be said to be a part of the animals.

[5] In fact, this will yield a somewhat more determinate and limited notion of participation than Plato relies on in the middle dialogues. Moreover, as Steve Strange reminds me (in written correspondence), in the *Topics*, Aristotle uses the term 'participation' (μέθεξις or μετέχειν) to refer to the relation species have to their genera, i.e., the various species will be said to *participate* in their genus or genera (see *Top.* IV, 1, 121ª10–19 and IV, 5, 126ª17–27). Indeed, Aristotle seems to go further, in thinking of participation as follows: if *y* is part of the essence of *x*, then *x* participates in *y* (see *Top.* V, 4, 132ᵇ35–133ª11; cf. V, 5, 134ᵇ18–22). Thus it would appear that the Academy, at least from a certain point onwards, is intent on *excluding* (what comes to be called) accidental predication as involving a kind of participation. Despite the fact that this Academic-Aristotelian usage is in direct conflict with the picture of participation presented in the body of the text, it does seem that that picture is in line with Plato's approach in the middle dialogues, where he seems primarily interested in using the notion of participation in connection with (what will later be thought of as) accidental predication: for example, think of ordinary, perceptible beautiful things which are said to be beautiful by participating in The Beautiful—they are not essentially beautiful, but only accidentally so. The shift between Plato's primary usage and the later

x participates in *y*. And *x* is called Υ, but is so called, not in its own right, but *after y*; in other words, *x* is called Υ derivatively.

Moreover, while this is not built into schemata (I) and (II) ab initio, in this second case, according to Plato, the item *y* is called Υ in its own right, nonderivatively. To see why, we should again recall that, in Greek, expressions formed from the neuter definite article + adjective are ambiguous in a crucial way, and hence can be used in (at least) two quite different ways—and are so used by Plato. Thus:

(1) 'The white' (τὸ λευκόν) refers to the color, white.

Or,

(2) 'The white' (τὸ λευκόν) refers to a colored thing, which is, or happens to be, white.

Or, to take an element familiar from various Presocratics and medical writers and, indeed, from Plato's *Phaedo*:

(1′) 'The cold' (τὸ ψυχρόν) refers to (what we would call) the quality, coldness; what they call *the cold itself.*[6]

Or,

(2′) 'The cold' (τὸ ψυχρόν) refers to a qualified thing, which is, or happens to be, cold.

We need to bring out some of what is going on with these two different uses of an expression like, 'the cold'.

(i) This expression applies primarily and in the first instance to the element, *the cold*. For *the cold* is what it is about whatever-is-cold that is cold—less cumbersomely, *the cold* is (as it were) the cause of being cold for whatever happens to be cold.[7] But *the cold*, the element, is cold in its own right, nonderivatively. So it is properly entitled to being called 'cold' or 'the

---

one will seem less peculiar, if Plato himself does not draw or rely on a distinction between (something like) accidental and essential predication with respect to sensible items, the participants.

[6] For the general point, see pp. 15–16 above and 120–21 below. In speaking of *the cold itself* (rather than, say, The Cold Itself) I mean to be offering a formulation that is neutral between Plato's language for Platonic Forms and the expressions certain Presocratics use for their elements.

[7] In Section 7, we will consider the thought that items like *the cold* are causes, and the force of the 'as it were' qualification.

cold'. Using the terminology of Part I, we could thus say that the expression 'the cold' should be thought of as the *proper name* of the element, *the cold*.

(ii) The expression can also be applied, secondarily, to any sensible cold thing, that is, any item in the world around us that can be said to be cold. The expression 'the cold' thus once more refers to something that is cold, but now to something that is not cold in its own right; it rather is cold by having a share of *the cold*. So it is called 'cold' in a derivative way, in virtue of having present within itself a share of the element, or as Plato and certain Presocratics sometimes put matters, in virtue of having a share of *the cold*. Since any number of things can be called 'cold' in this way—because any number of things can have a share of the element within themselves—we could say that the expression 'the cold' or 'cold' is a *common name* of each cold thing.

Let us return to the essentialist dictum. Suppose something *is* what it is and not another thing. What would this mean, given the present notions? We saw that if x is y, but being y was not (part of) what being x is, then y was something other than x, yet something to which x was appropriately related, by participation. So satisfying the essentialist dictum must involve schema (I) being satisfied, i.e., being y must be (part of) what being x is.

Of course we do not yet know all that is involved, if being y is part of what being x is. We would, for example, need to know what notion of *part* is being relied on in making this sort of claim. Nonetheless it seems trivially true that at least being x is part of what being x is.[8] So one way the essentialist dictum could turn out to be true is if x is x and is not any non-x, i.e., is not any non-x thing.

This gives rise to two obvious questions. To what does 'non-X' refer? What is being a non-x (item)? Once again, we seem to have two possibilities:

'Non-X' refers to anything and everything that is not-x.

Or,

'Non-X' refers to anything and everything that is incompatible with being x.

The relevance of this to Plato becomes clear as soon as we recall that self-predication (SP) sentences play a crucial role in Plato's metaphysical

---

[8] We will see that this seemingly trivial claim in fact proves not so trivial in certain cases; see p. 83 below.

reflections. For we know that, no matter how, in the end, these SP senten-ces are to be construed, if 'The X' refers to a Form, the sentence 'The X is X' must be true for Plato. But now we can ask, if 'The X' does refer to a Form, can *any* sentence of the form 'The X is Y' be true? It would seem that the answer must be: yes. Why? Because, according to Plato, each Form is, *inter alia*: one, the same as itself, different from the other Forms, eternal, unchanging, at rest, and so on. In short, there are a variety of things which are true of any Form simply insofar as it is a Form, and quite independently of which Form it is. Thus sentences like 'The X is Y' are also supposed to be true, for appropriate y's.

Yet now we face a problem. Although this is oversimplifying matters slightly, if we understand SP sentences in terms of the first construal of the essentialist dictum, it will turn out that all those things which are to apply to each Form, qua Form, cannot apply (except of course to the one eponymous Form).[9] Some examples will serve to illustrate the point. Is The Equal at rest? Qua Form, it ought to be. However, it would seem that being at rest is one way of being not-equal, or, of not being equal. (The delicate question of whether we should think of predicate-negation or sentence-negation in these contexts is one I wish to sidestep here.)[10] Is The Many one? Since The Many is one Form, it ought to be the case that The Many is one. But being one is surely a way of being not-many, and so it seems that The Many cannot be one. Thus, given the first construal, it seems that there is a contradiction at the center of Plato's thinking about Forms. Indeed, it may seem that Forms fail to satisfy a con-dition which anything at all must satisfy: each thing must be more than one thing in order to be (anything) at all; or, alternatively, any possible

---

[9] The oversimplification is the following: given the problems about self-predication, it is not clear *how* the eponymous predicate is to be predicated of the Form, hence it is not clear if it *can* be so predicated at all. On the perhaps most obvious and straightforward interpretation of these claims, we seem to end up with odd results. Thus Justice would have the feature of being just, The Many would the single(!) most multitudinous thing; Man (the Form) would itself be a human being; and so on. Notice that the SP sentences about Forms that correspond to features of all Forms sound less odd: 'The One is one'; 'Rest is (at) rest'; 'Eternity is eternal'; and so on. But given the oddness of the first set of claims, we should not take for granted that the second set will ultimately prove less odd. More precisely, we need analyses that treat the two kinds of SP sentences alike.

[10] J. McDowell's discussion of negation at *Sophist* 255e14 and 256a5 shows that Plato may have intended to distinguish predicate- from sentence-negation; see "Falsehood and Not-Being in Plato's *Sophist*," in *Language and Logos*, ed. M. Schofield and M. Nussbaum (Cambridge, 1982), p. 117.

subject of discourse must have more than one predicate predicable of it in order to be a genuine subject of discourse at all.

But is there any reason to think that we should interpret these sentences in the first way? Here a bit of Plato's technical vocabulary proves relevant. According to Plato Forms are *uniform* (μονοειδές).[11] The Beautiful, for example, is uniform. This seems to mean, The Beautiful is one in form, or is one Form, or is uniformly what it is, namely, beautiful. Let us suppose that we can always gloss 'The *X* is uniform' as 'The *X* is uniformly *X*'. This claim admits of two construals, which precisely parallel those given for the expression 'non-*X*' in the explication of the essentialist dictum:

'The *X* is uniformly *X*' means (or implies) that *x* is only *x* and is not anything that is not-*x*.

Or,

'The *X* is uniformly *X*' means (or implies) that *x* is *x* and is not anything incompatible with being *x*.

In the light of the difficulties adverted to just a moment ago, we might think that Plato must intend for us to follow the second option here. However, given the way the notion of uniformity is actually employed in the *Phaedo* and the *Symposium*, the first construal seems by the far the more natural one. This is not, I believe, a result of outright carelessness on Plato's part, nor is it simply a matter of his not choosing his words well. It is rather, at least in part, one consequence of Plato's not clearly distinguishing the two possibilities, at least in the middle dialogues.

The problem adumbrated is a well-known problem that seems to arise in connection with SP sentences about Platonic Forms. But since self-predication sentences are questionable in any event (see note 9 above), and since Forms independently seem like extremely dubious entities, our difficulty may seem like one more difficulty to be added to the legion of problems Plato already faces. Thus it may be a problem we could simply dismiss, if we reject Platonism—more specifically, if we reject Platonic Forms. But as we will see (in Sections 15 and 16), the present difficulty extends, or can be extended, in two directions; and once extended, it will be less easy to dismiss along with Platonism. First, it can be made to apply

---

[11] See *Phaedo* 78d5, 80b2, 83e2; *Symposium* 211b1, 211e4; and perhaps more controversially, *Theaetetus* 204d4. The notion of uniformity and its counterpart, multiformity, are discussed in more detail below, in Section 7.

to other sentences, in addition to SP sentences; and secondly, it can be made to apply to items besides Forms. (We will see that those items include natural kinds, and those sentences, sentences referring to natural kinds.) These additional sentences, and these additional items will, however, prove far less suspect than Platonic Forms.

At this point, however, let us ask if there is anything to say about particulars, that is, those items Plato sometimes calls the *participants* (τὰ μετέχοντα), because these items are (whatever they are) by participating in something *else*. We will see that the essentialist dictum bears on them as well, albeit in a surprising and completely different way.

Plato at times says that these things, strictly speaking, *are not* (whatever they 'are'), but only *become* (some of what they are said to be). Though this will require considerable argument—to be provided in Sections 3–14—it seems clear to me that Plato wishes to draw the following sort of distinction with respect to our ordinary use of the verb 'is'. Consider again the difference between schemata (I) and (II):

(I) 'X is Y' is true, because x is y in virtue of its own *nature*.

(II) 'X is Y' is true, because x is y, but *not* in virtue of its own nature.

Plato wishes to reserve 'is' for only the first of these cases, and to use 'becomes' in the second! That is, 'X is Y' in sense (I) is to be read as

(I′) X **is** Y.

But 'X is Y' in sense (II) is to be *replaced* by,

(II′) X **becomes** Y.

Plato's claim that everyday things make up a realm of becoming, wholly separate from the realm of being, should be understood as follows: everyday things are not, strictly speaking, i.e., are not whatever they are ordinarily said to be. Or alternatively, everyday things are not *really* or are not *purely* (whatever they are ordinarily said to be). Now it is because they are not really or are not purely, that ordinary things, in a way, both are and are not. And it is on account of their, in a way, both being and not-being that Plato wishes to say that, strictly speaking, everyday things merely become (whatever they are ordinarily said to be).

The claim that everyday things make up a realm of becoming thus also is not the claim that everyday things are always changing, in every way;

the view rather is that ordinary things are not stable, genuine things at all, hence they are always *subject* to change, in every way. To put the point in still another way, it is not the case that ordinary things have the nature: to be subject to change, in every way; rather, because ordinary things lack natures, they are subject to change, in every way. (This last formulation will no longer seem like arbitrary terminological legislation, once we recall that *natures* must be principles of stability, order, intelligibility, and so on.)

In order to appreciate more fully the distinctiveness of Plato's claim that everyday things constitute a realm of becoming separate from the realm of being, it is useful to contrast it with a more familiar distinction. Suppose Socrates is a human being who also happens to be healthy. One might suppose that Socrates is essentially human, but only accidentally healthy. A simple bit of reflection seems to support this thought. Socrates could contract a disease and so become ill. Throughout these changes, though, *he* remains unchanged, *qua being human*. However, should Socrates perish, we are faced with a quite different change. The transition from living human being to corpse seems to be different in kind, not just in degree, from the transition from being healthy to being ill. Indeed, we might be inclined say that Socrates no longer exists, once he has died, because there no longer is any human being, any living thing, that is Socrates. Aristotle's distinction, in the *Categories*, between the *ousiai* and the various nonsubstantial items seems intended to capture the intuition that lies behind our thinking of the two sorts of cases as two genuinely distinct sorts of cases.

Yet for Plato, as we will soon see, at least in the middle dialogues and in the *Timaeus*, it would seem that there is no *metaphysically* significant difference here.[12] Why is that? Everyday things, according to the *Phaedo* (80b4; cf. *Rep.* 612a), manifest themselves as multiform (πολυειδές). But this, I will argue, means that they *participate* in many Forms, not that they *are* many things. And although everything is what it is, since sensible particulars, strictly speaking, are not, the essentialist dictum does not apply to them! And thus the seemingly trivial claim, that being x is part of what being x is, does not apply to participants, since for any y which is predicated of x, x only participates in y (or y-ness). In short, for any x which is (only) a participant, there is, strictly speaking, no such thing as being x.

---

[12] The example of Socrates ill versus Socrates healthy is, of course, from the *Theatetus* (see 159b2–d8); but there are questions about whether Plato is there speaking *in propria persona*, or dialectically, i.e., bringing certain unattractive consequences of the Protagoreanism-Heracleiteanism under consideration to light.

These are obviously striking, not to say strange claims. The task is to make them seem less strange. Thus I will next turn to the problem of becoming (in Sections 3–4); and to Plato's first use of a distinction between being and becoming, as well as its background in Greek (in Sections 5–6); in order to then return to the metaphysical questions (in Section 7 and following).

3. The Problem of Becoming

We encounter the contrast between being and becoming quite frequently, throughout a range of dialogues.[13] (See, for example, *Timaeus* 27d, 37e–38b; *Republic* 518c, 519b, 521d, 523c–524a, 525b, 526e; *Theaetetus* 152d–e; *Sophist* 248a.) At first glance, this is hardly surprising. 'To be' and 'to become' are, after all, different. And that is so, irrespective of whether we use these verbs in a syntactically incomplete or complete way.[14] Becoming (or coming to be) learned is one thing; being learned is another. Similarly, the generation—that is, the coming to be, the γένεσις—of, say, a cat is one thing; the being of a cat, or being a cat, is another. Traditionally, it has been supposed that when Plato draws his distinction, he has something very much like this ordinary distinction between being and becoming in mind. But here is one initial indication that Plato is using his distinction in a way that is different from the ordinary contrast between being and becoming: Plato uses it to partition everything into two *wholly disjoint* classes—those items that can always be said to be, but not to become; and those that can always be said to become, but not to be. Yet ordinary

---

[13] The contrast is between γίγνεσθαι or γενέσθαι and εἶναι. Sometimes this is put as a contrast between γιγνόμενα or γενόμενα and ὄντα, or between γένεσις and οὐσία.

[14] This distinction is itself more complicated than it initially had seemed (e.g., to G. E. L. Owen, in his "A Proof in the *Peri Ideōn*," *Journal of Hellenic Studies* 77 [1957]: 108–9.) At first, it just looks as if incomplete uses of verbs will involve complements, while complete uses will not. But if we allow (i) that an incomplete use is one "in which a subject expression and the appropriate form of the verb requires a complement in order to be a complete sentence, though in an elliptical sentence the complement may be omitted" (J. McDowell, *Plato: Theaetetus* [Oxford, 1973], p. 118), and (ii) that a complete use is not one "which neither has nor allows a complement" but rather one "where there is no complement (explicit or elided) but which allows a complement" (L. Brown, "Being in the *Sophist*: a Syntactical Inquiry" *Oxford Studies in Ancient Philosophy* 4 [1986]: 53), then the simple picture will not do. (On the distinction in general, see ibid., pp. 52–59.) Fortunately, these complications do not matter for the present issue. I will return to the issue of incompleteness in Section 12 below.

ways of thinking and talking presuppose that the *same things* can be spoken of as being *and* becoming. We can say of some thing that it is changing; but we can also say that *it*—that very thing—has changed and now is in a certain state or has a certain feature. Similarly, we can speak of the generation and maturation of a living thing, but also of *that* living thing— the same one—as having come to be and having matured and now being a fully-grown individual of its kind.

By insisting that 'being' and 'becoming' are never to be applied to the same items, Plato seems to be making clear his intention of giving up this familiar and everyday way of looking at, and talking about the ordinary world and its contents. In the *Theaetetus*, this point is made explicitly. There we are told that, when speaking about items of a certain kind, it is simply incorrect to say that one of these items *is*. We should rather say that it *becomes*. We of course know what the items are that are being partitioned in this way. On the one hand, there are the mundane things in the world around us—these are said only to become. On the other hand, there are things (somehow) wholly separate from these ordinary things, namely, the Forms—and they are said only to be.

However, so far this proposal says absolutely nothing about our ordinary use of 'becomes'. In fact, it seems that we can continue to use 'becomes' in all those cases where we had already been speaking of becoming or coming to be. The situation we find ourselves in thus is the following. Plato is asking us to distinguish between γιγνόμενα/γενόμενα (becomings) and ὄντα (beings) in such a way that if, in our ordinary way of speaking, we also draw the usual distinction between γίγνεσθαι and εἶναι, that will be a distinction *internal* to the class Plato is calling the γιγνόμενα/γενόμενα. (See the accompanying diagram.)

The fact that our ordinary, everyday distinction between being and becoming falls wholly on one side of Plato's great ontological divide not only invites but makes pressing the question: how are we to understand Plato's distinction? We frequently use sentences of the form 'X is Υ'. As already suggested, Plato wants to distinguish two wholly different kinds of claims that sentences of this form can express. For as we have already seen, in saying 'X is Υ', we might mean to be claiming either

(I) (a) *x* can be said to be *y*, and
   (b) it is a part of the *nature* of *x* to be *y*,

or

(II) (a) *x* can be said to be *y*, and
    (b′) it is *not* part of the nature of *x* to be *y*.

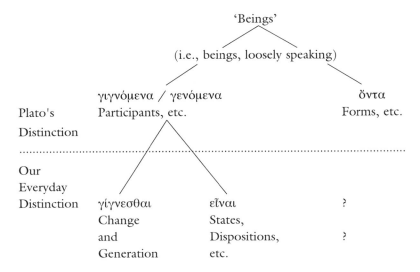

And Plato's proposed linguistic reform, if that is what we should call it, was that we use 'becomes' (γίγνεσθαι or γενέσθαι) rather than 'is' (εἶναι) in cases of type (II), and that we restrict our use of 'is' only to type (I) cases.

Before proceeding any further, four comments. First, obviously 'to be' as it occurs in clauses (a), (b) and (b′) cannot be the same as the being we are interested in contrasting with becoming. Rather, it is the ordinary language verb we have been using all along, in saying things like 'X is $\varUpsilon$'. Secondly, it is part of Plato's view that if 'X becomes $\varUpsilon$' is true, 'X becomes not-$\varUpsilon$' is also true, and vice versa. In the striking language of *Republic* V (479d), this is expressed by speaking of x's "rolling about" between being and not-being.[15] Thirdly, this notion of becoming is not essentially temporal, i.e., it does not refer to something's *changing* or *undergoing a process*. But becoming will turn out to be quite closely linked to these notions, because saying of some item that it becomes in this sense amounts to saying, *inter alia*, that it is *subject* to change, *subject* to

---

[15] If we wanted to work out the 'logic' of being and becoming, we would need to distinguish between (i) sentence-negation and predicate-negation, and (ii) strong and weak negation.

On (i): For example, $\neg$ (X becomes $\varUpsilon$) $\neq$ (X becomes not-$\varUpsilon$).
On (ii): Should we read '$\neg$' so as to get
    (a) $\neg$ (X is $\varUpsilon$) $\rightarrow$ (X is not-$\varUpsilon$), or so as to get
    (b) $\neg$ (X is $\varUpsilon$) $\rightarrow$ (X becomes $\varUpsilon$) v (X is not-$\varUpsilon$)?

Rules of inference will also need to be formulated delicately, so that the 'contradictoriness' of becoming does not infect being.

undergoing processes. Indeed Plato himself will sometimes revert back to temporal language and talk of change, etc.; but the close link between between becoming in his new sense and the familiar notions of change, processes, and so on, makes that reversion quite easy. Fourthly and finally, while we are not yet in a position to say what a *nature* is, it surely is the sort of thing something will have (or be) essentially, if it has one (or is one) at all. Hence I also want to refer to type (I) cases, as cases of strong or essential predication, and to type (II) cases, as cases of weak or nonessential predication.

Plato's distinction (as it is presented in the middle dialogues) partitions all the items that are loosely speaking called beings into, on the one hand, the beings strictly speaking, that is, the Forms; and, on the other hand, the becomings strictly speaking, that is, the participants. Given that partition, it turns out that *no* claims made about the participants are true in virtue of their nature. Indeed, as we will see, on Plato's view, the participants do not have natures at all.

In due course, we will consider the implications of that contention about the participants; but first we should briefly note that it has as its counterpart a contention about the Forms. For it seems that the *only* claims which can be made about the Forms are claims that are true of them in virtue of their own nature. Yet this principle about Forms leads to an immediate complication.

Suppose that there are three and only three just Antipodeans. Then the claim (S) 'Justice is instantiated three times in the Antipodes' looks like a counterexample to the principle proposed for Forms. For S appears to be about Justice, but surely it is not part of the nature of Justice to be instantiated three times in the Antipodes. A first attempt at a solution would be to suggest that we cannot take the surface grammar of sentences as a reliable guide to what makes them true. A proper understanding of S will show that it is true because sentences like (A1) 'Antipater is just', (A2) 'Antiphon is just', and (A3) 'Antisthenes is just' are true. These are of course all weak predications in the indicated sense.[16] However, this only

---

[16] This sort of account of the facts (or states of affairs) that underlie and ground sentences like S, is developed by C. Meinwald in light of the schemata for predication πρὸς ἑαυτό (in relation to itself) and πρὸς τὸ ἄλλο (in relation to another) that Plato provides in the *Parmenides*; see her *Plato's Parmenides* (Oxford, 1991). But I believe that even before he had produced this new account of predication, Plato would have given the suggested analysis of sentences, like S, whose truth appears to be grounded in facts about Forms that have nothing to do with their natures.

takes us part of the way. For even if the truth of S is to be explained in this way, it seems arbitrary to deny that S—or A1, A2, and A3, for that matter—are in at least some sense *about* the Form, Justice.

A different but not unrelated worry occurs with sentences like 'Justice is eternal', 'Justice is one', and so on, that is, all those sentences which predicate something of a Form qua Form, but not qua the Form that it is. For the nature of justice simply will be whatever is specified in a correct answer to the question, 'What *is* justice?'. In other words, the nature of justice will be rendered in the correct account or definition of justice. But being eternal will not be part of such an answer, for it will not be part of the definition. So the worry (which we have already encountered) simply is the question, how can Plato seem to be saying these two things: (i) Each Form x is *only* what it is.[17] And (ii), any Form x is y, z, . . . , where y, z , . . . belong to all Forms. For (i) suggests that 'X is X' is the only truth about the Form x, while (ii) suggests that 'X is Y', 'X is Z', and so on will also be truths about the Form.

I do not believe that Plato has an adequate reply to this in the middle dialogues. However, part of what motivates the πρὸς ἑαυτό/πρὸς τὸ ἄλλο (in relation to itself/in relation to another) distinction of the *Parmenides*,[18] and quite generally the so-called blending of Forms in the later dialogues, is wanting to have an adequate answer to the question: if a Form is only what it is, how can it also be other things, especially, all the other things all Forms are said to be? For example, Justice will be, say, Virtue + D_1 + . . . + D_n πρὸς ἑαυτό (where D_1, . . . , D_n are the relevant

---

[17] This also seems to be what M. M. McCabe has in mind when she speaks of Forms as "austere individuals" which are "just one"; see her *Plato's Individuals* (Princeton, N.J., 1994), p. 51. But she is not sufficiently clear about the problems this brings with it, viz., the tension between (i) and (ii); cf. also C. Meinwald's review of McCabe in *Archiv für Geschichte der Philosophie* 78 (1996): 66 and n. 2. In a similar fashion, N. Fujisawa writes, "only the Form, αὐτὸ τὸ καλόν, is always καλόν in the full sense by virtue of being nothing other than itself," in "Ἔχειν, Μετέχειν, and Idioms of 'Paradeigmatism' in Plato's Theory of Forms," *Phronesis* 19 (1974): 35. But he gives no indication of recognizing that, given (ii), there may well be problems with asserting (i).

[18] See 136a–c, 160b, and 166c (in 160b3 read ". . . καὶ πρὸς ἑαυτὸ καὶ πρὸς τἆλλα, καὶ τἆλλα ὡσαύτως" [. . . both in relation to itself and in relation to the others, and likewise for the others] rather than ". . . καὶ πρὸς ἑαυτὸ καὶ πρὸς τὰ ἄλλα ὡσαύτως" [. . . both in relation to itself and, likewise, in relation to the others] with Heindorf; for a defense of this emendation, see Meinwald, *Plato's Parmenides*, pp. 142–44; cf. *Parmenides*, tr. M. L. Gill and P. Ryan, in *Plato Complete Works*, p. 391 n. 17). This turns out to be the same distinction as the καθ᾽ αὑτό/πρὸς ἄλλο distinction of *Sophist* 255c12–13, on which see M. Frede, *Prädikation und Existenzaussage* (Göttingen, 1967), esp. pp. 12–37.

differentiae), and hence (i) will be satisfied. But Justice will also be eternal, at rest, one, and so on, πρὸς τὰ ἄλλα, hence (ii) will be satisfied. However, since the two uses of 'is' are now clearly identified as two *different* uses, (i) and (ii) no longer are in conflict.[19]

And as we have noted, this sort of problem also comes up in connection with the characterization of Forms as uniform (μονοειδές). Despite this major and deep problem, I believe that, in the middle dialogues, Plato does want to say that Forms are strictly speaking only what they are.

4. THREE DIFFICULTIES FOR THE PROPOSED ACCOUNT OF BECOMING

To return to our main argument. Before trying to determine the implications of this account of becoming for the participants, we need to confront some difficulties. For it may well seem quite bizarre to assert that what Plato's distinction between being and becoming amounts to is such a distinction between being a nature and having a feature. Obviously, a great deal would need to be said in order to make any interpretation along these lines so much as seem not wholly implausible. In particular, there are at least three considerations that tell strongly in favor of the traditional understanding of this contrast, so strongly that one might think one needs to stay with it, despite any problems it may face.

(i) First, while γίγνεσθαι is sometimes (especially in the aorist tense) used as the copula, there seems to be no reason for thinking that, on such occasions, it means anything other than εἶναι. Perhaps this first point is not as weighty as it might initially appear to be. Plato's remarks in the *Theaetetus* (152d–e and 157a–b) show that he is consciously innovating and going beyond, perhaps against, ordinary usage. Still, one is inclined to think that there should be *some* connection with previously attested uses. After all, why choose γενέσθαι to express weak predication rather than εἶναι qualified in some appropriate way?[20] The traditional interpretation, on the other hand, can rely on a well-established use of 'becomes'.

---

[19] Again, on the *Parmenides,* see Meinwald, *Plato's Parmenides*; on the *Sophist,* see Frede, *Prädikation und Existenzaussage.*

[20] Plato uses expressions like ὄντως (really), εἰλικρινῶς (purely), παντελῶς (wholly) and τελέως (completely) to qualify being. He could easily enough also use, e.g., ἐστὶ ἐνδεεστέρον (is, in an impoverished way), ἐστὶ φαυλότερον (is, in a more lowly way), or locutions like ἐστὶ κατὰ συμβέβηκος (is, *per accidens*) or ἐστὶ ὡς ἔπος εἰπεῖν (is, so to speak) for weak predication.

(ii) Secondly, this well-established use is one that had already played an important role in philosophy. Thus, whatever the obscurities surrounding Parmenides' argument may be, he does seem to seek to rule out generation (B 8.6–21) and change (e.g., B 8.22–33) on the basis of his principle:

It is and cannot not be.

A principle Jonathan Barnes has argued should be understood as:

Whatever is cannot not be.[21]

This would appear to rule out change in the following way. Suppose that some item is hot. Were it to become cold, it would change from being hot to not being hot. That would involve a transition from being to not-being, *because* it involves the transition from being hot to not being hot.[22] But not-being is impossible. Hence such a transition is impossible. Hence change is also impossible. And whatever doubts may remain about the proper interpretation of Parmenides' poem, it is quite clear that one of his two major Eleatic successors, namely, Melissus, offered this sort of reasoning against the possibility of change.

It is also generally agreed that various pluralists who succeeded Parmenides, notably Empedocles, Anaxagoras, and Democritus, meant to make room for generation and change, even though they accepted, at least to some extent or with some qualifications, Parmenides' principle.[23] They

[21] B 2.3. For taking 'it' as 'whatever', see J. Barnes, *The Presocratic Philosophers*, 2 vols. (London, 1979), 1:162. Barnes is part of a tradition of interpretation that goes back to G. E. L. Owen's classic paper, "Eleatic Questions," *Classical Quarterly*, n.s. 10 (1960), reprinted both in *Studies in Presocratic Philosophy*, vol. 2, ed. R. E. Allen and D. J. Furley (London, 1975), and in *LSD*. M. Furth's "Elements of Eleatic Ontology," *Journal of the History of Philosophy* 6 (1968), reprinted in *The Presocratics*, ed. A. Mourelatos (Garden City, N.Y., 1974), provides another very clear statement of this 'dialectical' reading of Parmenides. The groundwork for interpretations along these lines was laid by Karl Reinhardt, in his *Parmenides und die Geschichte der griechischen Philosophie* (Bonn, 1916). This reading's central tenet is that Parmenides' arguments are (as it were) a challenge to ordinary discourse and pluralist ways of thinking, and thus that the characteristic monism, etc., of Parmenides are arrived at through those arguments, not things to be assumed at the outset. (In mentioning Barnes, Furth, and Owen all together, I do not mean to suggest that they would agree about all, or even most, points of detail.)

[22] The correct interpretation of Parmenides is complicated and controversial, and I do not mean to prejudge anything as regards it. Yet it is also fairly clear that his argument was understood by his successors to have implications for change in this way.

[23] David Furley, in his important paper, "Anaxagoras in Response to Parmenides," *Canadian Journal of Philosophy*, suppl. vol. 2 (1976), reprinted in his *Cosmic Problems* (Cambridge, 1989), provides a clear and succinct statement of this standard view.

agreed that what is cannot not be and hence cannot change, but they sought to explain things in the world around us—things obviously subject to generation and destruction, and, more generally, to change—in terms of those things that are. To put the point another way: they agree with Parmenides that ordinary things have no claim to being called ὄντα (beings), but they then seek to explain these ordinary things in terms of what does have a claim to being called ὄν (being).

Now there is no reason to think that Parmenides or these successors of his used 'becomes' in any other way except to talk of change and generation. Plato was obviously familiar with their usage. Given this background, it would be surprising if Plato were suddenly to launch a new and unfamiliar use of 'becomes' without indicating that he is doing so. Yet if he is using 'becomes' in the way the traditional interpretation assumes, we can readily explain his interest in the distinction between being and becoming as arising out of a confrontation with his predecessors. Plato would be joining an ongoing debate.

(iii) Finally, in many places Plato does use 'being' and 'becoming' in the way in which these terms are ordinarily used, and he does, as a matter of fact, believe that the Forms are eternal, stable and unchanging, while the participants are not. Given this, and given the first two points, we would like to see him saying explicitly that 'being' and 'becoming' need to be understood in some other way—for example, in the way suggested—before we abandon the traditional interpretation.

5. Plato's Introduction of the Distinction between Being and Becoming

So let us ask: does Plato himself anywhere explicitly discuss the difference between being and becoming? Here we need to turn to the *Protagoras*. At a certain point in the dialogue, Protagoras comes to be dissatisfied with how the argument has been going—more specifically, with how he has been faring as the answerer in his question-and-answer exchanges with Socrates (335a–b). After an impasse which threatens to bring the dialogue to a premature end (335d–338b), Protagoras is persuaded to take over the role of questioner, and Socrates assumes the role of answerer (338d–e). And beginning at 339a, Protagoras chooses to ask, not about the nature or teachability of virtue—the subject of their previous question-and-answer exchange—but about poetry. In particular, he chooses Simonides 4 D (= *PMG* 542) as the subject for his questions.[24]

Protagoras sets up the dialectical trap by first asking Socrates if he thinks the poem is beautifully composed (Socrates says that it is—339b), and then asking: if the poet contradicts himself, is it a beautifully composed poem? (Socrates says that it would not seem so to him.) Protagoras, through a series of questions (339c–d), suggests that Simonides *is* contradicting himself in this poem, for in the very first line Simonides says:

It is hard to **become** good.

But only a few lines later, he *criticizes* Pittacus for saying:

It is hard to **be** good.

Protagoras is saying that Simonides is criticizing Pittacus for having said virtually the same thing he, Simonides, had said just before. And thus Socrates will be forced to withdraw his initial answer: the poem is not, given the criterion he himself has accepted, beautifully composed.

Before proceeding, we should recall that 'becomes' can function rather differently in Greek than in English. In English, the lines from Simonides sound like obviously different claims, and hence it appears as if there must be something contrived or perverse in Protagoras's insistence that these verbs mean essentially the same thing. But in Greek, as already mentioned, γίγνεσθαι, on many occasions of its use, in fact means the same thing as εἶναι. So there need not, automatically, be anything artificial or contrived about Protagoras's claim that Simonides is contradicting himself. Nor is it only Protagoras who thinks there is a contradiction. For once he points it out, the others who are present applaud, signaling their admiration for Protagoras (339d–e) and thereby agreeing with him that there is a contradiction in the poem. Thus Wilamowitz seems to have been correct

---

[24] This entire part of the dialogue—from 339a to 348b—is something of a puzzle. Since Socrates ends the discussion by saying that they ought to dismiss the interpretation of poetry, and since a great deal of his exegesis of the poem seems far-fetched, commentators have frequently thought that the whole episode is to be regarded as a parody of the Sophists' educational program, a reductio ad absurdum of one of their favorite instructional devices— the interpretation of poetry. It seems that because this is the general view of the passage, readers of the dialogue often neither look for, nor expect to find, anything of serious philosophical interest here. The implied dichotomy between parody and serious philosophy is surely much too primitive. At any rate, I will simply take it as given that the passage contains both. I discuss the role of 339a–348b extensively in my *Fighting with Words: Dialectic and Eristic in Plato's Protagoras and Euthydemus* (forthcoming).

with his observation—made in connection with precisely this poem—that in everyday Greek, no one would sense a difference between γενέσθαι ἀγαθόν and εἶναι ἀγαθόν, between becoming good and being good.[25] (In Section 6, however, we will see that Wilamowitz's observation needs to be qualified.)

Socrates, however, does not accept defeat in the dialectical exchange. He turns to Prodicus for help, in order to show that being and becoming are different, and thus to suggest that Simonides need not, after all, be contradicting himself (339e). (Here we should remember that Prodicus's special claim to fame was distinguishing meanings of words that ordinarily seem to mean the same, or almost the same thing.[26] He had already displayed his ability to do exactly that a bit earlier in the dialogue, at 337a–c. That Socrates turns to him may be additional confirmation of the fact that Protagoras does, at least prima facie, have a good case, or at any rate, a case of sufficient strength that the special expertise of a Prodicus is required, rather than simple familiarity with ordinary usage, to argue that Protagoras is mistaken in seeing a contradiction in the poem.)[27]

Prodicus, of course, insists that being and becoming are different (340b). In spelling out how Prodicus understands the distinction, Socrates turns to yet another poet, namely Hesiod. Hesiod agrees that it is hard to become good; he says, "the gods have placed sweat on the path to excellence (ἀρετή)" (340d). But he also thinks that it is *easy* to be good: "it [sc. ἀρετή] is easy to keep, hard though it was to achieve."

Socrates, in interpreting Hesiod, relies on the following construal of being and becoming: 'becoming' refers to a process or change, while

---

[25] U. v. Wilamowitz-Moellendorf, "Das Skolion des Simonides an Skopas," *Nachrichten der Königlichen Gesellschaft der Wissenchaften zu Göttingen*, phil.-hist. Kl. (1898): 210; reprinted, with minor changes, in his *Sappho und Simonides* (Berlin, 1913), p. 165. Since Simonides uses ἀγαθός (line 1; see 339b1) to make his claim while he quotes Pittacus as using ἐσθλός (line 7; see 339c4), it might seem that one possibility for avoidng the contradiction would be to find a difference in the meaning between these two adjectives (see Wilamowitz, locc. cit.). That, however, would be quite implausible; and since none of the participants in the dialogue even raises this as an option, much less makes use of it, it will be safe for us to ignore it as well.

[26] On Prodicus, see C. J. Classen, "The Study of Language amongst Socrates' Contemporaries," *Proceedings of the African Classical Associations* 2 (1959), reprinted in *Sophistik*, ed. Classen (Darmstadt, 1976).

[27] Cf. D. Frede, "The Impossibility of Perfection: Socrates' Criticism of Simonides' Poem in the *Protagoras*," *Review of Metaphysics* 39 (1985–86), who notes that "Socrates indirectly confirms . . . [the] implausibility" of the distinction, "by giving credit to his apprenticeship in Prodicus' art—indicating thereby that this is not a natural reading" (p. 739).

'being' refers to a state or disposition. Moreover, we are surely meant to see the state as the end point of the process, in short, becoming good leads up to being good. (This clearly is what Hesiod had in mind; see *Works and Days*, lines 286–92.) We thus arrive at a distinction between being and becoming; and if Socrates could show that Simonides is using the words in Hesiod's way, he would succeed in showing that Simonides has not contradicted himself.

Protagoras, however, objects, claiming in effect that it is completely wrong to say that *being* good is easy, because everyone would agree that being good is the most difficult thing of all (340d–e). Socrates accepts Protagoras's objections, but continues the exchange, proposing now to give his own interpretation of the poem instead (341e ff.). It will depend, as we might by now expect, on how being and becoming are to be understood.

Socrates' interpretation has been the subject of considerable controversy. We should, however, notice that his construal of the two key verbs is subject to two constraints. First, Socrates cannot have 'being' and 'becoming' meaning essentially the same thing—for that would leave Simonides contradicting himself, just as Protagoras had charged. Secondly, and even more importantly, Socrates' first, Hesiodic proposal for how these verbs are to be understood also needs to be abandoned. For that understanding—relying on the contrast between states and processes—has led to Protagoras's objections. Plato is thus making clear that we need yet a *third* interpretation of the contrast between being and becoming, one that avoids the shortcomings of the other two. Socrates' crucial remarks are the following:

> A little further on Simonides says, as if he were developing an argument, that although to become a good man is truly difficult, it is possible, for a while at least; but having become good, to remain in this state and *be* a good man—which is what you were speaking of, Pittacus—is impossible and not human (ἀδύνατον καὶ οὐκ ἀνθρώπειον). This is the privilege of a god alone. (344b6–c3; tr. W. K. C. Guthrie)

How then does Socrates understand being and becoming? At first, we might think that all he is saying is that the process of becoming good is broken off, reversed, or whatever; in other words, the process never reaches its end point, the *state* of being good. (And Socrates will, in fact, a little later go on to provide examples which suggest that things interfere with and bring about changes away from goodness.) Yet presumably such interruptions in the process of becoming good will be accidents, i.e., matters that only happen contingently. Thus it should not, in principle, be impossible for there to be a person who becomes good and does not meet with any such misfortune.

Yet could this person be said to *be* good? We might at first think that the answer ought simply to be: yes. But in fact it seems that such a person should not be said to be good—if we take the words "impossible and not human" seriously. Why not? The suggestion appears to be that it is simply not part of human nature to *be* good.[28]

This encourages us not to construe becoming as involving a change or process aiming at some end (whether that end is reached or not), nor should we take being as the state arrived at by undergoing the process. Rather, 'becoming good' amounts to *displaying* or *manifesting* goodness—which mortals, if they are lucky, are able to do, sometimes and in some circumstances. That is to say, they can on some occasions or in some situations, act or behave in the way in which a being that truly *was* good (viz., a god) would, on all occasions and in all situations, act or behave.

Alan Code, however, has insisted that Socrates, in fact, does not claim that it is impossible to be good. His interpretation of 344b6–345c3 relies explicitly on his construal of two important verbs (διαμένειν in 344b8 and διατελεῖν in 345c1), and implicitly on a contrast between being F (for a while) and being F (continuously). Code argues as follows:

> Socrates tells us (344b6–c3) on behalf of Simonides that becoming a good man is, in truth, difficult, but possible—however, what is impossible is this: having become good, to remain (διαμένειν) in that condition and be a good man. In order to remain in that condition it is necessary first to *be* in that condition. Hence Socrates is not claiming that it is impossible to be good. What is impossible is not *being* a good man for a short time, but (as Socrates puts it) *continuing* to be good (διατελοῦντα ἀγαθόν, 345c1).[29]

Despite the many difficulties the whole passage presents, it is clear that Code's view cannot be correct. For in 344e4–6, Socrates attributes this to Simonides:

[28] The adjective ἀνθρώπειος certainly suggests that human nature is being thought of. And Socrates' use of this adjective to mark a striking difference between gods and human beings (344c2–4) reinforces that suggestion. Compare also the discussion of man and god (and the human and the divine) in *Republic* IX (588b–590e).

[29] A. Code, "Reply to Michael Frede's 'Being and Becoming in Plato,'" *Oxford Studies in Ancient Philosophy*, suppl. vol. (1988): 59–60. Frede's view is very similar to the one I

But you, Pittacus, are saying that it is hard to be noble. In fact, however, it is hard to *become* noble, yet possible; but to *be* noble is impossible. (τὸ δ' ἐστὶ γενέσθαι μὲν χαλεπόν, δυνατὸν δέ, ἐσθλόν, ἔμμεναι δὲ ἀδύνατον.)

That is, Socrates precisely does say, on Simonides' behalf, that it is impossible to be good. We thus need a different interpretation of 344b7–c3 and 345c1–2. We also need to see what basis, if any, there is for supposing that Socrates means to distinguish being good (for a while) from being good (continuously).

In 344b7, Socrates has Simonides saying that to become good is truly hard, yet possible.[30] However, Socrates immediately qualifies this possibility, by continuing "at least for a time" (μέντοι ἐπί γε χρόνον τινά, 344b8). What then is it that is possible for a time at least? If Code were right, it should be: *being* good. But the reference can only be to what was mentioned just before, that is: *becoming* good. Hence what is possible for a human being is "to *become* good, for a time at least." (Leave open, for the moment, what exactly that is.) Next Socrates wants to talk about what is impossible:

> But having become (sc. good), to remain in this state and to be a good man . . . is impossible and not human. (γενόμενον δὲ διαμένειν ἐν ταύτῃ τῇ ἕξει καὶ εἶναι ἄνδρα ἀγαθόν, . . . ἀδύνατον καὶ οὐκ ἀνθρώπειον, 344b7–c3)

In order to interpret these lines correctly, it is critical to know the force of the words, "to remain in this state." In effect, Code's argument is that remaining (διαμένειν) presupposes being (εἶναι). And that construal would seem to require taking "in this state" to be referring to the state of being good. Code may have been encouraged to understand these words in this way by taking becoming in the conventional way: the *becoming* referred to in 344b7 is the process; the *having become* referred to in 344b8 is the end point, that is, the process of becoming is now over.

However, the order of the infinitives in 344b7–c1 tells strongly against this reading. For if Code were right, we should expect: "but having become good, **to be a good man** and to remain in this state . . . is impossible and not human." In the sentence as it actually is, the state of being good has not yet been spoken of. Thus it is much more natural to understand the

---

am advocating here; see his contribution to the same volume, "Being and Becoming in Plato," an article from which I have learned much.

[30] χαλεπόν in 344b7 corresponds to χαλεπόν in 344e5; οἷόν τε in 344b8 to δυνατὸν δέ in 344e5 and to οἷόν τε in 345c2.

words "in this state" as referring to the state, condition, or situation of becoming good, i.e., as I would argue, a situation in which goodness is manifested or displayed.[31]

What these lines suggest is that it is only by being good that one can manifest goodness continuously, that one can always act virtuously. Hence always acting virtuously will also be a *sign of* actually being good, even though it is *not* the same thing as being good. So the criticism of Pittacus could be paraphrased as follows:

> To display oneself as a virtuous person, to behave virtuously, is truly difficult. Yet it is possible, at least for a time. What is impossible is, having acted virtuously, to persist in this (viz., acting or behaving virtuously) and actually to be good, because such persistence is only possible for someone who *is* good. [Note that the two key verbs, διαμένειν and διατελεῖν, can certainly be understood in this way.]

The important contrast thus also is not between being good (for a while) and continuing to be good, but it is rather between becoming good (for a while) and continuing to become good (i.e., becoming good, continuously). However, given the close connection between being good and continuing to become good—the latter is a reliable sign of the former—this can also be expressed, more simply, as the contrast between becoming good and being good.

The general distinction, then, that Socrates is gesturing towards is the following. On the one hand, there is taking on (at some time or in some circumstances) certain characteristics or features. But these features are not constitutive of the thing whose features they are; for the thing could just as well lack them—for example, at other times or in other circumstances. On the other hand, there is having features or characteristics in such a way that the thing whose features they are could not just as well lack them. Thus I am inclined to believe that in the *Protagoras*, Plato really does wish to move away from taking 'becomes' as a mere variant for 'is'—as on Protagoras's interpretation—and from taking 'becomes' as referring straightforwardly to changes and processes—as on the interpretation arrived at with the help of Prodicus and Hesiod. The interpretation suggested, in terms of *natures*, seems to me to capture what Socrates is aiming at.

---

[31] Perhaps we should even read ἐν ταὐτῇ [τῇ] ἕξει rather than ἐν ταύτῃ τῇ ἕξει in 344c1, that is, "in *the same* state," rather than, "in *this* state."

There are, however, two complications, which may threaten this conclusion. First, in the course of his analysis of the poem of Simonides, Socrates seems to backtrack and, at least in part, to revert to the Hesiodic construal of becoming (345a–c). Secondly, given that the entire discussion of the poem is in large measure an ad hominem piece of dialectic directed against Protagoras, we might in any event want to hesitate before placing any substantial interpretive weight on this passage. Perhaps these complications suffice for showing that the *Protagoras* passage cannot represent a fully worked-out presentation of Plato's later thoroughgoingly metaphysical distinction between being and becoming. But that is hardly surprising. It also in no way undercuts the fact that already in the *Protagoras* (where the grand metaphysics of the middle dialogues is not in view), Plato has the resources for articulating the kind of distinction I have described. Indeed, in the next section, we will see just how well Socrates' interpretive maneuvers in the *Protagoras* fit with established Greek usage.

6. The Background to Plato's Special Use of 'Becoming'

We have just seen that Plato, as a matter of fact, explicitly discusses the distinction between being and becoming, even if in a context that may prove to be somehow problematic. In doing so, he is not putting forth an account of the contrast between being and becoming that is wholly novel or without precedent. In actual fact, he would have been able to draw on, and as the *Menexenus* shows, did draw on, a well-established use of 'becoming' in Greek—in particular, of the phrase, 'becoming good'—that is of great importance in funerary inscriptions, in the extant funeral orations, and in patriotic contexts more generally.[32] (This fact also should go a long way towards minimizing the force of any doubts one

---

[32] My discussion of the material that follows is heavily indebted to the work of a number of classicists, all largely ignored by philosophers. The essential point was, in a way, already made by Wilamowitz; see "Das Skolion," p. 221 and n. 2 (*Sappho und Simonides*, p. 176 n. 3; cf. also pp. 141 n. 3 fin). It was clearly stated by Eduard Schwartz in his *Das Geschichtswerk des Thukydides* (Bonn, 1925), pp. 351–56; cf. also his comments in the posthumously published *Ethik der Griechen* (Stuttgart, 1952), pp. 19–25. The observations of Schwartz are developed brilliantly both by Nicole Loraux, in *The Invention of Athens* (Cambridge, Mass., 1986), pp. 98–118; cf. also her "La 'Belle Mort' spartiate," *Ktema* 2 (1977), and by Jeffrey Rusten, in "Structure, Style and Sense in Interpreting Thucydides: The Soldier's Choice (Thuc. 2.42.4)," *Harvard Studies in Classical Philology* 90 (1986).

might have about the *Protagoras* passage taken only on its own.) Let us begin again by considering two texts. The first is from the seventh-century Spartan war poet, Tyrtaeus:[33]

> For a man is not good in war (ἀγαθὸς γίγνεται)
> if he has not endured the sight of bloody slaughter
> and stood fast and reached forth to strike the foe.
> This is excellence (ἀρετή); this is the noblest prize
> and the fairest for a young man to win.
> This is a common good, both for the city and her whole people,
> when a man stands firm in the forefront
> without ceasing, and making heart and soul abide,
> forgets shameful flight altogether and heartens by
> his words the man he stands next to.
> Such a man is good (ἀγαθὸς γίγνεται) in war.
> (Tyrtaeus 9 D, 10–20, tr. J. M. Edmonds)[34]

The second is from a speech of Lysias:

> But surely we ought to remember that already in the past, when we have supported others who were the victims of injury, we have established many trophies over our foes on foreign soil, and so ought now to act as valiant defenders of our country and of ourselves (ἄνδρας ἀγαθοὺς περὶ τῆς πατρίδος καὶ ἡμῶν αὐτῶν γίγνεσθαι). (Lysias 34.10, tr. W. R. Lamb)

For Tyrtaeus, becoming good in war is obviously a matter of acting or behaving in a certain way. And in the speech of Lysias, this seems so clearly to be what is meant that W. R. Lamb simply writes, "and so ought now to act as valiant defenders," where the more literal rendering would have been, "and must become good men."

However, each of these passages leaves open what the relation between the behavior and any settled habits, dispositions, or states of character might be. Indeed while it would surely be a mistake to attribute to Tyrtaeus any worked-out contrast between the character of a person and his actions, it does seem plausible to think that he believes that the sort of young man he is describing is able to *become* good, because he *is* good. More simply,

---

[33] The authenticity of all the poems (but especially 9 D) transmitted under Tyrtaeus's name has been challenged. On 9 D, however, see W. Jaeger, "Tyrtaios über die wahre ἀρετή," *Sitzungsber. d. Preuß. Akad. d. Wiss., Berlin*, phil.-hist. Kl.(1932); reprinted in his *Scripta Minora*, vol. 2 (Rome, 1960).

[34] I have made a few minor changes in his translation, but not in the translation of lines 10 and 20.

the young man is able to perform brave acts in virtue of being brave. The Lysias text, by its reference to past behavior, also suggests that there is some underlying character which would enable the audience to act in the way the speaker is recommending.

Thus in these texts, while there may be an implied or at any rate a potential contrast between being and becoming, the two go together in an obvious way: it is by being good that one can become good.

But now let us turn to some passages from the Funeral Oration of Pericles in Thucydides which suggest that this simple picture of the relation between being and becoming needs to be complicated. At II.35.5, Pericles reflects on the task that is before him, of giving the funeral oration, and says:[35]

> To me, however, it would have seemed sufficient, when men have proved themselves brave by valiant acts (ἀνδρῶν ἀγαθῶν ἔργῳ γενομένων), by act only to make manifest the honours we render them.[36]

A bit later, in II.42.2–3, Pericles turns to reflect on what type of men these were that are being honored by him and the Athenians:

> And it seems to me that such a death as these men died gives proof enough of manly courage (ἀνδραγαθία),[37] whether as first revealing it or as affording its final confirmation. Indeed, even in the case of those who *in other ways fell short of goodness*, it is but right that the valour with which they fought for their country should be set before all else. For they have blotted out evil with good, and have bestowed a greater benefit by their service to the state than they have done harm by their previous lives. (Emphasis added.)

The whole point of the funeral oration is to honor the dead soldiers for their *action*—they acted bravely. But Pericles is also acknowledging explicitly that these soldiers may not all have been virtuous men; they may have had any one of a variety of failings. In saying this, Pericles is clearly committed to there being a distinction between a person's character and that person's actions. Yet he also is committed to a certain picture of the

---

[35] The translations of all the passages from Thucydides are from C. Foster Smith's Loeb edition.

[36] See Lysias II, "Funeral Oration," 24–25 and 51; Plato *Menexenus* 237a6; 242b6–c1; 247d4–6; Hyperides VI, "Funeral Oration," 9 and 28–30; Demosthenes LX, "Funeral Oration," 1 for similar uses of ἄνδρες ἀγαθοὶ γενόμενοι.

[37] Compare Pausanias's use of ἀνδραγαθία (I.29.4), in reporting the inscription for the dead at Marathon.

relation between character and action. For Pericles needs to rule out any view according to which we can, in general, infer what a person is truly like merely from inspecting (even certain crucial) actions of his. Thus from the fact that a soldier performs brave acts, we cannot conclude that he *is* brave or good (where this is to be understood as something like: is the sort of person who does brave acts *because* he is brave or virtuous; or is the sort of person who does them *in the way* the brave or virtuous person would do them; and, perhaps, is the sort of person who will be brave and good in *all* circumstances, from *all* points of view.)

We know that distinguishing between behavior and underlying character will be of great importance for both Plato's and Aristotle's moral psychology. The point of Pericles' remark, though, is not to give an account, much less a worked-out philosophical theory, of the difference between behavior and character. Nor, obviously, is it to call into question the legitimacy of any such distinction. His point rather is that, however important we may think such differences are in general, on this particular occasion, because of these particular circumstances, it does not matter what these men were *really* like; all that matters is how they acted.

Here, then, the contrast between being and becoming is not merely implied or potential. For it seems that the two no longer need to go together; indeed, they can come apart: someone can become good *without* being good.

· · · · ·

Another illuminating example of such a use of 'becomes' in Thucydides can be found in the speech of the Plataeans in III.54 and in the Thebans' response in III.64. However, since the proper construal of 'becomes' in III.64 has been the object of a controversy between Michael Frede and Alan Code, it will be necessary to examine these passages very closely.[38] In III.54.3, the Plataeans say:

τὰ δ' ἐν τῇ εἰρήνῃ καὶ πρὸς τὸν Μῆδον ἀγαθοὶ γεγενήμεθα . . .

They are saying that they acted correctly, both during the Persian Wars and in the subsequent peace. Moreover (and this is made clear by the whole context), they are claiming that this behavior of theirs at that time is indicative or revelatory of what they were, and are, actually like. Thus Charles Foster Smith translates: "in the wars against the Persians and

[38] In the articles cited; see n. 29 above.

during the peace which followed we have *proved* ourselves good and true men" (emphasis added).

The Thebans (not the Spartans, as both Frede and Code inexplicably say) feel compelled to reply to the Plataeans' speech (see III.60).[39] They, of course, want to reject the claims of the Plataeans. But it is important to be quite clear about what, exactly, is being rejected. Code writes as follows on III.64.4:

> When the Spartans [*sic*] say to the Plataeans καὶ ἃ μὲν χρηστοὶ ἐγένεσθε, ὡς φατέ, they are referring back to III.54.3 where the Plataeans had said ἀγαθοὶ γεγενήμεθα (as the ὡς φατέ indicates). The Spartans [*sic*] are not endorsing the claim made by the Plataeans. They are rejecting it: you *say* that you proved yourself good back then, but you did nothing of the sort.[40]

And from this, Code wishes to infer that " 'becoming F' and 'being F' do *not* come apart in such a way as to form a contrast" in Thucydides III.64.

His remark about what the Thebans are saying in III.64.4, however, is not sufficiently precise. This becomes evident as soon as we consider two passages Code neglects: III.64.1–2 and the continuation of the sentence from III.64.4 which he has already quoted in part. In III.64.1–2, the Thebans say:

> You have, therefore, made it clear that even then it was not for the sake of the Hellenes that you alone of the Boeotians refused to medize [= collaborate with the Medes, viz., the Persians], but merely because the Athenians also refused to medize while we did not, and you preferred to act with the one party and against the other. And now you expect to be rewarded for virtuous behavior that was due to the inspiration of others! (καὶ νῦν ἀξιοῦτε, ἀφ᾽ ὧν δι᾽ ἑτέρους ἐγένεσθε ἀγαθοί, ἀπὸ τούτων ὠφελεῖσθαι.) But that is unreasonable.

The Thebans are not denying that the Plataeans did not medize. Nor are they saying that the Plataeans, in not medizing, qua not medizing, acted badly or inappropriately. In fact, they concede that the Plataeans "became good" at that time. But the Thebans are also saying that they did so δι᾽ ἑτέρους, i.e., because of others (viz., the Athenians), and not because of what they themselves were (or are) really like. Hence, however good or

---

[39] As well they might. See Herodotus VI.108–16 for the Plataeans' role at Marathon, and for their difficulties with the Thebans. On the Thebans' *medizing* (sc. collaborating with the Persians), see, e.g., Herodotus IX.67.

[40] Code, "Reply," p. 58.

virtuous their *conduct* may have been, it is revelatory of nothing as regards their true character, their real *nature*. That their real nature is what is at issue emerges clearly from the whole sentence in III.64.4:

> Furthermore, those noble qualities which, as you claim, you once displayed you have now made plain were not properly yours, but your *nature* has been put to the proof and shown in its reality. (καὶ ἃ μέν ποτε χρηστοὶ ἐγένεσθε, ὡς φατέ, οὐ προσήκοντα νῦν ἐπεδείξατε, ἃ δὲ ἡ φύσις αἰεὶ ἐβούλετο, ἐξηλέγχθη ἐς τὸ ἀληθές.) (I have slightly modified Forster Smith's translation here.)

The Thebans are claiming that the Plataeans' true nature is at odds with the behavior they had exhibited in the past (though not at odds with their true motivation for that behavior). But again, they are not actually calling the goodness of the behavior, qua behavior, into question. The point can be restated in the language of being and becoming. The Plataeans said that they *became* good then (sc. in the Persian Wars). And they appeal to this fact to support the claim that they *are* good. The Thebans concede that the Plataeans became good, but deny that they are, or ever were, good.

Thus I am inclined to believe that Code is simply mistaken in holding that it is a "misreading of the passage" to see a contrast between being and becoming in Thucydides III.64.[41] On the contrary, we need to suppose that the distinction between being and becoming advocated here (or something very much like it) is at work in order to make sense of the passage.

· · · · · ·

The words 'having become good men' or 'having become a good man' are also used in inscriptions to honor those who died in battle.[42] Indeed, the phrase 'having become good' often functions simply as a euphemistic circumlocution for 'having died in battle'.[43] Now in these inscriptions, just as in Pericles' speech, what is being commemorated is not lifelong virtue, is not *being* good. Rather what is being commemorated is a *single*

[41] Ibid., pp. 57–8.

[42] For the inscriptional evidence, see J. Gerlach, ΑΝΗΡ ΑΓΑΘΟΣ (Munich, 1932), pp. 7–14. An inscription from Thasos suggests that the war dead could even, on occasion, simply be called: οἱ Ἀγαθοί (The Good). See J. Pouilloux, *Recherches sur l'histoire et les cultes de Thasos*, vol. 1 (*Etudes Thasiennes 3*) (Paris, 1954), no. 141, pp. 371–79. (I have this reference from Rusten, "Structure, Style and Sense," p. 72 n. 76, where he also refers to Demosthenes *De Corona* 308.)

[43] See Loraux, *The Invention of Athens*, p. 101.

event or episode in the past: the action(s) that led to the war heroes losing their lives for their country.[44] And in these funerary contexts, the point is precisely that even *without* having been good in one's life, one can earn the right to be called ἀγαθός by acting appropriately in this single decisive moment.[45]

This funerary use of γενέσθαι (if we may call it that) is admittedly rather specialized. But it is clearly related to the more general use we have already seen. Thus, in the Lysias text, the injunction is not to die for one's country, nor is it to transform oneself so as actually to be a good person; rather, the injunction is to fight bravely—as in the translation quoted. We find quite similar uses in, e.g., Thucydides V.9.9 and VII.77.7. And if we look

[44] The fact that single past occasions are being referred to explains the frequency with which the aorist is used. Schwartz, though, was wrong to insist that *only* the aorist is used in contexts of this sort; see Rusten, "Structure, Style and Sense," pp. 72–73, and esp. n. 77. But the difference in *verbal aspect* or *Aktionsart* between the aorist and the imperfect, and even between the aorist and the perfect or pluperfect, is undoubtedly important here. Such a difference in aspect is also exploited by Euripides to poignant effect, when he has Hippolytus contrasting Phaedra with himself: ἐσωφρόνησε δ᾽ οὐκ ἔχουσα σωφρονεῖν, ἡμεῖς δ᾽ ἔχοντες οὐ καλῶς ἐχρώμεθα (*Hippolytus* 1034–35). (Literally: "she acted virtuously, even though she did not have being virtuous as her own; I have virtue, but did not use it well." In other words: "she acted virtuously, even though she was not virtuous; I actually am virtuous, but did not act virtuously.") See Rusten, *Structure, Style and Sense,*" n. 79, and also Euripides, *Hippolytus,* ed. W. S. Barrett (Oxford, 1964), p. 336 ad loc.

[45] Here it is relevant to recall that ἀγαθός was a term originally reserved for the aristocracy, that is, only an aristocrat could *be* good. Thus L. Kurke, in a paper on Alcaeus and, among other things, his relation to Pittacus, observes: "His [sc. Pittacus's] famous quip . . . that it is 'hard to be good' is nonsensical within the confines of strict aristocratic ideology: either you are *esthlos* [cf. n. 25 above] or you are not. If you are born noble, you simply are; if you are not, no amount of working at it will make it so" ("Crisis and Decorum in Sixth-Century Lesbos: Reading Alkaios Otherwise," *Quaderni urbinati di cultura classica* 47 [1994]: 84). But this might not preclude that the right sort of behavior, on the part of a nonaristocrat, could lead to his being *called* good. *Becoming good* (in sense discussed) thus would be *acting* like an aristocrat (i.e., as an aristocrat would act, or could be expected to act, in virtue of what he is, viz., good). This might be possible even for a nonaristocrat who, however, just could not (by definition, so to speak) become good in the sense of actually coming to be an aristocrat. Of course, someone with ultra-aristocratic sympathies, say, an Alcaeus, might find unacceptable and outrageous even this weaker suggestion—for Alcaeus may well hold that a nonaristocrat can in no meaningful way resemble an aristocrat. Consider also the following comment of Pausanias: "It was surely a just decree . . . when the Athenians actually allowed slaves [sc. certain ones killed in combat during the Persian Wars] a public burial, and to have their names inscribed on a slab which declares that in war they proved themselves good men (ἀγαθοὺς . . . γενέσθαι) and true to their masters" (I.29.7), tr. W. H. Jones in *Pausanias* (Loeb Classical Library), vol. 1 (Cambridge, Mass., 1918).

at various Greek authors more closely, we find that 'becomes' is used rather frequently in the sense of 'display', 'manifest', 'take on a role', or 'act in a certain way', and so on.[46]

While the verb 'becomes' is not available for such a role in English, there is an analogous phenomenon: the contrast between the *simple present* and the *present progressive tenses*. For example, it may be perfectly true for me to say 'I speak German', while continuing to speak English; but it would be incorrect, on such an occasion, for me to say 'I am speaking German'. The simple present seems to point to a standing capacity, ability, or disposition, the present progressive to its actual exercise.

Consider now the contrast between the simple present and the present progressive in the case of the verb 'to be': 'She is being kind'/'She is kind'; 'He is being extremely nasty'/'He is extremely nasty'; 'Your cat is being annoying'/'Your cat is annoying'; and so on. While there is no doubt some variation, and while there may be some contexts in which the generalization does not hold, it seems we are again inclined to use the

---

[46] See, for example, Herodotus V.2.1; VII.224.1; IX.71.1; IX.75; Thucydides I.86.1–2; Lysias XII, "Against Eratosthenes," 97; Aeschines III, "Against Ctesiphon," 154. Two observations about these and similar passages: (i) Saying that someone became F of course does not in general *mean* (a) that this person *merely* became F—but was not really so—as opposed to (b) that he became F because he really was F. Thus it will always be necessary to decide on the basis of the context whether (a) or (b) is the correct construal. (ii) Code ("Reply," p. 58) may very well be right that it is only a fairly narrow range of evaluative adjectives and nouns (e.g., ἀνήρ—which, as opposed to ἄνθρωπος, can be evaluative; cf. Latin *vir* and *homo*) that are used with γίγνεσθαι in this way.—There is yet one further complication. Passages like Xenophon *Anabasis* III.2.39 and Lysias II, "Funeral Oration," 24 (and there are many others) show that εἶναι is sometimes used in this way as well. Or, as we might say, putting matters in an exaggerated and paradoxical way, εἶναι is sometimes used in place of γίγνεσθαι. This, however, does not undercut the distinction. Rather it shows that in ordinary Greek, 'Be good!' or '. . . is good' can be used to cover both (i) being good in the strict sense, as well as (ii) behaving or acting well on an occasion. (Similarly in English, we do not say things like 'Don't be stupid!' to those we think really are stupid—or if we do say it to those we think really are stupid, we do not say this intending the person(s) addressed to *change*, so as to cease being stupid—rather we typically say such things to exhort those who we think are not stupid not to *behave* stupidly.) We will again need to rely on the context to decide which construal is appropriate. But an exhortation to fight bravely—"And whoever among you desires to see his friends and family again, let him remember to *be a good man* (ἀνήρ ἀγαθὸς εἶναι)" (*Anab.* III.2.39)—should hardly be understood as a recommendation or command to acquire a new character; such a remark is rather urging and commending a way of acting in the specific situation. Thus the Xenophon passsage is strictly parallel to passages where we find γίγνεσθαι used, like Thucydides V.9.9 or VII.77.7.

simple present to refer to a standing disposition, feature, or characteristic of the subject, while the present progressive is used to refer to behavior or to the display of a feature, on an individual occasion.[47]

Now although it may be tempting to suppose that any such display is in fact a manifestation of an underlying capacity or disposition, in certain contexts it remains an open question whether or not the display actually corresponds to the relevant underlying characteristic. Indeed on some occasions, one might use the present progressive precisely to indicate that what is being attributed to the subject is *not* some more or less permanent feature but an uncharacteristic display of something at odds with the basic characteristics, call it the nature, of that subject. Thus, 'He is being a bad boy', said of a child who is basically well-behaved, does not indicate that the child has changed his disposition to behave well, but rather indicates something about the way he is behaving in the present circumstances or situation. Similarly, we might say of someone reading Vergil aloud that he is reading Latin, even if the person in question does not know Latin, and we know perfectly well that he does not know Latin.

The claim thus is that when 'becoming' is being contrasted with 'being' in the Greek passages considered, it plays a role similar to this use of the present progressive of 'to be' in English. That is to say, if x becomes y, it need not be the case that x (actually) is y. What is being claimed is that x is being y, where this is compatible with the possibility that x may (actually) not be y.[48]

So we have the following results. First of all, it is clear that, in the *Protagoras*, Plato explicitly contrasts his understanding of the distinction between being and becoming with other available construals of the distinction. Secondly, it is even clearer that his (special) understanding of it has a real basis in well-attested Greek usage. However, the texts we have examined or adverted to in Sections 5 and 6 do not in any way prepare us for a suggestion which we have already encountered, namely, that some items *only* become (whatever they become) and *never* are (anything). No claim

---

[47] B. Comrie's *Aspect* (Cambridge, 1976) is a concise introduction to the topic of verbal aspect. For more on aspect and *Aktionsart* in English, see L. Brinton, *The Development of English Aspectual Systems* (Cambridge, 1988); chaps. 1 and 2 provide a useful overview of various proposed analyses of the contrast between the progressive and simple present, and between the progressive and the perfect.

[48] C. Kahn, in his *The Verb 'Be' in Ancient Greek* (Dordrecht, 1973), also notes that, in Greek, *is* and *becomes* differ in aspect; but he offers a rather different account of that difference (see pp. 194–207).

to this effect would be part of any ordinary understanding of becoming. Indeed, taken by itself, we have trouble seeing what that could even mean. Clearly, if Plato is committed to making this claim, it must be as the result of his theoretical reflection; and so we must look to Plato's philosophy to give it content.

In the next eight sections, I would like to consider Plato's picture of the participants (in the middle dialogues), as well as the philosophical background against which he proposes it, to try to understand why he wants to make this startling sounding claim. What leads him—what could lead him—to say that ordinary things, strictly speaking, never are (anything at all), but only become (some of what, loosely speaking, they are said to 'be')? Against that background, we will then, in Section 15, be able to see how the metaphysical picture of the Late-Learners is a striking alternative to Plato's.

7. The Participants: Plato and Anaxagoreanism

It will be useful to begin our investigation of Plato's picture of the participants by turning to the so-called affinity argument from the *Phaedo* (78b ff.). There Plato again divides all the things that can, loosely speaking, be called beings into two classes; the one comprises Forms, the other participants.[49] Moreover, in the course of that discussion, Plato attributes a fairly large number of systematically related features to the items in each of the two classes. At the very start of the passage, we hear:

(A1) x is not subject to dispersal, if it is incomposite; and
(A2) x is subject to dispersal, if it is composite.

And from the immediately following lines, despite some textual worries, we can conclude:

(B1) x is incomposite, if it is immutable; and
(B2) x is composite, if it is mutable.

Finally, at 78d we learn:

(C1) x is immutable, if it is uniform (μονοειδές).[50]

---

[49] See 79a–b: δύο εἴδη τῶν ὄντων (two kinds of beings). Note that we here have nontechnical uses of both ὄν (being) and εἶδος (form).

[50] 78d5–6: ἢ ἀεὶ αὐτῶν ἕκαστον ὅ ἐστι, μονοειδὲς ὂν αὐτὸ καθ᾽ αὑτό, ὡσαύτως κατὰ ταὐτὰ ἔχει καὶ ... The expresssion, μονοειδὲς ὄν, clearly is explanatory or justificatory—see, e.g., Heindorf (*Platonis Dialogi Selecti*, vol. 4 [Berlin, 1810], p. 100, ad loc.), who

And from the discussion at 80b, we can see:

(C2) *x* is mutable, if it is multiform (πολυειδές).

Obviously, A1, B1, and C1 are about features of the Forms; and A2, B2, and C2 are about features of the participants.

It has frequently been thought that Plato is claiming, in this passage from the *Phaedo*, that the participants have these features because they are *material* objects, while the Forms can be characterized in the way they are characterized, because they are *immaterial*. However, Plato does not in fact use the notion of matter or materiality here; and as we will see, matter quite irrelevant to the argument. Since it is uniformity and multi-formity that explain or give rise to the other features, it will be best to begin with them. In what way, then, is a participant multiform?

. . . . .

The answer to this question will be clearer if we first look at Anaxagoras's 'theory' of participation.[51] Anaxagoras also posits two classes of what can, loosely speaking, be called beings:[52]

(I) The *elemental quasi-stuffs*, and

(II) *Mixtures of portions* of the elemental quasi-stuffs.

---

writes: "*quatenus simplex est* (since it is simple)"; cf. G. Prauss, "Ding und Eigenschaft bei Platon und Aristoteles," *Kant-Studien* 59 (1968), p. 104. This is completely obscured in some translations (e.g., Hackforth's "or does each one of these uniform and independent entities remain always constant and invariable"), and is not sufficiently clear in others (e.g., Gallop's "Or does *what each one of them is*, being uniform alone by itself, remain unvarying and constant" [emphasis in the original]; cf. Grube's "being uniform by itself"). For a similar use of μονοειδές, see *Symposium* 211b1 and 211e4.

[51] One might suppose that *participation* is a technical notion from Platonic metaphysics, and so find it objectionable to speak of Anaxagoras's theory or view of participation. However, since Anaxagoras uses the language of participation, such an objection will be misplaced. The question will rather be, how are we to understand that language. For μετέχειν (have a share of) in Anaxagoras, see B 6 (DK, p. 35, 16); B 12 (p. 37, 18 and 21); and for ἔνειναι (be in), see B 4a (p. 34, 5); B 4c (p. 35, 4); B 6 (p. 35, 19); cf. Plato's frequent use of παρουσία (presence in). For uses of ἔνειναι and παρεῖναι in authors besides Plato see also H. C. Baldry, "Plato's 'Technical Terms,' " *Classical Quarterly* 31 (1937), esp. pp. 145–46. It is perhaps worth noting that Baldry seems to be following F. M. Cornford on these matters.

[52] The question of where Νοῦς (Reason or Mind) fits into this scheme is certainly important for a complete understanding of Anaxagoras. Obviously it will belong either into class I or into a separate class, all its own. Fortunately, Νοῦς does not matter for those issues in Anaxagoras' physical theory with which we are concerned here, so it can be ignored safely.

Before examining some of the details about the items in these two classes, two cautionary points. First, as soon as one speaks of stuffs, however qualified, it may be tempting to suppose that *matter* is in fact being spoken of. And since Aristotle does interpret Presocratics like Anaxagoras as if they were trying to give an account of the being of things in terms of their material constituents, it is easy to slip into thinking that these thinkers themselves see the issue in this way. The stuffs then would appear to be things denoted by mass-terms (construing that notion narrowly).[53] But this is a mistake. For it leaves open, and may even invite, a contrast between the *stuffs* (like water), on the one hand, and the *features* or *properties* of the stuffs (like the water's wetness), on the other.

Jonathan Barnes, for example, in his otherwise very useful discussion of Anaxagoras, writes:

> I propose that we read Anaxagorean 'things' [sc. χρήματα] as stuffs; and I claim that the proposal is fundamentally Aristotelian. What of the obvious objection, that 'the hot', 'the cold', 'the wet' and so on are not stuffs? Here again I side with Aristotle: according to him, Anaxagoras *mistakenly* [my emphasis] treats properties, like 'the hot', as substances; the criticism seems to me to be just, for the fragments reveal Anaxagoras doing exactly that.[54]

In a note to this paragraph, he asks, "Why not simply say Anaxagorean things are both stuffs and qualities?"[55] Barnes answers his own question, "But then Anaxagoras' theory is inelegant; and *he* gives no hint that his 'things' fall into two classes."

Of course Anaxagoras gives no such hint, for from his point of view the quasi-stuffs do not fall into two classes, stuffs (i.e., material substance stuffs) and properties.[56] Rather, the single class of what I have been calling

---

[53] O. Jespersen, *The Philosophy of Grammar* (London, 1924), seems to have introduced the term 'mass-word' (see pp. 198–201) to cover both material items (e.g., water, butter, etc.) as well as immaterial ones (e.g., success, leisure, justice, etc.). By a narrow construal, I simply mean, restricted to material substances. The literature on mass-terms is vast. In thinking about the issues in these essays, I have found the following especially useful: T. Parsons, "An Analysis of Mass Terms and Amount Terms," *Foundations of Language* 6 (1970); G. Bealer, "Predication and Matter," *Synthese* 31, nos. 3/4 (1975); P. M. S. Hacker, "Substance: The Constitution of Reality," *Midwest Studies in Philosophy* 4 (1979); and P. Simon, *Parts: A Study in Ontology* (Oxford, 1987), pp. 153–62.

[54] *The Presocratic Philosophers*, 2: p. 20.

[55] Ibid., p. 295 n. 9.

[56] As H. C. Baldry, following F. M. Cornford (see n. 51 above), remarked: "It is generally recognized . . . that the majority of fifth-century thinkers made no distinction between 'substances' and 'attributes', but vaguely regarded qualities as 'things', on the same level as

quasi-stuffs is characterized by certain features (on which, more below) that serve to demarcate class I from class II. It is only from the perspective of Aristotelian and post-Aristotelian metaphysics that this will look like an illegitimate conflation of heterogeneous ontological categories. The elemental quasi-stuffs Anaxagoras and others speak of should therefore instead be thought of as what is denoted by certain *non-count terms* quite generally, and not just by mass-terms, narrowly construed. (I take the expression 'non-count term' from Hacker.)[57] Most simply, a term X will be a count term, if we can speak of *many*, or *few*, or precisely *this number* of X's, and thus can ask, 'How many, or how few, X's are there?' A term Y will be a non-count term, if we can speak of *much*, or *little* of Y, but *not of the number* of Y's, and can thus instead ask, 'How much, or how little of Y is there?' But to be a non-count term, a term need not be a mass-term, in the sense of referring to a material stuff. (The general distinction should be clear, despite the fact that certain English words can function as both count and non-count terms.)[58] The relevance of this to Anaxagoras and other Presocratics is that the hot, the wet, or the white will be elemen-

---

other 'things' " ("Plato's 'Technical Vocabulary,' " p. 145). The example of Barnes shows that this remains far from being generally recognized. More importantly, in formulating his remark, Baldry (perhaps not surprisingly) resorts to Aristotelian terminology. But this blunts the force of his fundamentally correct observation: the πϱάγματα or χϱήματα of the Presocratics cannot be qualities masquerading as things, nor vice versa—for neither things nor qualities are on the scene yet (so to speak).

[57] See his "Substance: The Constitution of Reality."

[58] However, in many (maybe most) cases where expressions can be used as both count or non-count expressions, they can actually be used in only one of the two different ways in a given context, with that context determining *which* of the two that is. Contrast, for example, 'I want some more goose' with 'I want some more geese'! (The word 'goose' is being used as a non-count expression in the first sentence, but as a count term—with an irregular plural—in the second.) Another example: if we say that there are many cheeses in the cheese shop, this means there are many kinds or varieties of cheese (*not* that there are many pieces of cheese, or even, many whole cheeses); while if we say that there is much cheese in the refrigerator, we are treating 'cheese' as a non-count term, and not distinguishing the kinds or even the pieces of cheese in the refrigerator. (Thus there might be much cheese in the refrigerator, even if there is only one kind of cheese, and even if there are not very many pieces—provided the pieces that are there are large ones; think of a large wheel of Emmenthaler, etc.). Similarly, a term like 'duck' is normally a count term, though sentences like 'Duck is one of her favorite foods' or 'The dinner was good, except there wasn't enough duck for everyone' shows it can be used as a non-count term. Moreover, by adding expressions like 'piece of', 'bit of', 'portion of' and so on, we can easily form countable units, even of things which are designated by non-count expressions (consider, e.g., 'periods of leisure', 'moments of quiet', or 'strokes of good fortune'; and 'a piece of gold', 'a puff of smoke', or 'a share of the whole').

tal—members of class I—in the same way, and to the same extent, that water, air, or earth are. Whether further stuffs, like gold, wood, bone, or blood, are also elemental for Anaxagoras, as had traditionally been supposed, has come to be disputed.[59] In what follows, I will be assuming that all such items are elemental. But the logical or structural point is not affected by being less, rather than more inclusive about which quasi-stuffs are elemental. All that matters is that Anaxagoras countenances as elements both items we would treat as stuffs and items we would regard as properties. And that he surely does do.

Thus I believe we should not start out by supposing that Anaxagoras is confused about mass-stuffs and their features in the way that Barnes and Aristotle suggest. Nor should we suppose that he simply treats properties as things (viz., stuffs), and things as properties. We should rather recognize that Anaxagoras is innocent of this distinction. Having recognized that, we should try to become as clear as possible about his ontological picture on its own terms, and only then go on to consider how well it solves the metaphysical problems it needs to solve. Of course here it may well turn out that, ultimately, Aristotle's distinction—or something relevantly similar—is necessary for any adequate solution of even those very problems. With this proviso in mind, I will for the most part simply speak of the elemental quasi-stuffs as stuffs, that is, as stuffs in the Anaxagorean, not the Aristotelian sense.

Secondly, as soon as one speaks of stuffs (again, in whatever sense), it may be tempting to think that objects *constituted out of* or *from* the stuffs are also being thought of. Here as well, the analysis that Aristotle provides of objects, as composites of matter and form, encourages us to think in this way. But again this would be a mistake. For once one thinks of the relation between objects and stuffs as one of constitution, it is natural to see the objects as independent of the stuffs to at least this degree: it will be intelligible to ask, about some object, could *this object* be constituted of different stuff than the stuff from which it is actually constituted? (Consider questions like: could *this statue* be made of different bronze than the bronze of which it is made? Indeed, could *this statue* be made of a different metal altogether? And even, could *this person* consist of different flesh, blood, and bone than the flesh, blood, and bone of which she presently consists?) Pressing such a line of thought may well encourage us to look for, say, identity conditions of objects that do not directly invoke, or even

[59] See Malcolm Schofield, *An Essay on Anaxagoras* (Cambridge, 1981), especially chap. 4, "Seeds, Portions and Opposites," pp. 100–144.

111

depend on, the stuffs. Form plays this role in Aristotle.[60] But Anaxagoras did not have Aristotle's notion of form, nor does he employ any equivalent concept. And thus while the mixtures, in some way, are the ordinary things in the world around us, the objects of everyday experience, we should not think of these objects as being constituted out of the stuffs—they just *are* mixtures of bits or portions of stuffs. Again, it may turn out that, ultimately, this proves to be an inadequate way of thinking about them (perhaps for the sorts of reasons Aristotle offers). Nevertheless, we should first look to see what the theory is actually claiming.

So let us do just that. What more, then, is there to say about the two classes of beings? Class I contains a very large, perhaps an infinite number of stuffs like water, stone (B 16), or gold (A 41), silver, . . . , and flesh, bone (B 10), blood, . . . , but also the hot, the wet (B 4c), . . . , and white, black (Arist., *Phys.* 187^{b}5), ... These stuffs have the following characteristics:

(i) Any portion of an elemental stuff is the same stuff.
(They are, in Aristotle's terminology, *homoiomerous*; see *De Gen. et Corr.* 314^{a}18–20 or *De Caelo* 302^{a}31–^{b}3.)[61]

(ii) They are infinitely divisible into such portions, i.e., there is no least portion. (See B 3 and B 5.)

(iii) They are eternally and immutably what they are. (See, e.g., B 17; cf. B 10.)

(iv) They are wholly and purely what they are.

And it is because these stuffs are only (whatever they are) and never become (anything else) that they can be said to be beings, strictly speaking. The items in class I, in other words, are thought to satisfy Eleatic strictures on being.

---

[60] Other approaches are possible as well. For an extensive discussion of various contemporary approaches, see Simons, *Parts*, pp. 210–360. Mark Johnston's "Constitution Is Not Identity," *Mind* 102 (1992), is an elegant recent attempt to prise apart constitution and identity.

[61] In *De Gen. et Corr.* I, 314^{a}20 f., Aristotle characterizes the notion of 'homoioemery' in terms of *his* notion of synonymy: "He [Anaxagoras] posits the homoiomeries as elements—e.g., bone, flesh, marrow and those others whose parts are *synonyms* of the whole." In other words, homoiomeries are those wholes whose parts have the same name and the same account as the whole; recall *Cat.* 1^{a}6–8.

The mixtures, the items in class II, are the things we would call sensible particulars (and sensible stuffs). The features they have will be explained in terms of the elemental stuffs and by two principles. First, the Principle of Latency:[62]

Everything has a share of everything.
(See B 6, B 11, and B 12.)

This is usually taken to mean that every *mixture*, that is, every sensible thing, has some portion (however tiny) of every *elemental stuff* within itself.[63]

Anaxagoras seems to want this principle in order to explain all 'change' (and 'generation' and 'destruction') in the ordinary sense, as the result of the remixing and recombining of the (immutable and indestructible) stuffs that are already present (see B 17). (Clearly, a change in the location or distribution of some elemental stuff is not to count as a bona fide change.) Thus, because there is some small portion of stuff S in a mixture M, M can be said to be S (at least latently). Hence a 'change' from M being overtly not-S to its being manifestly S will really be an episode of adding more of S to the portion of S that is already present in M.[64] If there had been no S at all in our mixture M, such a 'change' would really have been a *change*—from M not being S in any way to being S. But that is precisely the sort of change Parmenides was thought to have shown to be impossible. With his Principle of Latency, then, Anaxagoras is able to maintain, with Parmenides, that no new beings come into being, and no old beings pass out of being.

Yet if everything has a share of everything, why aren't all things alike? The answer comes in two parts. In the beginning, that is, before the cosmos in its present form existed, all things were alike, in a kind of cosmic slurry. Now, of course, there are differences among things. All of these differences are to be explained by the second principle, the Principle of Predominance:

---

[62] I take the names for these principles from D. J. Furley; see his "Anaxagoras in Response to Parmenides," p. 68 (= *Cosmic Problems*, p. 53).

[63] For this interpretation of the Principle of Latency, see, for example, C. Strang, "The Physical Theory of Anaxagoras," *Archiv für Geschichte der Philosophie* 45 (1963), reprinted in *Studies in Presocratic Philosophy*, vol. 2, ed. R. E. Allen and D. J. Furley, (London, 1975), and D. J. Furley, "Anaxagoras in Response to Parmenides."

[64] This, of course, can be accomplished either by directly adding something that has a higher proportion of S in it (a purer instance of S) or by removing some of what is not-S from M.

An item will manifest itself as those elemental things that predominate in the mixture.

(See, e.g., B 12 fin.; cf. Aristotle *Phys.* 187^{b}2–7.)

(This predominance or preponderance need not be a purely quantitative matter. Think of how even small variations in the spices can affect the character of the dishes in which they are used. Secondly, the things over which a given thing can even in principle predominate must be restricted in some rough and ready way. For example, the wet can predominate over the dry, and vice versa, but not over the hot or the cold. It would be very natural to see the traditional opposites of Greek thought as being some of the groupings that appropriately restrict the range of possible predomination. Others will no doubt be needed as well.)[65]

The relation between the mixtures and the elemental stuffs thus has the following characteristics. First, the mixtures clearly are derivative items; for they depend on there being elemental stuffs. But there is no reason why, in principle, there could not be only elemental stuffs and no mixtures at all. Secondly, the mixtures literally have a share of—participate in—the elemental stuffs; conversely, the elemental stuffs literally are present in the mixtures. (In other words, the elemental stuffs will be *wholes* of which the bits that are present in the mixtures are *parts*. These bits are also *parts* of the *wholes* that are the mixtures.) Thirdly, the mixtures are called what they are called on account of the elemental stuffs that are in them, while the elemental stuffs are called what they are called in their own right. For example, a gold crown is said to be gold (viz., phenomenal gold) because gold (viz., elemental gold) is its predominant ingredient.[66] But the gold that is in the crown is said to be gold because that just is what it is. Fourthly, the mixtures are not eternally or immutably whatever they are

---

[65] If various metals count as elements, then gold could perhaps predominate over lead, in things that are gold (and lead over gold, in things that are lead). Since there are obviously more than two kinds of metals, the constraints on the range(s) of possible predominance will be more complicated. The idea would have to be that a metal is not even a candidate for predominating over, say, spices.

[66] Someone might want to urge that the crown should be said to be 'golden', not 'gold'. That someone is Aristotle. Indeed, as *Metaphysics* VII, 7 shows, Aristotle wants to go further: quite generally, if *x* is made of a certain kind of *matter*, we should not say that *x* is *that* (ἐκεῖνο)—sc. that matter—but *thaten* (ἐκείνινον; 1033^{b}6–7); that is to say, in case we do not have an existing term, like 'golden', Aristotle wants us to coin new ones. (Cf. the whole of 1033^{a}5–23; see also *Phys.* 245^{b}9–12 and *Met.* IX, 7, 1049^{a}18–27.) These neologisms will make it less likely that we identify a thing with its matter. Anaxagoras seems to take no note of such differences; nor, as we shall see, does Plato (at least not before the *Theaetetus*).

said to be. Finally, the mixtures are only impurely and partially what the elemental stuffs are really and fully.

Now on this Anaxagorean view, participants (i.e., the mixtures) will in fact present a multiplicity of aspects: we can see that they are more than one thing, simply in virtue of the fact that they are mixtures. So from the very fact that they present themselves as having several features—as being *multiform*—we can tell that they are composite and hence subject to change. And because they are composite, they are dissoluble (that is, the ingredients in the mixture can be redistributed) and hence subject to dispersal. (Strictly speaking, of course, no ingredient will ever be removed totally—recall the Principle of Latency. Nevertheless, enough of any ingredient can be removed, or enough of some other ingredient can be added to predominate over it, in order to make the mixture not merely 'change', but 'cease to be'.)

On the other hand, the elemental stuffs (which, according to Anaxagoras, *we* never actually do encounter in an unmixed state) are *uniform* in the relevant way. For since they are only one thing, they would present themselves only as what they are. Because they are only one thing, they cannot change. (Such a change would involve generating a new being and, perhaps, destroying an old one.) They are also clearly not composite. Hence, according to the theory, they are not dissoluble, not subject to dispersal.

Here it is absolutely crucial to recognize that *two very different notions* of dissolution or division, and thus also of part or portion, are at work in the picture. It was after all part of the very definition of the elemental stuffs that they *can* be divided homoiomerously—just as we can scoop out cups of water from the ocean or draw a glass of port from a cask, and each cup will be water, and a portion of the water that was in the ocean, and each glass, a glass of port, indeed some of the port that had been in the cask. So this cannot be the sense of division that is being ruled out.

The elemental stuffs are indivisible in another sense: not only can we not physically extract any portion of them that will not be the same as they are, we cannot even *conceptually* distinguish such a portion or part. It is this second sort of divisibility that is at issue. And *no* elemental stuff will be divisible in this way (not being so divisible is simply part of being elemental). But of course *any* mixture, simply in virtue of the fact that it is a mixture, will consist of more than one thing. Hence it will be divisible in this second way, even if it should not turn out to be divisible in the first way.

In light of this, we might wonder if the elemental stuffs and the mixtures are wholes in the same sense; and likewise if the bits, which are parts of both the stuffs and the mixtures, are parts in the same sense. Anaxagoras does not address this in the extant fragments, and we may well doubt whether he did so at all. We will see a similar question arising in connection with Plato's Forms.

How good, then, is Anaxagoras's response to Parmenides?[67] From the evidence we have considered—even if only briefly—it seems that he can account, first of all, for what Aristotle would call qualitative change (alteration); secondly, for growth and diminution (e.g., phenomenal flesh grows by the addition of elemental flesh); thirdly, for one of the kinds of substantial change (e.g., some phenomenal water can change into phenomenal air, if elemental air comes to predominate in that mixture); and fourthly, as we already have seen, change of location is not to count as a bona fide change at all and thus is unproblematic. For all these kinds of changes Anaxagoras has explanations, and, given the sorts of views his is competing against, not unattractive ones.

However, it looks as if he cannot meet Parmenides' challenge when it comes to the generation and perishing of living organisms. Thus while we can fairly easily see, at least in principle, how, say, flesh, blood, and sinew come to be out of what is (only latently) flesh, blood, or sinew, and hence why none of these is a case of something coming to be out of what it is not (in any way), how are we to explain the coming to be of *whole* organisms: cats, human beings, and so on? As David Furley succinctly observes, unless Anaxagoras has something to say at this juncture, he will only have "postponed the problem, not . . . solved it."[68]

Now Anaxagoras does have something to say, but it is by far the least satisfactory component of his picture. He holds that there are (latently) everywhere *seeds* for everything, i.e., for all living things. These seeds need not, and presumably should not, be thought of atomistically, that is, as being discrete particles. Rather, think of them as portions of *seed-stuffs*.[69] We need to imagine that a portion of human seed-stuff "contains, latent within it, small quantities of all the parts of the adult body, and these are 'separated out' as nutrition adds to them."[70]

---

[67] In speaking this way, I do not mean to suggest that Parmenides himself would regard any of Anaxagoras's position as acceptable.

[68] Furley, "Anaxagoras in Response to Parmenides," p. 66 (= *Cosmic Problems*, p. 51).

[69] See Barnes, *The Presocratic Philosophers*, 2:21; compare also the views Aristotle discusses at *De Gen. Animal.* IV, 769ᵃ6–35.

[70] Furley, "Anaxagoras in Response to Parmenides," p. 75 (= *Cosmic Problems*, p. 58).

But it is easy to feel, with Furley, that "the mechanism creaks here a little".[71] For while (phenomenal) bone grows by the addition of more (elemental) bone, a (phenomenal) human being does not grow by the addition of more (elemental) human being—nested like Russian dolls— but precisely by the addition of (elemental) bone, blood, and so on. Thus even if Anaxagoras is in a position to say that a human being comes to be from what is (latently) a human being, and hence not from what is not (in any way) a human being, he seems to have no account whatsoever of the *relation* between the human being—the whole organism—and the flesh, blood, bone, sinew, and so on that it has. Surely, however—and Aristotle will press this point—we want such an account. Once again, we will see that we encounter a similar problem in Plato.

. . . . .

The parallels to Plato's view of Forms and participants are clear—even though he does not want to construe part, portion, and participation in such literal terms.[72] Plato was obviously familiar with Anaxagoras (as we can see from the *Phaedo* itself; cf. 97c) and with some medical views that are quite similar to Anaxagoras's view of physical things.[73] One of the

---

[71] Ibid., p. 81 (= *Cosmic Problems*, p. 63).

[72] This is at least suggested by *Phaedo* 100d3–6, which speaks of the relationship between Form and participant as "presence in, communion with, or *whatever* it is" (or if we accept Wyttenbach's conjecture here, "*whatever* it should be called"; my emphasis, both times). Yet why would Plato even raise this terminological issue, if a literal, Anaxagorean understanding of an 'element' being present in a 'participant' seemed perfectly in order to him?

[73] The question of the relationship between medical theory and Plato is obviously much too complex to be considered in any detail here. However, it is quite certain that Plato takes medicine seriously. Consider only (i) Plato's remarks about Hippocrates in the *Phaedrus* (270c ff.); (ii) the prominent place the doctor Eryximachus occupies in the *Symposium* (on which, cf. L. Edelstein, "The Role of Eryximachus in Plato's *Symposium*," *Transactions of the American Philological Association* 76 [1945], and D. Konstan, "Eryximachus' Speech in the *Symposium*," *Apeiron* 16 [1982]); and perhaps most importantly, (iii) the 'medical passage' in the *Timaeus*, which shows Plato's familiarity with medical theorizing even if it is not, as was once thought (e.g., by M. Wellman, *Fragmente der sikelischen Ärzte* [Berlin, 1901]), a direct reflection of Philistion's theories.—As far as Anaxagoreanism is concerned, the use made of the hot, the cold, the wet, and the dry at *Symp.* 188a, and the use made of earth, fire, water, and air at *Tim.* 82a–b should be compared with, e.g., [Hippocrates] *The Nature of Man* iii, 19–34 or *On Ancient Medicine* i; xiii; xv. These passages suggest that at least certain medical theorists made the hot, the cold, the wet, and the dry the principles of their theorizing about health and illness. *The Nature of Man* vii, 52 ff. shows that these were sometimes conceived of as more general principles as well (that is, not just principles of health or of living things). *The Nature of Man* i, 1 ff. shows that it was easy to pass from talk of fire, water, etc., to talk of the hot, the wet, and so on (cf. *On Regimen* I, iv, 1 ff.

117

members of the Academy, namely, Eudoxus, even went on to offer an Anaxagorean view of the Forms (see Aristotle *Met.* 991ª14–19 or 1079ᵇ16–22, and especially, Alexander *In Met.* 97, 27–98, 24).⁷⁴ Thus it seems quite plausible to suppose, as has in fact often been suggested, that Plato's picture of Forms and participants and, indeed, the very language of participation owes a great deal to Presocratic views like those of Anaxagoras and the medical thinkers.⁷⁵ Hence I would like to suggest that in

---

and Philistion Fr. 4 Wellman). *On Ancient Medicine* xv shows that it was easy to move from talk of hotness or coldness to talk of the hot or the cold, and vice versa (in other words, the abstract noun and the definite article + neuter adjective constructions are interchangeable here as well). The criticisms Diocles of Carystus directs at certain doctors show that, even after Aristotle, medical writers did not universally distinguish between stuffs, like water, and their features, like wetness; some continued to think in an Anaxagorean way. (On Diocles, see W. Jaeger, *Diokles von Karystos* [Berlin, 1938], and his "Diocles of Carystus: A New Pupil of Aristotle," *Philosophical Review* 49 [1940].) Connections between medical theory and Anaxagoras himself are especially clear in [Hippocrates] *On Regimen* I, iv, 23–35, which has long been thought to have been influenced by Anaxagoras. Similarities in technical vocabulary between *On Ancient Medicine* and the fragments of Anaxagoras are noted most usefully by G. Vlastos, in his review of F. M. Cornford: *Principium Sapientiae*, reprinted in *Studies in Presocratic Philosophy*, vol. 2, ed. D. J. Furley and R. E. Allen (London, 1970); see pp. 45–46 n. 4. A useful discussion of the philosophical issues raised by *On Ancient Medicine* is provided by H. Diller, "Hippokratische Medizin und attische Philosophie," *Hermes* 80 (1952). His post-Platonic date for the treatise, however, has been widely rejected; see J.-H. Kuehn, *System und Methodenprobleme im Corpus Hippocraticum*, *Hermes Einzelschriften* 11 (1956), and G. E. R. Lloyd "Who Is Attacked in *On Ancient Medicine*?" *Phronesis* 8 (1963). Lloyd also discusses many more passages from the Hippocratic Corpus that contain this sort of Anaxagorean language or reflect this way of thinking.

⁷⁴ Aristotle writes: "But they [sc. the Forms] do not help . . . towards their [sc. sensible particulars'] being, if they are not *in* the things which participate in them; though if they were, they might be thought to be causes, as the white <is a cause of being white>, when it is mixed in something white. But this argument, which first Anaxagoras and then Eudoxus (and some others) used, is upset too easily" (*Met.* 991ª12–18).

⁷⁵ In addition to G. Prauss's "Ding und Eigenschaft bei Platon und Aristoteles" and D. J. Furley's "Anaxagoras in Response to Parmenides," see J. Brentlinger, "Incomplete Predicates and the Two-World Theory of the *Phaedo*," *Phronesis* 17 (1972), and N. Denyer, "Plato's Theory of Stuffs," *Philosophy* 58 (1983). Denyer offers a very spirited defense of this sort of interpretation of the *Phaedo*, see sect. 3, pp. 316–21. A. L. Peck, in his "Anaxagoras: Predication as a Problem in Physics," *Classical Quarterly* 25 (1931), laid important groundwork for this line of interpretation. It is curious that R. Dancy, in his careful and extensive discussion of Anaxagoreanism (which he calls 'Immanentism') in Plato, does not consider the Affinity Argument from the *Phaedo*. See his *Two Studies in the Early Academy* (Albany, N.Y., 1981), "Study 1. Predication and Immanence: Anaxagoras, Plato, Eudoxus, and Aristotle," pp. 3–59. Perhaps this is because Dancy, in part, is responding to G. Fine's "Immanence" (*Oxford Studies in Ancient Philosophy* 4 [1986]), which is totally silent on the Affinity Argument.

the passage from the *Phaedo* with which we began this section, Plato means essentially the same thing by 'uniform' and 'multiform' that Anaxagoras would have meant (had he used these terms).[76]

Sensible particulars are multiform because they 'are' (though only derivatively) a variety of different things.

Forms are uniform because they **are** (that is are really and nonderivatively) only what they are.

[76] In effect, this was suggested long ago by Ludwig Heindorf (*Platonis Dialogi Selecti*, 4:100), who writes: "μονοειδὲς ὄν, *quatenus simplex est*, i.e. non ex diversis concretum elementis, sed *sincerum* nihilque habens alieni admixtum, velut aurum μονοειδὲς γένος appellatur in Timaeus p. 59 B. Aliud est τὸ ἀσύνθετον" (being uniform, *since it is simple*, i.e., not put together out of various kinds of elements, but *pure* and having nothing other mixed within itself, just as gold is called μονοειδὲς γένος at *Tim.* 59b. Alternatively, it is also τὸ ἀσύνθετον [what is incomposite]) (Heindorf's emphases). Immanuel Bekker, in his edition of the *Phaedo* (London, 1825) expands on Heindorf's observation and provides, with his note to this passage (p. 123), what is perhaps the best discussion of the force of 'uniform': "The Latins (Latini) call it *simple* (*simplex*), or alike in kind (ὁμογενές). Take care lest you think that what is simple is the same for Plato as it is for us, who add the notion of immateriality to this word (huic verbo notionem immaterialitatis subjiciunt); for it means, what has nothing mixed within itself that is either disparate or dissimilar to it (quod nil habet in se admixtum, vel dispar sui atque dissimile), as a passage from Cicero *Academica* I. 8 shows: 'Earum qualitatum sunt aliae principes, aliae ex iis ortae; principes sunt uniusmodi et simplices. Itaque aer et ignis et aqua et terra, prima sunt'. [Of these qualities, some are primary, others arise from these; the primary ones are alone and simple. And so air and fire and water and earth are each primary.] Compare *Cato Major* 21. In another place, Cicero describes what is simplex thus: what has 'nihil concretum, nihil copulatum, nihil coaugmentatum, nihil duplex' [what has 'nothing compounded, nothing joined, nothing added, nor anything twofold'] (*Tusc.* I. 29). Cf. ibid., c. 10: 'nec sit quidquam nisi corpus unum et *simplex*' [nor is there anything except for body, single and *simple*]. Thus [in Latin] what is *simplex* is opposed to what is *mixed* (*mixto*), and to what is put together out of several sorts of elements (ex diversis elementorum generibus concreto), but not to that which has parts (quod habet partes). . . . In this sense, Vergil speaks of the soul (*Aeneid* VI, 747). [See the whole of 724–751, especially 745–47: donec longa dies perfecto temporis orbe/concretam exemit labem, *purum* relinquit/aetherium sensum atque aurai *simplicis* ignem. (until the long day, having completed Time's circle,/takes out the clotted stain, leaving in its *pure* state/the ethereal sentient power and the fiery, *simple* breath). Cf. P. Vergili Maronis *Aeneidos: Liber Sextus*, with a commentary by R. G. Austin (Oxford, 1977), pp. 229–231, ad 743 f.] See also Servius, who has some true things to say. . . . The true force of the word is manifest when it is attributed to inanimate things, like gold, which is called μονοειδὲς γένος, *uniforme* [i.e., a uniform kind], in the *Timaeus* [see 59b]. . . . In the *Symposium* [see 211b], the beautiful (τὸ καλόν) is called μονοειδές, i.e., εἰλικρινές (pure), καθαρόν (pure), ἄμικτον (unmixed), as it had been called earlier. Compare . . . also the *Republic* [see 612a]. What these passages teach us is that τὸ μονοειδές is what is unmixed (ἄμικτον), pure (sincerum), having nothing different from it mixed within it (nihil alieni sibi admixti habens), but being

119

8. SELF-PREDICATION

Before returning to being and becoming, we should note how this picture of participation bears on the troubling issue of self-predication. (Once again, I would like to stress that in using the expression 'self-predication', I mean only to be labeling sentences of a certain form, and not *thereby* to be making any claims about their proper interpretation.) We all know that Plato frequently uses sentences of the form, 'the *X* is *X*' or, '*X*-ness is *X*'; but it has often been thought that he accepts these odd-sounding claims because they are consequences of his metaphysical theory. However, as noted in the introduction, SP sentences make their first appearance in the *Hippias Major*, *Lysis*, and *Protagoras* and are there accepted by various figures—who surely should not be thought of as believers in Platonic Forms—as trivially and obviously true.

Thus, as suggested at the outset, it would be desirable to have an account of these SP sentences that does not depend on Plato's own metaphysics. Moreover, we should want an account that avoids forcing us to interpret the SP sentences in the objectionable way, that is, as involving confusing being an object with being a property, or being a property with having a property, and thus as wrongly attributing a property to a property.

We have already seen that an expression of the form 'the *X*' (= neuter definite article + adjective; see pp. 15–16 above) can be used in at least three important and importantly different ways. It can refer, first, to a particular (instance of) *x*; secondly, to particular *x*'s (instances of *x*) in general; and thirdly, to something general, *x*-ness, which can also be referred to by the corresponding abstract noun, '*X*-ness'. Indeed, we should regard abstract nouns as merely lexical variants for such constructions.[77] But these are not three independent uses of 'the *X*'. The diagram, which considers the examples of the white (τὸ λευκόν) and the beautiful (τὸ καλόν), may help to show how these uses are systematically related.[78]

We have (ii) and (ii′) because of an assumption that seems to be made implicitly. Suppose something is white. Any ordinary thing that is white

---

of a single kind (sed unius generis). From these notions . . . it is not possible to extract the notion of *immateriality*. . . ."—Compare also *Theaetetus* 205c4–205d2. (Emphases in Bekker's text are his own; in the Vergil quotation, they are mine.)

[77] In general, abstract nouns start appearing in the Greek language later than the definite article + neuter adjective constructions.

[78] I owe these formulations to Michael Frede. See also Meinwald, *Plato's Parmenides*, pp. 15–16.

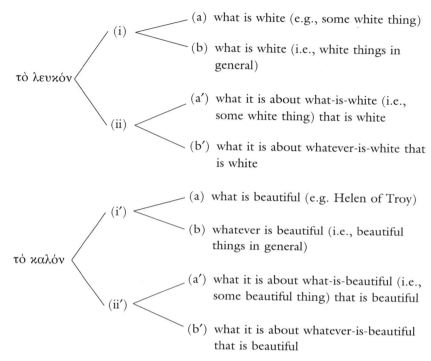

τὸ λευκόν

(i)
(a) what is white (e.g., some white thing)
(b) what is white (i.e., white things in general)

(ii)
(a′) what it is about what-is-white (i.e., some white thing) that is white
(b′) what it is about whatever-is-white that is white

τὸ καλόν

(i′)
(a) what is beautiful (e.g. Helen of Troy)
(b) whatever is beautiful (i.e., beautiful things in general)

(ii′)
(a′) what it is about what-is-beautiful (i.e., some beautiful thing) that is beautiful
(b′) what it is about whatever-is-beautiful that is beautiful

will, of course, be many other things as well; it is after all not only white. Hence one might ask, what about it is white, or, what in it is white? (As opposed to, say, what about it is hot, or, what is hot in it?) Part of the assumption seems to be that there must be something like that—leave aside, for the moment, just what that actually is—or else the thing would not be white in the first place. Thus it seems that, whatever this *nescio quid* may turn out to be, it will be responsible for the thing's being white, in the sense that it is at least a necessary condition for the thing's being white. (The claim that Platonic Forms are *causes* of the participants' being what they 'are' is a specific version of this general idea.) And if one assumes, as Socrates surely does, that what it is about a white thing that is white will be the same for all white things, (ii a′) simply collapses into (ii b′).

Similarly, suppose someone (more fortunate than us, who can no longer do so) looks at Pheidias's statue of Zeus at Olympia and reacts in the way Dio Chrysostom describes: "whoever is completely burdened in his soul, having had many misfortunes and much grief in his life, and not having attained sweet sleep, even he, I believe, if he stood before this image, would forget all the terrible and hard things one must suffer in human

121

life. Such a sight (θέαμα) did you [Pheidias] devise and fashion" (XII.51–2). Yet even this surpassingly beautiful statue is many things besides beautiful. And so we might well be prompted to ask, what about this statue is beautiful?—as opposed to asking, say, what about this statue is sublime? (The answers to both questions may of course turn out to the same; recall and compare Socrates' doctrine of the unity of the virtues.) Again, the assumption is that if there were nothing like that, the Zeus of Pheidias would not be beautiful. (Note the affinity of this picture with the 'safe' view of the *Phaedo*, the view Socrates begins outlining at 99d ff.)

. . . . .

Now to self-predication. It is perfectly clear why the SP sentences corresponding to (i) and (i') are true. Let us take (i a) as an example. From the very fact that we have identified some thing as a white thing, it follows that it is white; 'What is white is white' is true. But that just is to say that 'The white (sc. thing) is white' is true as well. The predicate, in the SP sentence so construed, adds nothing; that is why the sentence is trivially true. The same account, mutatis mutandis, applies to (i b), (i' a) and (i' b).

But it also applies to the SP sentences corresponding to (ii b') and (ii' b'). For as soon as we speak of 'what it is about whatever-is-white that is white', we have again, in effect, *already* predicated white. Thus the predicate in the sentence, 'What it is about whatever-is-white that is white, is white' (however difficult this may be to parse), also is adding nothing.[79] Hence figures like Protagoras and Hippias can accept the SP sentences as readily as they do.

(We will need to consider whether this means that SP sentences are identity statements, as has sometimes been held. I would like to defer considering this extremeley important question until Section 16, where we can then consider it together with the corresponding question about the Late-Learners' sentences.)

Of course nothing said here answers the substantive questions: what, then, is this that is white about whatever-is-white; what, then, is this that is beautiful about whatever-is-beautiful? (Hence I allowed myself the expression *nescio quid* a few lines back.) Calling that *quid* the beautiful,

[79] For a somewhat different, but not wholly unrelated account of SP sentences, see A. Nehamas "Predication and Forms of Opposites in the *Phaedo*," *Review of Metaphysics* 26 (1972–73); "Plato on the Imperfection of the Sensible World," *American Philosophical Quarterly* 12 (1975); and "Self-Predication and Plato's Theory of Forms," *American Philosophical Quarterly* 16 (1979).

or beauty (the white, or whiteness), is merely using an expression as a placeholder; it is not providing an informative account of the relevant stuff, or nature, or Form, or whatever, that gets labeled by the placeholding expression. (Again, note the affinity with the 'safe' view of the *Phaedo*. The 'safe' answers Socrates gives there to the 'What is *X*?' question are similarly uninformative; they too must be placeholders for fuller answers.)

Let us consider what, given a picture like that of Anaxagoras—and indeed given any Presocratic view that does not distinguish properties from objects, but only what is general from what is particular—these sorts of trivially true claims actually amount to. The wet itself, for example, is obviously wet. Indeed it is only wet and nothing else besides. Of course we can also say of some ordinary thing, for example, a sponge, that it is wet. And it will be a wet thing because it has a portion of the wet itself present within itself. Again, we can go on to ask: what about the sponge is wet; what is it that makes the sponge wet; what is present in the sponge that is wet? (As opposed to asking: what about the sponge is ochre; what is it that makes the sponge ochre; what is present in the sponge that is ochre?) Here the answer simply will be, that very portion of the wet itself; this is what is wet.

Now the wet itself is wet in and of itself (καθ' αὐτό); it is wet in a primary and fundamental way. And while the sponge is also wet, it is so *only* in virtue of having a share of the wet and thus is so *only* in a derivative way. This is no more mysterious than saying that ochre paint is ochre and that something painted with this paint is also ochre. Only, think of the paint as nothing but ochre; and the wet, nothing but wet. (One might very reasonably object that this is not merely very difficult, but impossible to do. This may well be right, but it points to a difficulty Plato, at least in the middle dialogues, is faced with as well, a difficulty he will later try to address. See also pp. 80–1, 88 above.)

Thus all the things we would be inclined to treat as properties are treated as portions or parts. Since Plato—unlike Anaxagoras, or so it would appear—also wants to talk about the equal, the large, the beautiful, and the just (and other such items), he needs to, and does, move away from a purely physical or spatial interpretation of part, portion, and participation. Yet he continues to use the *language* of participation. A good many of the difficulties we face (and Plato faced) in connection with the so-called middle-period 'theory' of Forms, it seems to me, can be traced back to this need to interpret these originally physical and spatial notions of part, portion, and participation in nonphysical, nonspatial terms.

Finally, in holding that the SP sentences can be construed in the way suggested, I do not mean to imply that they cannot be construed in the objectionable way. Indeed, as the *Parmenides* famously shows, Plato himself saw—or came to see—that these sentences can lead to trouble. The claim is only that they need not have been objectionable right from the start. Of course, it may also well be the case that once the problematic reading has been focused on, a more refined understanding of the SP sentences will be needed, in order to *block* that reading. No doubt part of that refinement will involve new interpretations precisely of the notions of part, portion, and participation. But, again, all this does not show that *before* the problematic construal had explicitly arisen, the SP sentences could not have been construed in the (more) innocuous way.

9. THE BEING OF THE PARTICIPANTS: PRELIMINARIES

We are now in a position to return to the question concerning becoming. Why are the participants only becomings, not beings? Again, it is relatively easy to see why this should be so on Anaxagoras's picture. The elemental stuffs just are what they are in virtue of themselves; they cannot be anything else. But we saw that whatever the mixtures 'are', they 'are' that, *not* in virtue of themselves, but in virtue of those elemental stuffs that predominate in them. Yet any stuff that predominates could just as well not predominate. Hence the mixtures are subject to change. Thus a mixture that 'is', say, wet, only manifests itself as wet, without really being wet. But this simply means that it becomes wet, given the recommended account of what becoming is. And what is true of the mixture's wetness is true of everything else that it manifests itself as.

The point could also be put as follows. There really are no genuine things, because there is nothing to being such a particular 'thing' besides being a certain mixture. So any time the mixture is changed, we have a new 'thing' (because the proportions of the elemental stuffs in the mixture are different). But each mixture can be thus changed in every way.[80] Hence there is no genuine alteration (as opposed to substantial change); rather,

---

[80] Anaxagoras does not expressly say this. But it seems like a reasonable inference to attribute it to him, because, first, he, like Empedocles, seems especially impressed with the *variety* of change, and secondly, a large component of Aristotle's criticism of Presocratics like Anaxagoras is that they do not account for the systematicity and regularity of change, i.e., the patterns in which changes occur. In Anaxagoras's case, this is no doubt related in part to his inadequate account of the relation of whole organisms to their parts.

all cases of what we ordinarily take to be change are really instances of the generation or perishing of mixtures, in other words, instances of rearranging the eternal, elemental stuffs. And hence there also is nothing the 'thing' actually *is*. Whatever it 'is', it merely *becomes*.

Plato, it seems to me, has essentially this view of ordinary things. Indeed, as John Burnet noted in 1914, "a particular thing is *nothing else* but the common meeting place of a number of predicates, each of which is an intelligible form" (emphasis added).[81] Before exploring this suggestion further, however, we need to consider two very general sorts of objections that will be raised against it.

First of all, there is an obvious difficulty. For it seems that (at least some) objects can persist even when some of their features change: thus Socrates, for example, endures even if some of his features change. And there seems to be a difference in kind, not just in degree, between the healthy Socrates and the ill Socrates on the one hand, and between the living Socrates and the corpse on the other. It is perhaps most characteristic of the essentialism associated with Aristotle's name that he will press this line of thought. This will allow him to distinguish clearly between alteration and substantial change, between (mere) change and the full-fledged coming-to-be and ceasing-to-be of objects. Indeed in the light of this fairly obvious problem, it will be urged by some that Plato as well explicitly distinguishes between two sorts of properties, for example, between 'being tall' on the one hand, and 'being Simmias' or 'being (a) man' on the other (see *Phaedo* 102b–d), or between 'being soft to the touch' and things like 'being (a) finger' (see *Republic* 523b–524d). In other words—the objection would have it— Plato does recognize both a class of predicates that are crucial to the identity of the particulars of which they are predicated, and a class of predicates that are not crucial to the identity of those particulars. And so he is able to hold, and in fact does hold, both that there is something that, say, Simmias is essentially, namely, (a) man, and that there are some things he is only accidentally, e.g., tall.[82] This recognition allows Plato to regard some changes as mere alterations after all—because what Simmias *is* (namely, a man) endures throughout and beyond the change; thus Plato

---

[81] See J. Burnet, *Greek Philosophy: Thales to Plato* (London, 1914, repr. 1950), p. 165.

[82] A. Nehamas, both in his "Predication and Forms of Opposites in the *Phaedo*," see pp. 469–73, and in his "Plato on the Imperfection of the Sensible World," see pp. 108–9, provides clear statements of this very Aristotelian way of reading Plato. J. Annas, in her *An Introduction to Plato's Republic* (Oxford, 1981), holds the same view; see p. 209 and pp. 219–22.

is not forced to treat all changes as cases of some thing's coming to be or ceasing to be.

The second main problem concerns what has been called the question of the extent of Forms: just what is it, for which will there be Forms? The present account will seem problematic to two main groups of interpreters. On the one hand, those who think that Plato is only (or at any rate primarily) interested in positing Forms for what they call *incomplete* predicates, e.g., 'is half', 'is large', . . . , or 'is cold', 'is hot', . . . , or 'is just', 'is beautiful', . . . , will see too *many* Forms here.[83] For it looks as if, given the view I am advocating, there should be Forms for items like white, black, etc., and maybe gold, water, etc. as well. But on this view, the predicates corresponding to these things are supposed to be *complete* (in the relevant way), and hence are thought not to require Forms corresponding to them at all. On the other hand, those who are impressed by reading *Republic* 596a ff. in a certain way will think that, on the present account, there are too *few* Forms. For they urge that there will be Forms corresponding to every general term.[84] In particular, there will be Forms of artifacts like couches and tables (*Rep.* 596a ff.), or weavers' shuttles (*Cratylus* 389a–390b).

These objections are serious. In the next three sections, I will consider them in some detail. We will see that the problem of 'incompleteness' does in fact play a key role in deciding what Forms are required. But I will argue that the notion of incompleteness that is in play in the dialogues is rather different from the one which commentators have suggested is involved. We will also see that there is no requirement that there be Forms corresponding to every general term. In Section 13, I will take up yet another kind of objection to the present picture of the participants' becoming. This one will prove still more serious, but will also highlight the distance between Aristotle and Plato (and certain Presocratics) on the question of individual things.

In a way, then, Sections 10–13 serve as a very large excursus. But this excursus turns out to be no mere digression. For various issues will be set

---

[83] This is suggested by Owen ("A Proof," pp. 107–9). He speaks of the "exclusion [sc. of Forms for] such non-relative predicates as 'man' "—though he also holds that this exclusion is "plainly . . . not characteristic of later dialogues nor even of the last book of the *Republic*" (p. 109). Nehamas, in the articles mentioned, argues expressly that, at least in the *Phaedo*, Plato is committed to forms for *only* these kinds of predicates.

[84] See, for example, W. D. Ross, *Plato's Theory of Ideas* (Oxford, 1951) who thinks that Plato's theory of forms "was the theory that there is an Idea answering to every common name" (p. 24).

in sharper relief, so that when we return to Plato's picture of the participants in Section 14, we will be better positioned to see the full implications
of his views.

10. The First Objection: Does Plato Distinguish between Essential and Accidental Properties?

Let us begin with the first objection, that Plato actually does have a
distinction between essential and accidental properties for sensible particulars, for the participants. As far as *Republic* 523c–524d is concerned, it is
important to read this passage much more carefully than is customary, and
to read it in its whole context (going back to 521d).[85] Socrates is interested
in finding that study (μάθημα) which will lead the soul from the realm of
becoming to the realm of being (521d). In the course of trying to show
that "number and calculation" are this study, Socrates distinguishes between two kinds of perceptions (or objects of perception): those that draw
the mind to inquiry, because the perception (or thing perceived) does
not, on its own, yield a sound result, and those that do not draw the mind
to inquiry, because perception, on its own, is able to judge its object
sufficiently (523a10–b4).

Glaucon takes Socrates here to be alluding to various optical or perspecti-
val illusions, and he thinks that Socrates is contrasting these with ordinary,
clear perceptions, taking place under normal conditions, and so on. Socrates' language could certainly be used to mark that distinction. But it turns
out that Glaucon has misunderstood Socrates, thus Socrates needs to be
more precise about what he is aiming at.

It is at this stage of the argument that Socrates contrasts the perception
of a finger with perceptions of certain other things. *Perception* will always
say that a finger is (a) finger: ". . . sight never indicates to the soul that a
finger is the opposite of (a) finger" (523d5–6). But Socrates does not
conclude from this, what we would expect him to conclude if this first
objection were on the right track, namely, either that a finger is *essentially*
(a) finger, or is (a) finger in and of itself (καθ' αὑτό), or that some things
are such that they are, *by nature*, fingers. Rather his conclusion is that
"such a thing [i.e., either the finger or the perception of it] would not be
likely to call on or rouse reasoning (νόησις)" (523d8–e1).

---

[85] On this entire passage, see the sensible remarks of R. Patterson, in his *Image and Reality in Plato's Metaphysics* (Indianapolis, 1985), pp. 104–6. However, see n. 100 below.

But this leaves completely open whether, in the last and most complete analysis, the deliverances of these kinds of perceptions really are accurate and adequate. The point simply is that when we are *beginning* to try to turn away from the sensible world of becoming to the intelligible world of being (compare 521d2–3 with 524c4, 524d9–525a2 and 525c5–6), perceptions which seem perfectly adequate, that is, ones which do not suggest that there is anything deficient about the perceptible world, are not going to provide the stimulus for the soul to turn towards what is really real (ἐπὶ τὴν οὐσίαν). As Richard Patterson observes, "most people are not stimulated to inquire into the nature of a finger."[86] Certain other perceptions, however, are inadequate, in that they cause puzzlement and hence do provide the right sort of stimulus. For example, in the case of something hard, the perception of it "announces to the soul that it perceives the same thing to be both hard and soft" (524a3–4). This is what causes the soul to be puzzled: "Whatever does this perception mean (ση-μαίνει) by hard, if it says the same thing is also soft?" (524a7–8). Similar puzzles arise in the case of light and heavy (524a8–10), and in the case of small and large (524c3 ff.).

This puzzlement, in turn, leads the soul to inquire, with the help of reasoning, whether, in each of these cases, it is confronted with two things, or only with one. The suggestion is that νόησις will treat as different (ἕτερά, 524b7), separate (κεχωρισμένα, 524b10), not mingled (οὐ συγ-κεχυμένα, 524c7) and determinate (διωρισμένα, ibid.) what sight treats as one (524c1), not separate (οὐ κεχωρισμένον, 524c3–4), and commingled (συγκεχυμένον, ibid.). By thus separating and distinguishing them—better, by recognizing that they are separate and distinct—we are forced to ask: 'What then is the large?', and 'What then is the small?' (524c10–11). And so quite generally, when confronted with these sorts of puzzling perceptions of something *x*, we are compelled to ask the 'What is *X*?' question. Only at this point does Socrates return to the issue he is actually interested in; and it is agreed that 'one' (or 'is one') is problematic in exactly this way, "for we will see the same thing as both one and unlimited in number" (525a4).

Thus at no point in this whole explanatory digression does Socrates say what he is alleged to be saying, namely, that in the case of certain things we can see what they are (that is, see what they are in and of themselves, or are essentially) merely by looking at them or perceiving them through the other senses. The only possible support for an interpretation like that

---

[86] Ibid., p. 104.

of Nehamas—which holds that perception really is capable of answering the 'What is *X*?' question about some things—would be to read ἱκανῶς (523b1, 524d10) very strongly, i.e., as 'fully adequately' or 'completely sufficiently'. There is certainly no need to take the adverb that way.[87] In fact, I am inclined to agree wholly with the following comment of Patterson's:

> Socrates does not specify the purpose for which sight is "adequate" in the case of fingers and the like. It would seem to be adequate for non-problematic *identification* of fingers and the like. By contrast . . . this same thing—this finger, or perhaps the length of this finger—is both long and short. So sight's identification of things as long and short, even if correct, is problematic, because apparently contradictory. Now there is nothing in this to suggest sight is adequate for understanding, rather than just identifying, either fingers or things long or short.[88]

Indeed, there is simply no indication in our passage that ἱκανῶς should be read strongly. Moreover, the explanation given of why the perception of a finger is adequate (523d5–6) encourages a weaker and more moderate reading. Such a perception is adequate, qua perception, only in that it never signals that a finger is also the opposite of (a) finger.[89]

David Sedley has urged that this makes the adequacy claim much too weak, for even an illusion or a reflection could be 'adequate' in this (excessively) weak way.[90] I myself am inclined to think that illusions and reflections support the interpretation I am recommending. If we recall the analogy of the Cave, it seems clear that the shadows on the wall (and the sounds echoing from the wall, which seem to be produced by the shadows) appear to be real to the prisoners. That is to say, nothing about the shadows themselves suggests that they are deficient, that they, somehow, fall short of reality—the predicament of the Cave's inhabitants is precisely that they do not, and cannot, recognize the shadows for what they are, namely, shadows. It is only when a prisoner has been freed from his fetters and is forced to look on the puppets and the fire behind them, that he *is* able to see the shadows for what they are. Prior to his liberation and enlighten-

---

[87] Compare G. E. L. Owen's translation of ἱκανῶς at *Statesman* 277c2 and 286a4 as 'tolerable', i.e., 'tolerably satisfying', in his "Plato on the Undepictable," reprinted in *LSD*, p. 143; cf. p. 139 n. 5.

[88] Patterson, *Image and Reality*, p. 105.

[89] There is absolutely no warrant for saying, as Nehamas does, that "for the *definition* [my emphasis]" of a property like being a finger, "we need look at nothing other than the particulars which bear them," see "Predication and Forms of Opposites in the *Phaedo*," p. 468.

[90] He made this suggestion in a conversation during January 1992.

ment, his perception *would* suggest that what he perceives is adequate; his perception thus *would not* in any way rouse or call upon νόησις. This ought hardly to come as a surprise. The Cave-Dwellers predicament is, after all, supposed to be *ours* (see 515a). And just as we (ordinarily) fail to find anything wrong with the deliverances of our perceptions qua perceptions, so they too fail to find anything wrong with theirs. But, and this no doubt is the point of the analogy, *we* can immediately grasp that *they* are failing to see things as they really are, that *their* perceptions are misleading them in a radical and fundamental way. Grasping this should, or so Plato hopes, encourage us (as it were) to step outside ourselves and countenance the possibility—which our perceptions of ordinary things typically do not suggest—that we too are misled in radical and fundamental ways. Here it is also relevant to recall Socrates' remark that "in these kinds of cases, the soul of the many (τῶν πολλῶν) is not compelled to ask the understanding what a finger is, since sight doesn't suggest that a finger is at the same time the opposite of a finger" (523d3–6). Mentioning the many is surely no accident; of course perception will not compel *them* to ask the 'What is *X*?' question about ordinary, perceptible items.[91] Yet from their failure to ask, it hardly follows that there is no question to be asked. (Note that in one important respect, our situation is actually much better than that of the prisoners: the fact that we are able, in some cases, to perceive reflections and shadows *together* with the objects whose reflections and shadows they are, puts us in a position to draw a contrast between appearance and reality wholly *within* the realm of our perceptual experience. Thus at least potentially we are able to draw that contrast more generally. We can, so to speak, make our own way out of our own 'caves'.)

Finally, it would hardly be in keeping with the entire central portion of the *Republic* (i.e., 475e–540b) and its repeated emphasis both on the distinction between the visible and the intelligible, as well as on the inadequacy of the former, for Plato to say that, in some cases, the deliverances of sight are fully adequate after all.[92] Thus while Plato undoubtedly does distinguish between things like being a finger, and those like being

---

[91] Patterson's observation here is entirely to the point: "Coming from Plato, this [sc. Socrates' remark that the many are not led to inquire into the nature of a finger] hardly shows that he considered the non-enquirers to possess an account of the nature of a finger. . . ." *Image and Reality*, p. 105.

[92] See also R. Bolton, "Plato's Distinction between Being and Becoming," *Review of Metaphysics* 29 (1975–76): 79–80; and F. C. White, "Plato's Middle Dialogues and the Independence of Particulars," *Philosophical Quarterly* 27 (1977): 197.

hard, being small, or being one, his distinction here is between what is "soul-turning" (μεταστρεπτικός; see 525a1, c5, and cf. 521c5), and what is not soul-turning. But this is not the distinction between those predicates that are crucial to the identity of their subjects, and those that are not.

Yet how could a finger be anything other than (a) finger? First of all, what is (a) finger at one time (when the person is alive and healthy) will not be (a) finger at other times (e.g., if the finger is somehow cut off, or when the person has died). Secondly, any finger is flesh, blood, bone, sinew, and so on, arranged in certain ways; but these can and will be arranged in other ways (cf. *Sympos.* 207d–e). Thirdly, the finger is surely not (a) finger in and of itself (καθ᾽ αὑτό) but is only (a) finger because it is, in certain ways, related (πρός) to at least the whole organism.[93]

. . . . .

Now to the *Phaedo*. What of the suggestion that 'being Simmias' or 'being (a) man' might be predicates of that sort? Nehamas offers the following bit of strikingly Aristotelian reasoning:

> There is a peculiar asymmetry between asking 'Why is Simmias tall?' . . . on the one hand, and 'Why is Simmias a man?' . . . on the other. . . . Simmias may be tall because of his legs, or his head, or what have you, and if whatever accounts for his tallness were otherwise, Simmias might have been short. But if his constitution had been different, would *Simmias* not have been a man (but a woman, or a tree)? . . . He is not a man because of some isolated characteristics he happens to have, but because to be a man is (at least part of) what it is to be Simmias.[94]

Maybe not a tree. But in the *Timaeus*, we are told that a man's soul can be reborn in a woman, or even in a wild animal (42b5–c4; but see the whole of 41d4–42d2). Nor do we need to look so far afield; for in the *Phaedo*, the very dialogue Nehamas is interpreting and relying on for this point, we learn that the souls of human beings can be reborn in donkeys, wolves, hawks, bees, ants, etc. (81c8–82c8).[95] Thus (however strange this

---

[93] Thus I am inclined to think that *all* participants are in fact both *x* and not-*x* (for *all* values of *x*). More cautiously: in this passage from the *Republic*, Plato has given us no reason for denying that, in the case of some *x*'s, if a participant is *x*, it is also not-*x*. (Patterson's comments suggest that he might reject even this weaker formulation; see *Image and Reality*, pp. 103–6.)

[94] Nehamas, "Forms of Opposites," p. 472; see also Annas, *An Introduction to Plato's Republic*, p. 209.

[95] Cf. also *Phaedo* 83d4–e3, where we hear that a contaminated soul will not be able to enter Hades; rather it will quickly fall back into *another* (ἄλλο) body. These passages from

may sound to us) according to Plato, if a human being is to be identified with its soul, it will *not* essentially be a human being. Much less will a man (ἀνήρ not ἄνθρωπος) be a man essentially, as opposed to being a woman. And it is quite certain, both in the *Phaedo* and in the *Republic*, that a human being is not essentially the body it happens to have. A soul, or a self, can be a human being at one time, and not be one at another. More precisely: a soul—or a portion of Soul—can be *in* a human being for a certain time, but be *in* something else during other times.[96]

Thus when talking about those items we think of as sensible particulars, not only does Plato fail to draw the Aristotelian distinction between essential and accidental predicates, he says things that positively rule it out for what would appear, prima facie, to be a star case: being human.

The *language* of *Phaedo* 102a10–102d4 may, however, still suggest that Plato is at least gesturing towards, maybe even relying on the essence/accident distinction for particulars. One sentence is especially striking: "For surely it is not by nature (οὐ πεφυκέναι)[97] that Simmias overtops him, i.e., by *being* Simmias, but by the largeness he happens to *have*" (102c1–3).[98] The linguistic parallels to 103c10–104c6 are taken to confirm and reinforce the essence/accident distinction in this earlier passage.[99] For in the later passage, certain attributes are spoken of as belonging essentially to certain physical stuffs, or to certain groups of physical things: snow cannot but be cold while remaining snow; a group of three cannot but be odd while remaining three.[100]

---

the *Phaedo* and *Timaeus* are emphasized by R. Heinaman, "Self-Predication in Plato's Middle Dialogues," *Phronesis* 34 (1989): 59 n. 12, against views like that of Nehamas.

[96] An analysis of the final argument for the immortality of the soul in the *Phaedo* would take us too far afield. But I believe that Plato is not sufficiently clear as to whether human souls are bona fide individuals or are portions or parts of Soul. (Alternatively, we might say that he is not sufficiently clear about whether 'soul' is a count-term or a mass-term.) If the latter, establishing the immortality of soul would not suffice for establishing that *the* soul is immortal in the sense we care about, i.e., that there is some form of *personal* survival.

[97] φύω in its various forms need not imply a commitment to natures in any strong sense of nature. See also Owen, "Plato on the Undepictable," reprinted in *LSD*, p. 142.

[98] F. C. White, in his "Particulars in *Phaedo*, 95e–107a," *Canadian Journal of Philosophy*, suppl. vol. 2 (1976): 133, gives a clear statement of such a view.

[99] See, e.g., D. Gallop, *Plato: Phaedo* (Oxford, 1975), p. 192, and his other comments on the relevant passages.

[100] Patterson questions whether we need see an essence/accident distinction even in 103c–105c; see *Image and Reality*, p. 108. This is going too far: for the example of snow's relation to the cold (or to the-cold-in-it) surely does suggest that Plato is gesturing towards something like an essence/accident distinction.

But the differences between the two passages are at least as important as the parallels. In 102a10–102d4, we are not told that Simmias cannot but be human while remaining Simmias. In point of fact, *nothing* is said about what Simmias is necessarily or essentially.[101] And given that the contrast in 102c1–3 (between attributes that essentially belong to something, as long as it exists, and those that do not) is not developed or explored further, Plato is presumably only making the more modest claim that being large is (at least covertly) context-dependent, while being Simmias is not (or at least not obviously so).

This is not to deny that a reasonable way of developing Plato's point would be to introduce the essence/accident distinction; it is only to say that *Phaedo* 102a10–d4 does not already do so.[102] (Moreover, if Plato is drawing such a distinction at all, it seems to be a distinction that applies to stuffs, like snow, rather than to discrete, physical objects.)[103] However, denying that Plato relies on, or draws the full-fledged essence/accident distinction is not yet to answer either of two important questions. First, how then are we to understand things like being (a) man, or being (a) finger? Secondly, is there, or is there not, a Form corresponding to being (a) man? I would like to postpone both of these questions temporarily and rather turn next to consider the second objection; for the issues raised in addressing it will bear directly on the two questions just asked.

11. The Second Objection: The Extent of Forms (and a Methodological Digression)

We come now to the objection concerning the extent of Forms. Let us begin with the less difficult of the two possible forms this objection can take, the thought that the extent of Forms is quite wide, far wider than on the interpretation I am advocating. Here *Republic* 596a ff. is the crucial

---

[101] Cf. ibid., pp. 107–8.

[102] Alan Code observes, quite plausibly I believe, that *Aristotle* would have seen the essence/accident distinction at work here in the *Phaedo* (see his "Aristotle: Essence and Accident," in *Philosophical Grounds of Rationality*, ed. R. Grandy and R. Warner [Oxford, 1986], pp. 427–28).

[103] Using the terminology employed in the introduction, we could say that Plato gestures towards a distinction between *general objects* (like stuffs) and their *properties*. But that is not yet the distinction between bona fide *objects*, or *things* (i.e., those items Aristotle calls primary *ousiai* in the *Categories*), and their *properties*.

text. It is a striking, but also a strikingly anomalous passage. First of all, it is the only place where "Plato seems unequivocally to require a Form for every predicate."[104] And even this will depend on whether 'name' (ὄνομα) is in fact to apply to any predicate at all or only to a restricted class of them.[105] (Thus we might in any case wonder whether—as Aristotle appears to have charged—negated or privative expressions can be treated as names in the relevant sense, and thus be used as a basis for inferring that there must be Forms corresponding to them.) Secondly, this is the only passage where Plato seems ready to speak of separate, that is, Platonic Forms as being *created* by God (597a5–7).

Hence the safest path seems to be to suppose that Plato is speaking the way he is speaking here because of the specific issue he is considering, namely, artistic imitation, the sort of imitation characteristic of artists and artisans, and that this passage therefore has no import outside its context; or if that should seem excessively dismissive, to suppose that Plato is here addressing a somewhat different set of concerns than those which guide him in other passages dealing with Forms, concerns which do not necessarily link up very well with the sorts of issues he usually focuses on. And while Forms of artifacts are also mentioned in the *Cratylus*, one of the most striking features of the single stretch of text in all the dialogues where the assumption that there are Forms is explicitly thematized and reflected on, namely, *Parmenides* 130b ff., is that there is not even a hint of separate Forms for artifacts. (We will soon be considering some details from this passage.) And so although the *Republic* X and *Cratylus* passages do raise questions, probably even important ones, we should not hold the interpre-

---

[104] Owen, "A Proof," p. 107 n. 25.

[105] J. A. Smith has argued that *Republic* 596a6–7 *ought* actually to be translated quite differently from how it is usually translated, namely as follows: "for we are, as you know, in the habit of assuming [as a rule or procedure] that the Idea which corresponds to a group of particulars, each to each, is always one, in which case we call the group of particulars by a common name"; see his "General Relative Clauses in Greek," *Classical Review* 31 (1917): 70. Thus even this sentence would not be asserting that there is a Form corresponding to every general expression. In their replies to Smith (*Classical Review* 32 [1918]), both E. A. Sonnenschein ("The Indicative in Relative Clauses," pp. 68–69) and A. W. Mair ("General Relative Clauses in Greek," pp. 169–70) show conclusively that Smith was wrong to maintain that the sentence *must* be translated as he recommends; but Sonnenschein and Mair have not shown it to be impossible to construe 596a6–7 as Smith does. Thus the *possibility* of so translating the sentence remains. However, even with all that being said, the more usual translation—"We are accustomed to assuming one Form in each case for the many particulars to which we give the same name" (Grube)—seems somewhat easier.

tation of the picture of Forms which we find in the middle dialogues hostage to these texts.

. . . . .

Before proceeding to consider incompleteness, we should reflect a bit, by way of a methodological digression, on why the question concerning the 'extent of Forms' is one of the more vexed and controversial questions that arises in interpreting the dialogues. The difficulty is due to various factors. It is, no doubt, due in part to the fact that Plato does not have a *theory* of Forms, or if he does, we do not find it in the middle dialogues. Let me explain very briefly. It is clear that Forms are theoretical entities, both in the sense that positing them is the product of theoretical reflection, and in the sense that whatever grasp we will have of them will involve operations of the mind and not be a matter of sense perception. Yet the various things Plato says about Forms hardly add up to a theory. For we expect a theory, at a minimum, to provide a systematically articulated structure, with first principles and derived results; with a clear domain of application, i.e., things that are to be accounted for, made sense of, or whatever by that structure; and with some explanation of, or guidance about, its central notions. (In the case at hand, we would surely want to see the notion of participation elucidated.) Plato's comments about mathematics and astronomy show that he was perfectly familiar with theories or prototheories in this sense. Thus denying that he presents a theory of Forms in the dialogues is not a matter of holding Plato to some inappropriately stringent or anachronistic standards for what is to count as a theory.

The absence of a real theory is, I believe, no accident, nor a matter of Plato's having been unable to formulate that theory; this absence is rather bound up with the nature of the dialogues themselves. For they are not, ultimately, dogmatic statements of doctrine, presented ex cathedra, but are rather hortatory (παραινητικός) and protreptic, and this in two ways. First, in each of the principal middle dialogues, there is some issue or set of issues that we can be supposed to have an antecedent interest in: the immortality of the soul, the nature and benefits of justice, the role and nature of beauty or love—to mention only some of the most prominent ones. These topics are all ones someone might be deeply concerned about—but be concerned about in a way that involves nothing like an (initial) commitment to philosophy in Socrates' and Plato's sense. Yet Plato endeavors to show that as soon as we try to consider any of these matters in a serious way, we will find that in order to make satisfactory

135

progress, either with the questions that had troubled and provoked us initially, or (equally) with new ones that have arisen, we will need to engage in quite a bit of metaphysical inquiry. Once we actually have done that, we will, ideally, be able to answer our questions, but failing that, we will at least be closer to answering them. Suppose, for example, that we are interested in what justice is, and in whether it really is beneficial for us to be just (the question that guides the *Republic*). If we are shown that the answers (indeed, also the proper understanding of the questions) depend on a whole host of metaphysical issues, we will have been provided with reasons, with some rational motivation for engaging in metaphysical inquiry. And these reasons will be reasons for us, quite independently of whether or not we had any antecedent interest in metaphysics, in fact, quite independently of whether or not we still have no independent interest in metaphysics. So the dialogues exhort us to engage in these kinds of studies, and by giving us reasons to do so, turn us towards them.

But they are protreptic in another way too. For the dialogues are not, after all, devoid of metaphysical inquiry and reflection. Thus with respect to Forms, what we find is the assumption that there must be something like them in order for anything like a satisfactory theory to be so much as possible. This assumption remains fixed throughout Plato's works. Plato continues to insist on it even after having given arguments which seem—to many commentators—to demonstrate the incoherence of his own 'Theory of Forms'. But that can hardly be the end of the matter. For in the passage that *immediately* follows those arguments, he has Parmenides say that doing away with Forms will "altogether destroy the capacity for reasoned discourse" (*Parmenides* 135b5–c3).[106] And in the rest of the *Parmenides* (as well as in, e.g., the *Sophist* and the *Philebus*) he develops a new picture of Forms, participants, and their relations to one another.[107] Thus what is required is an adequate understanding and account of the assumption that there must be Forms. But the picture of Forms Plato presents in the middle dialogues—by way of what are, in the end, relatively few remarks scattered throughout them—is not the theory and does not provide it. That picture rather constrains, or is meant to show constraints

---

[106] There is some controversy whether διαλέγεσθαι here really means reasoned discourse rather than something more specific and limited, e.g., dialectical discussion. This controversy does not matter for the present point: I see no room for *any* sense of διαλέγεσθαι in the dialogues according to which the destruction of the capacity to διαλέγεσθαι would not be an intolerable result for Plato.

[107] On this picture, see Frede, *Prädikation und Existenzaussage*, and Meinwald, *Plato's Parmenides*.

on, any fully worked out theory we may be able to construct and articulate. And as suggested in the introduction, such a theory will need to answer to, or incorporate, or perhaps, even go beyond the picture.

Let us note some of those constraints. In the first instance, Forms are meant to satisfy Eleatic strictures on being in such a way that we are not forced to say, with Parmenides, that all ordinary discourse is pure nonsense, that all ordinary experience is nothing but an illusion, and that all ordinary things are not (sc. anything, in any way). The development of Plato's relation to Parmenides' thought might, roughly and schematically, be put as follows. Parmenides had identified three roads:

(I)   It is and it cannot not be.
        (Whatever is, cannot not be.)

(II)   It is not and it is necessary for it not to be.
        (Whatever is not, cannot be.)

(III) It is and it is not.
        (Whatever is, also is not, and vice versa.)

For Parmenides, (II) is a "track beyond all tidings" (B 2), that is to say, (II) is utterly impossible and unknowable; (III) is the path that ignorant mortals stagger along on (B 6.4–9), but it too is similarly unacceptable.

I would suggest that in the middle dialogues, Plato is above all concerned to point out ways in which some sense can after all be made of (III). This is the realm of becoming, the realm of ordinary and familiar things. But it depends on (I) for its 'being', it depends on the realm of true being, which is is to say, it depends on the Forms. And in those dialogues, Plato agrees with Parmenides about (II)—this is quite hopeless and utterly unknowable.[108] Thus the protreptic aim of the middle dialogues is not simply to turn us towards metaphysical inquiry quite generally, but towards metaphysical theorizing which holds to these Eleatic constraints. And so the philosophical task is to work out, *inter alia*, the theory of Forms that is only hinted at in the dialogues.[109]

---

[108] By the time Plato comes to write the *Sophist*, if not already in the *Parmenides*, he finds even (II), if construed properly, unproblematic. For now absolutely everything will participate in Not-Being, even the Form of Being itself. More precisely, the position is that, strictly speaking, *both* (I) and (II) prove unacceptable on their own, and that (III), properly understood, is the only path.

[109] Obviously a great deal would need to be said to defend this interpretation of the dialogues as hortatory and protreptic with anything like the requisite amount of detail. And one would need to address the always complicated and delicate issue of Plato's stance vis-à-vis writing. Two works which do undertake to do just this, and go some ways towards

In the light of these methodological suggestions, it is not at all surprising that the question, for what are there Forms, proves difficult. However, this question is also difficult because the one passage that does thematize it, and to which interpreters have hence flocked, is not as easy to interpret as they would hope. In the *Parmenides*, Parmenides asks Socrates, if, on his view, there are Forms for items in four different classes (in the dialogue, the classes are marked by four separate questions):

(I)   Likeness, unlikeness, one, many, motion and rest, all such things (130b3–5; cf. 129d6–130a1).

(II) The just, the beautiful, the good, and all such things (130b7–9).

(III) x(a) Man, or
       (b) fire or water (130c1–2).

(IV) Laughable things: hair, mud and dirt, and other undignified and lowly things (130c5–d1).

Socrates has no hesitation about answering 'yes' for (I) and (II); he is puzzled whether to say 'yes' or 'no' for (III), and he is inclined to think that it would be just too absurd (130d4–5) to say anything but οὐδαμῶς (absolutely not) for (IV). But then he has some doubts about this, and wonders if it should not be the same for all (130d5–6); that is, maybe 'yes' is the correct answer for (IV) as well.

Parmenides suggests that Socrates' (undoubtedly genuine) reluctance about (IV) is misguided.[110] For our purposes, however, what matters is that Parmenides' remarks seem meant to suggest that classes (I)–(IV) should be treated alike. We will of course want to see why this should be so. But first, why do we have the division into four classes? And what, if anything, is the significance of Socrates' different responses?

---

succeeding, are K. Gaiser, *Protreptik und Paränese bei Platon* (Stuttgart, 1959) and W. Wieland, *Platon und die Formen des Wissens* (Göttingen, 1982); see especially chap. 2, "Die Ideen und ihre Funktion." Th. A. Szlezak, in his *Platon und die Schriftlichkeit der Philosophie* (Berlin, 1985), provides the most extensive and careful treatment of those passages where Plato seems to reflect on textuality, philosophy, and the relations between the two. His discussion is of great value, though we will hardly be likely to be convinced by his picture of an 'esoteric' Plato.

[110] "Parmenides said: you are still young, and philosophy has not yet grasped hold of you as much as—in my opinion—it will sometime in the future. Then you will not despise any of these things. Now, because you are young, you still look towards the opinions people have" (130e1–4). It is beyond the scope of the present inquiry to address the many questions this comment raises.

12. THE SECOND OBJECTION CONTINUED: FORMS AND 'INCOMPLETENESS'

At this point, we are finally ready to take up the issue of incompleteness, for this notion has been invoked precisely in order to answer these questions. The answer which Owen and his fellow travelers give goes something like this. In the *Phaedo* and *Republic*, Plato had had arguments only for there being Forms that correspond to incomplete predicates (which, as it turns out, themselves form a fairly mixed group). These predicates are contrasted, not surprisingly, with complete predicates, for which there are no Forms, at least not in these dialogues (again, excluding *Rep.* X). However, certainly by the time he comes to write the *Timaeus*, Plato also has (different) arguments for there being Forms corresponding to natural kinds and natural stuffs. But these arguments were never at the core of his concerns, never formed his primary reason for introducing Forms in the first place. Classes (I) and (II) comprise the incomplete predicates. Socrates' unhesitating readiness to say that there are Forms for them reflects Plato's own (earlier) views. Class (III) comprises natural kinds and natural stuffs, and Socrates' hesitation here reflects that they are not, after all, integral to the theory. (Let us ignore class (IV) for the moment.) Should we believe this story?

In order to evaluate Owen's suggestion, we obviously need a clearer sense of the notions of incompleteness and completeness involved. Now while Owen does not explicitly define incompleteness, we can see, at least roughly, what he must have in mind:[111] Υ is predicated incompletely of X (or Υ is an incomplete predicate in a sentence of the form 'X is Υ'), if there are further specifications that need to be provided before we can properly apply the predicate and thus say whether 'X is Υ' is true or false. Moreover, it is characteristic of these predicates that if one set of appropriate specifications makes 'X is Υ' true, there will also be another set, in its way equally legitimate, that makes 'X is Υ' false. (This is the κυλίνδησις, the rolling about, between being and not-being.) Examples: 'Simmias is tall'—taller *than* Socrates, true; taller *than* Phaedo, false. 'The (spinning) top is moving'—*with respect to* its circumference, true; *with respect to* its axis, false. 'Helen of Troy is beautiful'—*compared to* other mortals, true; *compared to* Aphrodite, false. 'Socrates is many'—many *things* (i.e., has many parts or aspects), true; many *men*, false. And Owen

[111] "A Proof," p. 108.

expressly, and rightly, notes just "how various such specifications will be."[112] However, as we shall see, even Owen may not have been cautious enough on this score.

Owen's characterization of incomplete predicates appears to fit well with the later Academic category of πρός τι (relative) predicates:

> Among things said to be πρός τι are all those which need some additional explanation (προσδεῖταί τινος ἑρμηνείας), for example, the greater, the quicker, the more beautiful, and those like these.[113] For the greater is greater than a lesser, and the quicker is quicker than something. (Diogenes Laertius III. 108–9)[114]

We should also remember that Xenocrates made τὸ πρός τι one of his two basic categories (Fr. 12 Heinze); and there can be little doubt that he too thought of these predicates in this way, that is, as relatives which are 'completed' by the specification of what the relative is related to.

If we now return to Plato and look at, e.g., *Republic* 438a7–e9 (but cf. *Charmides* 168b2–9),[115] we notice that Plato singles out several notions, e.g., the larger, the lesser, the half, the double, etc., which satisfy the following schema:

For certain *x*'s and *y*'s, if some *x* is (said to be) *y*,
there is a *z*, such that *x* is (said to be) *y* πρός *z*.

---

[112] Ibid. Others have tried to categorize and classify these sorts of specifications more exactly, although that seems to attribute a degree of precision and a kind of classification that is not present in the relevant texts and which overconcretizes what Plato has to say. We find this tendency in, e.g., Nehamas, "Forms of Opposites," Brentlinger, "Incomplete Predicates and the Two-World Theory of the *Phaedo*," or Denyer, "Plato's Theory of Stuffs," sec. 3.

[113] Translating the text I am tempted to read: οἷον τὸ μεῖζόν [τινος] καὶ τὸ θᾶττόν [τινος] καὶ τὸ κάλλιον καὶ τὰ τοιαῦτα· τό τε γὰρ κτλ. The bracketed words ("the greater *than something* and the quicker *than something*") seem like intrusive glosses that anticipate the γὰρ clause; without them its import is clearer.

[114] Compare also the division of beings by Plato's student Hermodorus (apud Simplicius *In Phys.* 247, 30 ff.). Sextus Empiricus *M* X.265 (but see all of *M* X.263–69) is clearly derived from a similar schema; *M* VIII.454 and, perhaps, *PH* I.136 also reflects this conception of πρός τι λεγόμενα. And Aristotle, both in the *Categories* (c. 7, but especially 8ᵃ35–ᵇ15) and in the *Topics* (e.g., at 142ᵃ28–31) speaks of πρός τι predicates in this way as well.

[115] The whole of *Charm.* 167b10–169a5 is relevant here. But 168b10–169a5 (especially 169a1–5—a very difficult passage) complicates the picture considerably.

And *Phaedo* 74a–e, 100a ff., *Republic* 331c, 479a–b, 523a–525a, and *Hippias Major* 288b–289b, among other passages, show that Plato holds that

If, for certain *x*'s and *y*'s, when some *x* is (said to be) *y*
and there is a *z*, such that, strictly speaking, *x* is (said to be) *y* πρός *z*,
then there *also* is a *z*′, such that *x* is (said to be) *not y* πρός *z*′.

Hence it does look as if there is good evidence that, in the middle dialogues, Plato recognizes a class of items which corresponds to Owen's notion of incomplete predicates.

Now of course Owen sees these predicates as contrasted with complete, i.e., καθ' αὐτό (*per se*/absolute/nonrelative) ones. What then are these complete predicates, and in virtue of what are they complete? Owen writes that "a finger can be seen καθ' αὐτό," as if this made being a finger a *per se* predicate.[116] But Plato himself does not say this; at best it could be inferred from *Republic* 524d10, and we have seen there is good reason to doubt that he meant this passage to be so construed. Owen also seems to take the fact that (in the *Peri Ideōn* fragment which he is concerned to analyze) 'man' applies strictly (κυρίως) to individuals like Plato or Socrates, as if this were some sort of evidence that man, or being (a) man is also predicated *per se* of those individuals.[117]

And here again he thinks that the later Academic account of καθ' αὐτὸ λεγόμενα captures what Plato is committed to. The passage from Diogenes Laertius III which we have just looked at, begins:

Of beings, some are καθ' ἑαυτά (*per se*), some are called <sc. what they are called> πρός τι (with respect to something). And things said to be *per se* are those that need no additional explanation. These are, for example, man, horse, and the other animals. For none of them gains by explanation. And among things said to be with respect to something . . . (see above).[118]

Yet when we return to Plato, matters are quite different from the way they had been in the earlier case. For nothing in the middle dialogues corresponds to *this* use of *per se*. And we have already seen that two passages (*Rep.* 523a ff. and *Phaedo* 102b ff.) which might be thought to rely

[116] Owen, "A Proof," pp. 108–9.

[117] See the whole section "καθ' αὐτό and πρός τι," pp. 107–10 of "A Proof."

[118] Once more, compare Hermodorus, loc. cit.; Sextus Empiricus *M* X.263; see also Aristotle *Cat.* 8ᵇ15–19 (but in 8ᵇ18–19 we should surely read: . . . οὐκ ἔστιν <ἀναγκαῖον> εἰδέναι ὡρισμένως with Ackrill). Xenocrates' other principle category was τὸ καθ' αὐτό.

on this notion of being (something) *per se* do not in fact do so. Thus while Plato does, in the relevant places, mark certain things as having a πρός character, he does not contrast them with things that are καθ' αὐτά in the way Diogenes Laertius describes. Moreover, Owen's caution on just how to spell out the conditions for being incomplete seems well taken.

At first it looks as if all the incomplete predicates are somehow relational; indeed, this is what the later Academic tradition's construal and usage of πρός τι would suggest. But in fact it seems that Plato wants to analyze '. . . is larger than . . .' in terms of '. . . is large' (alternatively, things are *larger* by the presence of Largeness), rather than the other way around (i.e., things are not *large* by the presence of a supposed Form, Largerness).[119] So even predicates which seem as if they could be assimilated to straightforwardly relational predicates are not so assimilated; hence their incompleteness cannot consist in their being relational. In addition, it is obvious that any number of evidently nonrelational predicates can be incomplete, and turn out to be that in any number of ways. Now while they can all be completed by the addition of some relevant specifications, we do not have available, in advance, a schema for the specifications. Indeed, Nicholas White argues quite plausibly that a statement like 'This is hard' itself "makes no reference to the surrounding circumstances," although a statement of "the conditions of its acceptability must make such a reference."[120] Yet that suggests that not only are matters more complicated than Owen had supposed, but that we should seek to understand the relevant πρός-character of these predicates rather differently.

The first suggestion I would like to make is that the class of items predicated πρός τι is open-ended, in fact, sufficiently open-ended that we cannot antecedently rule out whether things like water, fire, . . . , but also, man, horse, . . . are not πρός τι after all, *only not as obviously so* as the examples Plato uses, which are the ones commentators have fastened on. Together

---

[119] This is stressed by F. C. White, in his "The Compresence of Opposites in *Phaedo* 102," *Classical Quarterly*, n.s. 27 (1977); see pp. 306–9. And N. White observes that "it is far more difficult than Owen supposed to explain the positive forms in relational terms"; see "Perceptual and Objective Properties in Plato," *Apeiron* 22 (1989): 50. N. White (ibid.) also refers us to some contemporary literature on attributives, including J. Wallace, "Positive, Comparative, Superlative," *Journal of Philosophy* 69 (1972), and S. Wheeler, "Attributives and their Modifiers," *Nous* 6 (1972), to substantiate his claim that "straightforward paraphrases" of expressions like 'large G' are hard to come by."

[120] N. White, "Perceptual and Objective Properties," p. 51; but cf. the whole discussion in pp. 51–65.

with this suggestion, I would like to suggest, secondly, that what makes the various πρός τι items πρός τι is not their syntactical or semantic incompleteness (viz., the incompleteness of the expressions used to introduce them into discourse); instead it is the following fact:

An item will be a πρός τι item, if it depends for its being on there being something else, different from it.

This dependence, however, *manifests* itself most clearly in the case of items that are referred to by overtly relational predicates. For example (as Plato explicitly points out), something can only be equal, by being equal to something. Hence its being equal is not some independent, self-standing fact about it, but is rather something that depends, at a minimum, on there being some other thing, to which it is equal.[121] And if we look at Plato's favored examples, we can see that in all cases, the specifications that are added specify other things, contexts, factors, or whatever, which these 'incomplete' items depend on for their being. In addition, these favored examples from the middle dialogues all have in common that the dependence at issue is *easy to recognize*—it is grasped either by perception or by fairly simple reflection.

Other things might of course also depend on something different from them for their being, but it might be much more *difficult to recognize* that this is so. (Again, think of the relation between the shadows and the puppets and the fire, from the point of view of the prisoners in the Cave. The shadows clearly depend for their being—that is, for their being what they are—on the puppets and the fire. Thus they are dependent beings; more specifically, they are things which have their being πρός the puppets and the fire. But prior to being unchained and literally turned around, no prisoner can see that the shadows are dependent things, rather than independent ones, things that are what they are in their own right.) Now all such dependent beings could very reasonably be called beings πρός

---

[121] I say 'at a minimum' deliberately. For Plato takes this sort of dependence to show that there is another, more important sort of dependence involved as well. For any equal thing will depend on The Equal Itself, and hence can also be said to be equal πρός The Equals Themselves. (Plato seems to attribute no significance to the different formulations; cf. N. White's remarks in his "Forms and Sensibles: *Phaedo* 74B–C," *Philosophical Topics* 15 [1987]: 205.) The dependence in question and the relation indicated by πρός will obviously be different. But this need not *eo ipso* be a problem. For πρός signals relationality quite generally, not necessarily any particular relation. Which relation is in fact involved will be determined by the context. On πρός, see also Meinwald, *Plato's Parmenides*, pp. 49–53.

ἕτερα (with respect to other things) or beings δἰ ἑτέρους (through other things).[122]

Yet if each and every thing were to depend on something else for its being, we would end up with either a circle or an infinite regress of ontological dependence. Thus the following ought to be the case:

There are some items that do not depend for their being on there being something else, different from them.

Such independent beings could very naturally be called beings καθ' αὑτά. Yet notice that this would leave us with *another* contrast between καθ' αὑτά and πρός τι (viz., πρὸς ἕτερα). Indeed the later Platonic tradition recognizes this contrast as well. Plutarch distinguishes between what is (what it is) *per se* and what is (what it is) δἰ ἕτερον; and it is clear from the context that the things that are (what they are) in and of themselves are Forms, while the items that are (what they are) through, or because of, something else, are the participants (*Adv. Colot.* 1115 E). And just a bit later, he speaks of what is (what it is) καθ' αὑτό and what is (what it is) πρὸς ἐκεῖνο, i.e., what is (what it is) with respect to that which is (what it is) in and of itself (*Adv. Colot.* 1115 F).

Yet is this not the very same distinction between *per se* and relative predicates which, it was just argued, is not operative in the dialogues? It is not. And this for the simple reason that things that are nonrelational (whether we construe 'relational' widely, with Hermodorus and Xeno-crates, or narrowly, with Aristotle) are not, simply in virtue of that, things that do not depend for their being on there being something else, different from them. Thus we have a *basic* division of beings into two classes, as shown in the small diagram. And then we locate, *within* the class of πρὸς ἕτερα beings, the distinctions of Hermodorus and others; the completed tree can be represented by the larger diagram.

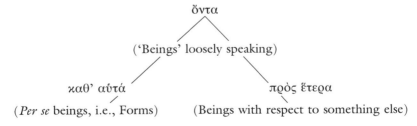

ὄντα

('Beings' loosely speaking)

καθ' αὑτά   πρὸς ἕτερα

(*Per se* beings, i.e., Forms)   (Beings with respect to something else)

---

[122] Cf. H. Cherniss, *Aristotle's Criticism of Plato and the Academy* (Baltimore, 1944), p. 283 n. 191, who observes that πρός τι can have the sense of 'dependent upon'.

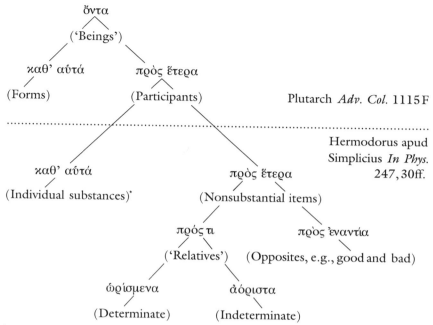

ὄντα
('Beings')

καθ' αὑτά
(Forms)

πρὸς ἕτερα
(Participants)

Plutarch *Adv. Col.* 1115F

Hermodorus apud
Simplicius *In Phys.*
247,30ff.

καθ' αὑτά
(Individual substances)*

πρὸς ἕτερα
(Nonsubstantial items)

πρός τι
('Relatives')

πρὸς ἐναντία
(Opposites, e.g., good and bad)

ὡρισμένα
(Determinate)

ἀόριστα
(Indeterminate)

*Simplicius citing Porphyry citing Dercyllides citing Hermodorus gives *man* and *horse* as examples.

Given the terminology, the potential for confusion or conflation is great.[123] And given the interest, from at least the time of the *Categories*, in individual *ousiai*, it is easy to see how only part of the tree could have come to seem to be the whole tree, in other words, how the classification of only part of the beings could have been taken to be a classification of beings quite generally. (Aristotle's own classificatory schema would, of course, make the bottom portion of the whole tree look rather different.)

Now it will be urged that this may all be well and good so far as concerns Plutarch, but what does any of it have to do with Plato's middle dialogues, much less with the problematic passage from the *Parmenides* with which our discussion began in the previous section?

Plato obviously uses the expression καθ' αὑτό to characterize the being of the Forms—that is, their kind or way of being—throughout the dia-

---

[123] The question of what the distinction between determinate and indeterminate relatives comes to is one that we, fortunately, do not need to settle here. Merlan suggests that 'double—half' is a determinate relation, while 'many—few' is an inderminate one. "Beiträge zur Geschichte des antiken Platonismus," *Philologus* 89 (1934), p. 43 n. 7.

logues. And he uses this expression to indicate their independence from other things, to indicate that they, unlike the participants, are (what they are) in and of themselves. Hence it seems to me that Plato's usage corresponds to, and in all likelihood was the basis for, the sense of καθ' αὐτό we have just seen in Plutarch.

But this reinforces the suggestion that, in our *Parmenides* passage, the contrast between classes (I) and (II) on the one hand, and (III) and (IV) on the other, is not based on the distinction between incomplete and complete predicates, at least not as it is usually understood. For in this sense of καθ' αὐτό, the following is true:

No sensible item is (what it is) καθ' αὐτό.

Thus it should come as no surprise to find, in the later tradition, the phrase τὰ πρὸς τὰ εἴδη being used to refer to the sensible particulars, for they are the things (that are what they are) with respect to the Forms.[124] So it turns out that, in fact, in the relevant sense of πρὸς ἕτερον, man, fire, water, hair, mud, and dirt are *all* πρὸς ἕτερα, for they all are what they are by being appropriately related to something other than themselves.

However, why then does Parmenides divide them into four classes in his questions, and why does Socrates offer different responses to those questions? It is characteristic of the things in classes (I) and (II) that their dependent character is exhibited fairly easily (this is one of the principal lessons of the middle dialogues). While one might endeavor to give a subtle account of why (I) and (II) are separate classes, not just a single one, the events in the dialogue could explain their separateness sufficiently. Zeno's arguments were concerned with the items in class (I). Socrates had responded to those arguments by suggesting that there are Forms for these things (128e–130a). So it is only natural for Parmenides to take up Socrates' comments, and to begin his questions as he does. Proceeding to class (II), then, need reflect nothing more than an everyday sense that those moral/aesthetic predicates are different, in some obvious, intuitive, and nontechnical way, from the ones in class (I).

In moving on to ask about class (III), Parmenides does not so much as hint that different sorts of considerations would need to underlie positing Forms in these cases. And Socrates' hesitation need not reflect his (i.e., Plato's) lesser confidence in these different sorts of considerations, or

---

[124] See, e.g., Alexander *In Met.* 56, 1–6; 58, 12–13; 97, 10–12; cf. 123, 10–11 (cited by Cherniss, *Aristotle's Criticism of Plato*, p. 283 n. 191); compare Alexander's use of τὰ πρὸς τὰς ἰδέας ὄντα, e.g., at 90, 5–12 and 106, 15–107, 13.

strategies for argumentation; nor need it reflect a sense that, in some way, Forms for *these* items are not really integral to the theory. Rather, his hesitation may simply signal that it is more difficult to *recognize* that Forms are required for such items as well.

The fourth class is obviously the most difficult, for any account.[125] But it is important to note that Owen's suggestion—that here we can see exactly what each of these is καθ' αὑτό—cannot be correct.[126] The reason is that in 130d3–5, Socrates says, "but these at least, what we see <them to be>, that they also are (ταῦτα καὶ εἶναι)"; Socrates does *not* say, 'but these at least, what we see <them to be>, that they also are *in and of themselves* (ταῦτα καὶ καθ' αὑτὰ εἶναι).'

Nor is it clear why Socrates would say we can see clearly what hair, mud, and dirt are *per se*, but *not* also say the same thing about man, fire, and water. Moreover, while it is, in a sense, correct to speak of Socrates as "unready to admit Forms" (so Owen) for the items in both (III) and (IV), this is a misleading way of putting matters. In fact, Socrates is puzzled about (III), but thinks there surely are not Forms for the items in (IV). Finally, if one of the star examples of a καθ' αὑτό item is man, and if this is perfectly clear from perception, why is Socrates puzzled about man at all? It seems to me that if Owen were right, we should expect Socrates rather to be puzzled about the items in (IV), but to have no hesitation at all about saying 'no' for (III).

To arrive at the correct account (if there even is such a thing) for Socrates' response about (IV) is a task beyond the scope of the present inquiry. But we should consider seriously the possibility that here too we are not faced with something particularly theory-laden, but rather that neither Zeno nor Socrates had concerned themselves with these sorts of items, nor would it be immediately obvious why anyone ought to concern himself with them; and so Socrates, overhastily, dismisses them, recognizing however that this dismissal may, in the end, not be justified. For it might be "the same concerning all" (130d6). That is, all the items mentioned (and implied) in (I)–(IV) may be dependent beings, beings that are (what they are) because other things are (what they are) in and of themselves.

---

[125] To begin with, why does Parmenides call these things laughable? Secondly, each of these terms can also refer to other things besides those which they are standardly translated as; θρίξ: hair, but also wool or bristles; πηλός: mud, but also clay of various sorts; ῥύπος: dirt, but also, it would seem, sealing wax (see LSJ). Are these facts relevant here? Thirdly, it is not clear why hair—surely something beautiful in the case of, say, Aphrodite—should be thought to be undignified and lowly.

[126] Owen, "A Proof," p. 109.

Thus the two difficulties (broached on pp. 125–26 above) do not stand in the way of the two suggestions made in Section 9. Recall what those suggestions had been. First, that for Plato, being a participant (i.e., what we would think of as a sensible particular) is something like being an Anaxagorean mixture—something like, rather than exactly like—because when we speak of justice and beauty, or, even worse, of largeness or unity, these can hardly be thought of as concrete, physical ingredients in, or parts of, the mixtures that are the participants. Secondly, that in characterizing the participants as becoming (and not as being), Plato is indicating that whatever they 'are' (said to be), they 'are' that not in their own right, not independently, but derivatively; hence they are also subject to change in every way.

13. A THIRD OBJECTION: CAN FORMS BE 'INGREDIENTS'?

But an even greater difficulty has been looming all along. It is easy enough to think of earth, air, fire, and water as ingredients. And we have seen that, given Anaxagoreanism, exactly the same is true for the hot, the cold, the wet, and the dry. However, even if we could come to be persuaded to think of beauty and justice, and perhaps also (but here still more reluctantly) of largeness or plurality, as being ingredients in some relevant extended, analogical, or metaphorical sense of ingredient,[127] it still seems quite impossible to think of certain things for which there do seem to be Forms in this way at all. Consider the Form, Man. First, there is no whole—no quasi-stuff—of which instances of Man are parts; secondly, even if there were a whole of some appropriate sort, such a whole simply could not be an ingredient. Thus Alexander of Aphrodisias says (perhaps quoting or paraphrasing Aristotle): "a part of Man cannot be a man, as a part of gold is gold" (οὐ γὰρ οἷόν τε τὸ μέρος τοῦ ἀνθρώπου ἄνθρωπον εἶναι, ὡς τὸ τοῦ χρυσοῦ μέρος χρυσόν; In Met. 98, 8–9).[128] Now while the target

---

[127] We do after all say things like 'she gathered all her strength', 'his courage drained away', and so on. Thus at least at the level of metaphor, we seem willing to treat some properties in an Anaxagorean way and use the expressions referring to them as non-count terms. Does this reflect a level of 'archaic thinking' that is still with us?

[128] This is part of a longer passage (97, 27–98, 24) often thought to derive from Aristotle's now lost "Περὶ Ἰδεῶν" ("On the Forms" or "On Ideas"). Dancy (Two Studies, pp. 32 ff.), following H. Karpp (see his Untersuchungen zur Philosophie des Eudoxos von Knidos [Würzburg-Aumühle, 1933], pp. 28–35), argues that much less of the whole passage than is commonly supposed—including the sentence quoted—goes back to Aristotle. G. Fine ("Critical Notice" [of Dancy's monograph] Canadian Journal of Philosophy 22 [1992]:

of this criticism is often thought (primarily) to be Eudoxus, we will also want to see how Plato can meet this objection.

The way around the first difficulty will involve a more fine-grained sense of exactly which aspects of Presocratic metaphysics Plato is seeking to retain. That he cannot retain it all, and would in any event not want to retain it in the form in which Anaxagoras and the medical writers had presented matters, is clear. The key insight Plato means to hold on to, I believe, is not the notion of infinite *homoiomerous* divisibility, it is rather the weaker notion of *homonymous* divisibility. What is the difference between the two?

In the case of homoiomerous divisiblity, we are to think of certain uniform wholes (the elements) as being divisible into portions or bits, which then go into the multiform mixtures (the ordinary things). Here the uniformity in question clearly is physical homogeneity, or something relevantly similar, so that each element will be wholly and only what it is. Thus a portion of elemental water is itself elemental water; and if we impose Anaxagoras's other constraints (including the denial of atomism and infinite divisibilty), *any* portion of elemental water, no matter how small, will itself be elemental water.

In the case of homonymous divisibility, certain uniform, incomposite wholes (the Forms) have homonymous parts or participants. This notion of uniformity is weaker. For here uniformity is presumably not to be thought of as matter of physical homogeneity, but rather as something like: consisting of a single aspect. That is why, if The Just Itself is a relevant whole, 'The Just Itself is just' is true. Now, as we know, some just individual, not identical to The Just Itself, is called 'just' in virtue of participating in The Just Itself.

398–401) maintains that Dancy is too sceptical here (although she does not address Karpp's arguments); and in her *On Ideas: Aristotle's Criticism of Plato's Theory of Forms* (Oxford, 1993), she endorses H. Cherniss's verdict (*Aristotle's Criticism of Plato and the Academy* [Baltimore, 1944], p. 531) that Alexander gives 'the arguments only in the incomplete and compressed form of an abstract' (see p. 256 n. 24). Fortunately, it does not matter for our purposes whether the objection comes from Aristotle or not; because even if it is not his, it is thoroughly Aristotelian in spirit. What is of far greater importance is how, exactly, to translate the sentence. Dancy (*Two Studies,* p. 31) has "the part of a man can't be a man, as the part of gold is gold"; while Barnes and Lawrence have "For part of man cannot be a man, as a part of gold is gold," in *The Complete Works of Aristotle,* 2 vols. (Princeton, N.J., 1994), 2:2440. This is better; but given that the context is one where Forms are under discussion, the objection would be most to the point if the Form, Man, were being referred to. I have thus translated accordingly (but note that only a few lines earlier, at 98, 5, Alexander refers to the Form, Man, as αὐτοάνθρωπος, i.e., Man Itself).

Before proceeding, we need to take note of a complication. For it seems that there are potentially *two* different ways we could conceive of this participation. (i) We might think that the person himself, say, Socrates, participates in The Just Itself. Or (ii) we might think that what, looked at in one way, is a part of Socrates—namely exactly that part which accounts for his being just—is, looked at in another way, also a part of The Just Itself. In case (i) is the proper way to construe matters, Socrates himself would be a part of The Just Itself, by participating in the Form. In case (ii) is the proper way, it is rather Socrates' justice which would be a part of The Just Itself. Plato's language often suggests (i). But when he describes the participants as themselves being multiform composites, as he does in the *Phaedo*, Plato may seem to be suggesting that (ii) is, strictly speaking, the proper picture.[129] Notice that a question analogous to the one about (ii) versus (i) can be raised for Anaxagoras: (i′) is it a given mixture that itself participates in an elemental stuff, or (ii′) is it a part of the mixture—namely, the S part—that is a portion of the elemental stuff, S? The fact that these questions can be raised, and that there is some unclarity about how to answer them, is one further symptom of the fact that neither Plato nor Anaxagoras (and other thinkers adopting such an approach), have a clearly formulated conception of particular things as opposed to the features those things can have.

To return to the main line of argument: there are two indications that homonymous divisibility is the aspect of Anaxagoreanism that Plato is committed to. First, Plato does not so much as hint that he is concerned to maintain the *infinite* divisibility of the wholes into parts, the parts into still further parts, and so on. Secondly and more importantly, the notion of *wholeness* used to characterize the wholes as wholes is less restrictive than Anaxagoras's. Any whole that is privileged in the right way, and that has homonymous parts,[130] can be a relevant whole. Obviously, this would allow Plato to retain all the Anaxagorean elements as wholes (though he might want, for other reasons, to deny elemental status to some or even

---

[129] There may well be some tension between (ii) and the thought that the participants are rolling about between being and not-being. For (ii) would suggest that the just (part) in Socrates is just, while everything else that is in Socrates in an analogous way, i.e, what we would think of as his other characteristics, is not just. But in that case, is there any longer a *single* item that both is, and is not just?

[130] As we have noted earlier (pp. 47–8 above), Plato does not, in the middle dialogues, distinguish between homonymy and what Aristotle calls paronymy. While Plato does distinguish them in the *Theaetetus*, in the *Phaedo* and *Republic*, paronymy is assimilated to hom-

to all of them). Yet not every Platonic whole of the relevant sort could count as an Anaxagorean stuff. Why not?

The reason is that Plato can also count as wholes genera (γένη) and species (εἴδη). Saying this is not to claim that, in the middle dialogues, Plato already has a notion of genera and species along the lines we find developed in the late dialogues. The point rather is that the conception of εἶδος (form) which is in play—such that things alike in form have a share of, or particpate in *the Form*—is insufficiently determinate between things like quasi-stuffs had in common, and kinds. Thus there is also no reason for thinking that, when Plato, in the late dialogues, comes to conceive of the Forms as kinds, he is changing the meaning of the term εἶδος. He is rather focusing on, and articulating, a use for which it had been available all along. Now in the course of working out that use more precisely, and becoming clearer about what all is involved with that understanding of Form, it may very well also become clear that certain aspects of this new, more articulated use are incompatible with other uses, ones that had, however, been more prominent in the earlier work.

Now the reason why that notion of form is insufficiently determinate, and hence the reason why genera and species can in fact count as wholes (of the appropriate sort), is that the parts of these genera and species also have the same name as they do (e.g., 'man' is *the* name for the species and *a* name for Socrates). Indeed, on Plato's view, the parts (participants) are named as they are *after* the wholes, the Forms or species.[131] (This precisely parallels the Anaxagorean view.) Thus Socrates is a part of Man, the species; and he is called (a) man because he is such a part. Justice is a part of Virtue, or equivalently, Justice is a species of Virtue; and it is called (a) virtue because it is such a part or species. White is a 'part' of color, that is, White is a color, or is one of the colors, or is a kind of color; and it is called (a) color because it is such a part or kind. And so on. (Of course, once again it is not clear whether, in case Socrates is just, it is Socrates who is a part of Justice, or whether it is Socrates' justice—the just part of Socrates—which is a part of Justice.)

While turning to homonymous rather than infinite homoiomerous divisibility goes some way towards addressing the first problem, the second one

---

onymy, it seems. Thus, for example, a just thing can be a homonym of the Form, irrespective of whether the Form is called The Just Itself or Justice.

[131] See, for example, *Phaedo* 102b2, c10; 103b7–8; *Parmenides* 130e5–131a2; and *Timaeus* 65b5; 83c1–3.

still looks like a glaring difficulty. Suppose we do think of Socrates as a mixture or quasi-mixture. On the Anaxagorean-Platonic view, we will think of his complexion, his justice, his size, his health, and so on as each being a part of him. Now if this were applied across the board, then man (i.e., a part of the Form, Man) should also be a part of him. Yet it seems that either Socrates, the man, just *is* all those other things, or that Socrates, the man, is *composed out of* or *from* those other things. But however we decide between those two possibilities, it seems perfectly clear that Man can hardly be another part or ingredient alongside of, and on a par with, all the others: to put the point tendentiously, the expression 'his man' does not refer to his being human, but to his servant or slave; 'his pallor', on the other hand, refers to his being pale.

This problem, it seems to me, lies at the heart of the matter. Yet we need to decide if it is a problem with the interpretation advocated here, or a problem with the view itself. First of all, we saw a quite similar difficulty in Anaxagoras. For it was not clear how an individual organism (or its seed-stuff) was related to the other things (e.g., the flesh, blood, and bone) that went into the mixture that is the entire organism. If Plato's view derives from Presocratic thinking like that of Anaxagoras, it would not be surprising if his view is subject to similar difficulties.

Secondly, as we can see from Aristotle's critique of Platonism (especially in *Metaphysics* VII, 17 and VIII, 3), there does in fact seem to be a problem of this sort. For while Aristotle praises Plato and the Platonists for recognizing that a formal component is needed for satisfactory explanations, and while he acknowledges that their views thus represent an advance over those of their 'materialist' predecessors, he also thinks that they have an inadequate conception of how a form can be part of a hylomorphic compound. For the form is supposed to explain why the compound is a genuine unity, and not merely a heap (of stuff, or whatever). But if this is so, one cannot treat the form as yet another part of the compound, alongside of, and on a par with, all the others. That is because doing so leads to an infinite regress: for now another form will be required to explain why all those things, together with the first form, constitute a genuine unity; and so on. Hence a form should either not be thought of as a part of the compound at all, or it needs to be thought of as being a part in a very different way of being a part.

Before continuing, we should note that we may be faced with a potentially significant disanalogy here. Aristotle is relying on the following notion of form: that which unifies various *material constituents* in a hylomorphic compound. The role just envisaged for the Platonic Form, Man, however, was to unify the various *features* in a particular human being, like Socrates. But, it will be objected, material constituents and features are fundamentally different sorts of entities, so Aristotle turns out to be equivocating on the notion of form, by equivocating on the kinds of entities that are to be unified, and hence on the kind of unification that is at issue.

Such an objection would be premature. Given that Plato's view of features is a quasi-Anaxagorean one, a key role for the Form, Man, must be that of unifying the different bits of the different quasi-stuffs (viz., what we would call the properties) present within a particular human being into *that* particular human being. Thus Aristotle is not simply equivocating on the notion of form. In fact, *composing* something out of quasi-stuffs and *constituting* an object out of matter prove to be parallel notions. In each case, Aristotle holds, that which is to do the composing or constituting must yield an entity of a different type, indeed, an entity on a different ontological level, from the entities that compose or constitute the new, unified entity.[132] If the operations of composing or constituting yield entities of the same ontological type as the entities that are being composed into, or that constitute, the new entity, then those operations will be subject to the objections Aristotle presents. This part of Aristotle's critique of Platonism thus amounts to the charge that Plato's view is an exact counterpart of the materialists' view in its failure to recognize that a particular object must be of a different ontological type than its features.

Moreover, in *Metaphysics* VII, 10–11, Aristotle undertakes a painstaking inquiry into the question of the priority of parts to wholes, and wholes to parts, in the cases of forms, compounds, and definitions. As we might

---

[132] This way of speaking may suggest that the item or items (i.e., the matter) that constitute some further item (i.e., the hylomorphic compound) are present, or exist *before* the operation of so constituting (i.e., 'enforming') them takes place. It may similarly suggest that the item or items (i.e., portions of the quasi-stuffs) that are composed into some further item (i.e., the mixture) are also there *before* the opertion of so composing them takes place. On Aristotle's own considered view of these issues, however, in a genuine hylomorphic compound, the matter is *not* there before the formation of the compound. Indeed, the difference between living things and artifacts in part comes down to exactly this: in the case of artifacts, there may be a sense in which the matter is prior to the artifact, precisely because it is present before the artifact is manufactured (consider the bronze as the matter for the statue); but nothing analogous is true in the case of organisms and their material constituents (consider the flesh and blood of the living person). Thus the formulation in the body of the text should be taken as being merely a *façon de parler,* not as the description of the actual sequence of 'enforming' any genuine hylomorphic compound, like a plant or an animal.

expect, he is there concerned to distinguish different senses, or ways, of being a part or a whole, as well as different kinds of priority. And the examples considered as well as the explicit reference to Socrates the Younger (a member of the Academy) make clear that Aristotle is considering the questions he is considering, not only out of a sense of their general importance, but because becoming clear about them bears directly on the Platonists' ontology and their conception of it.

To take just one example, Aristotle is concerned to distinguish between those things which fall apart into their parts when they cease to be, and whose parts hence are prior to them, and so can also, in some sense, be regarded as the principles (ἀρχαί) of these things; and those things which do not fall apart into their parts when they perish, and whose parts thus are not prior to them. In fact Aristotle is able to differentiate among a whole range of notions of part and whole. But the very care and extensiveness of his analyses in these two chapters suggests that there really are difficulties for Platonism on this point, difficulties that need to be worked out. Thus if we are inclined to think that Aristotle is being at all fair-minded here, it would again come as no great surprise to find related difficulties in Plato's dialogues.

And there is reason to think that Aristotle is being at least somewhat fair-minded. For in the *Parmenides*, the problem is raised whether Forms are present as *wholes* in the things participating in them, or as *parts*. This dilemma is developed with the Form Large, not Man. Parmenides (i.e., Plato) no doubt thinks that this particular Form presents other acute paradoxes, whichever option one chooses, but especially if one says that it is a part of The Large Itself that is present in a large thing—for such a part is presumably smaller than The Large Itself, but then it seems that something small accounts for the participant's being large. Socrates is forced to concede that it seems that participants do not have a share of either the whole or a part of the Form (131a–e). (It is sometimes suggested that Plato's target, in the part-whole dilemma, is Eudoxus. The fact that the Form, Large, is chosen, however, shows that the target cannot be *only* Eudoxus, if he is a target at all. For Forms like The Large had played a prominent role in Plato's own picture of Forms, for example, in the *Phaedo*.)

The initial dialectical worry is of course not the end of the matter. It indicates that we need a much clearer sense of the notions of part and whole, before we start applying them to Forms and participants, and that we cannot simply carry over our most straightforward understanding of these ideas, which just is to say, we cannot simply understand these notions in their usual physical or spatial sense. In the second part of the dialogue, Plato goes some way towards providing the needed (revised) conceptions of part and whole. Indeed, I believe he was, in part, motivated to construe Forms as *kinds* precisely in order to deal with the problems arising from any overly concrete or simplistic understanding of the notions of part and whole. If this is correct, it again makes perfect sense to suppose that there are corresponding difficulties (or at any rate, unclarities) in the earlier works.

Thirdly, we need to remember that for Plato, genera and species cannot be identified with the classes of particulars falling under them. This is one consequence of the arguments in the *Parmenides* and *Sophist* which show that, e.g., one and many, and same and different, apply to absolutely everything. This means the *extension* of all of them is the same. Yet surely, for example, what it is to be one is not the same as what it is to be many, and vice versa. (The same point, mutatis mutandis, obviously applies to all of these Forms/species.) Hence the Form/species One (i.e., The One Itself) comprises not only all the things that can be said to be one. In addition to the extension, there will also be something that corresponds to the answer to the question, 'What is (it to be) one?' (We might label whatever this turns out to be: the *principle of unity*.) And while it would be simply absurd to think of the extension of Man as a part of, e.g., Socrates—he rather is part of the extension—it is less clearly absurd, though perhaps problematic in other ways, to think of this nonextensional component, this principle, as a part of him. In the dialogues that we are interested in here, Plato of course has not yet worked out this bipartite conception of Forms/species. But given that in those dialogues, he is not yet regarding any part of the Form as a class or collection, it is even less likely that he had a purely extensional view of Forms there.

All of this hardly shows that thinking of Man—whether construed as an Anaxagorean element or a Platonic Form—as being a part of each and every individual human being is not misguided and even seriously mistaken; still less does it suffice for showing that this (somehow) is a satisfactory way of conceiving things, after all. But it does suggest that we are not faced with a simple or straightforward confusion. And so the fact that Man is a Form for the Platonic tradition (and probably was one for Plato himself) does not stand in the way of the interpretation proposed here; it rather points to aspects of the metaphysical picture about which we would need to achieve far greater clarity in order to see what, precisely, has gone wrong. (I have suggested that Aristotle holds that Plato's failure to distinguish objects from properties is the source of the difficulties we have just noted.)

It may be useful briefly to consider (what turns out to be) another version or formulation of the same problem. In criticizing views like that of Burnet—that the participants are bundles or clusters of Form-instances— F. C. White charges that this would (i) commit Plato to a doctrine of *bare particulars*, because (ii) "properties are aspects *of*, qualities *of*, individuals or particulars."[133] But White holds that the idea that there should be bare particulars—i.e., individuals that are not, in their own right, characterized as anything other than being *this* or *that* individual—is incoherent; and that "[i]t is easy to talk as if there were no difficulty about the existence of properties on their own, but in fact properties can no more exist except as properties *of* individuals than the latter can exist unless they are individuals *with* properties."[134] Let us grant that bare particulars are deeply problematic pseudo-entities. But what of the second contention? On the one hand, it would be easy to reply that White is simply begging the question against *bundle-theorists*. For such theorists precisely deny what he takes as uncontroversial, namely, that properties must be the properties *of* something.[135] But White's discomfort is symptomatic of a post-Aristotelian way of looking at things (as is his talk of individuals, particulars, and properties). Such discomfort, I am suggesting, simply does not arise for Anaxagoras, or for Plato. And if sensible particulars are mixtures or quasi-mixtures, there is no reason to think that so construing (what we have come to think of as) properties commits Plato, or Anaxagoras, to bare particulars. For there is no reason to think that a mixture or quasi-mixture is anything indepedently of what is mixed in it. Yet it is exactly at this point that the objection we have been considering can be made telling. For whatever it is that makes, say, a human being be a human being seems to be of a different sort than what accounts for that human being being pale, or just, or tall, and so on. In the *Metaphysics*, Aristotle will maintain that his analysis of objects into compounds of form and matter, compounds which (then) have properties, accounts for that difference. In the *Categories*, as we will

[133] "Plato's Middle Dialogues and the Independence of Particulars," *Philosophical Quarterly* 27 (1977): 202 f, 204.

[134] Ibid.

[135] On theories of this sort, see: J. Van Cleve, "Three Versions of the Bundle Theory," *Philosophical Studies* 47 (1985).

see in Part III, he simply *insists* that objects must be specified as the *kind* of objects they are, and that both the objects and the kinds need to be distinguished from the properties. In both cases, Aristotle is repudiating something Anaxagoras and Plato (it seems) just take for granted. To make real philosophical progress with the underlying issues, we would thus need to find a neutral standpoint from which we could try to adjudicate matters. The foregoing considerations should have helped to show that this would be a far from trivial task. (Undertaking that task with anything like the requisite care would obviously also involve going far beyond the confines of the present inquiry.) But having considered and reflected on these various objections, we can now, at last, return to the participants and their being, that is, their becoming.

14. THE PARTICIPANTS: BEING AND BECOMING

Following Burnet, the claim had been that the participants are something like mixtures. More precisely, they are like mixtures to the extent that any change they undergo results in what is, strictly speaking, another mixture. And because they can change in every way, they *are* not anything, strictly speaking. Plato thus agrees with Parmenides, at least about ordinary things. Nevertheless, Plato parts company with Parmenides and insists that we can make some sense of the things they, i.e., the mixtures, are (ordinarily) said to be. For it turns out that even if they *are* not any of the things they are said to be, they still *become* at least some of them. This means, first of all, that the participants appear, manifest, or display themselves in various ways, and secondly, that their 'ability' to appear or to display themselves depends on there being other things that are—that is, are really, or are intrinsically, or are in their own right—all of the things the participants only become. We should now return to the dialogues to see how this picture of the participants manifests itelf.

Let us begin with the *Theaetetus*. There, in the course of trying to explicate the epistemological thesis which had been attributed to Protagoras—that knowledge is perception—Plato introduces a strange view, the so-called Secret Doctrine of Protagoras. There is every reason to believe that this Secret Doctrine has nothing to do with the views of the historical Protagoras. In fact, as has often been noted, it rather is remarkably similar, in many ways, to views Plato presents in the *Republic* (see 475e–480a, 521c–

525d) and in the *Timaeus*.[136] Socrates describes the Secret Doctrine as follows:

> I will tell you, this is certainly no common, everyday account. It says that nothing is one thing in and of itself (ἕν αὐτὸ καθ' αὑτό), and that you cannot correctly call <anything> anything, or even say that it is qualified in any way, . . . it rather, due to motion and change (κίνησις), and the mixture (κρᾶσις) of things with each other, becomes all the things which we say it is, not expressing ourselves correctly. For it never is, but always becomes. (152d2–e1)

And after having discussed the implications of the Secret Doctrine for perception, Socrates summarizes:

> Thus the result of all this is, just what we were saying at the beginning: nothing is one thing by itself (ἕν αὐτὸ καθ' αὑτό), but always becomes for someone. And 'to be' ought to be excluded everywhere—not that we haven't been compelled, by habit and lack of knowledge, to use it often. But we ought not to, . . . nor ought we to admit 'something', 'someone's', or 'my' or 'this' or 'that', nor any other name that fixes things. . . . (157a7–b8)

It is sometimes suggested that Socrates speaks the way he does in this part of the dialogue, because of the relativity of *perception*, which is certainly central to Protagoras's theory and to the Secret Doctrine. That suggestion is actually quite puzzling: for why should we switch verbs and introduce the other restrictions to make the point about relativity? Someone could, after all, perfectly well say, 'the wind is cold for me, but it is hot for you'; or 'this is good for me, but it is bad for you'. How would substituting 'becomes' for 'is' help—either in presenting or in defending the relativism?

Something else must be going on. John McDowell, of recent commentators on the dialogue, has most strongly emphasized the relevance of Eleatic constraints on being in these passages. If we have accepted those constraints, we will not be in a position to say, of some *x*, that it both is (something, e.g., hot) and is not (something, e.g., cold). Yet it is characteristic of everyday things that we will be compelled to say such things, if we are to say anything at all. As McDowell observes, "it seems plausible that any statement about anything involves saying that it is ____, where the gap is filled according to what the statement is."[137] Now when we come to the relativized perceptions, we will *still* be compelled to say such

---

[136] See, for example, McDowell, *Plato: Theaetetus*, pp. 122–29, ad *Theaet.* 152d2–e1.
[137] Ibid., p. 127.

things about them; and the relativizing supplements ('. . . for me', '. . . for you', '. . . for the Gods', '. . . for mortals') do *not* remove, as we might believe they would, the contrariety or contradiction.

Why not? The things being talked about are such as both to be (something, for someone) and not to be (something, for someone); but this simply means that, despite the relativizing supplements, we are still speaking of being and not-being. But speaking of being and not-being is precisely what had been ruled out. Thus, either we will be able to say nothing about these relativized items as well, or we will need to find some other verb to use in place of 'is'. McDowell suggests that 'becomes' or 'comes to be' "*might be pressed into the same service,*" to do duty for 'is'.[138] But if we understand 'becomes' in the usual way, there would be something quite unnatural and contrived about doing that—as is suggested by the very language of "pressing into service" McDowell uses. Yet if we recall that 'becomes' can in any event be used as the copula, and if we recall the special variant of that use (which we examined earlier) that Plato had focused on and developed further, then insisting on using 'becomes' in all those sentences where we had, *incorrectly*, been using 'is' seems like a perfectly natural move; it is not a matter of pressing the verb into a service for which it is ill suited.

In the *Timaeus*, Plato seems to go still further. But before considering some passages from that dialogue, we need to remind ourselves that it presents special problems of intepretation. To begin with, there is the curious fact that in so overtly dogmatic and systematic a work, Plato repeatedly introduces notes of caution which undercut that dogmatism significantly. Thus Timaeus emphasizes that the account he is giving is, at best, a likely, not a true one (29c7–d3; cf. 48d1–e1 and 49b6–7). At various points, important details are omitted, e.g., (as commentators have often noted) the retrograde motions of the planets are left as a topic to be explored further, on some other occasion (38d6–e3). Moreover, Timaeus observes that a crucial part of the picture—the way in which The Receptacle

---

[138] Ibid.; emphasis in the original. M. Burnyeat, in the introduction to *The Theaetetus of Plato*, tr. M. J. Levett, rev. M Burnyeat (Indianapolis, 1990), does not directly discuss the meaning of 'becomes' in 152d–e and 157a–b. (Hereafter this will be cited simply as Burnyeat, "Introduction.") But on his preferred account of the dialogue, the Heracleitean view of becoming underlying the Secret Doctrine should be construed as a "metaphsyical" rather than "physical" theory (pp. 16–18). The present interpretation of becoming is likewise a metaphysical one; but I have tried to offer reasons for thinking that the verb 'becomes' is well suited to play this role.

is modified or characterized by the items that come to be present within it—is "difficult to describe" (50c5–6). Indeed, Timaeus warns that his whole exposition might not be entirely consistent (29c5–7)!

This caution seems well taken. Consider only two difficulties. (i) On the one hand, The Receptacle is supposed to be *entirely* featureless (50b8–c4; d7–e1; 51a7); on the other, it is supposed to contain *traces* (ἴχνη, 53b2) of the fire, air, water, and earth that are to come to be within it, and so it seemingly proves *not* to be entirely featureless after all.[139] (ii) The account of the four elements at 31b–32b suggests that they will be directly comparable to each other—in terms of the geometrical progression outlined—and thus also transformable into each other. But the later account of them, at 54b ff., emphasizes that earth cannot be transformed into the others, nor they into earth, since earth consists of triangles of one sort, while fire, air, and water consist of triangles of a different sort (where the two sorts are not transformable into each other, because not directly commensurable with each other).[140]

But the question of the relative *chronology* of the dialogue may seem most pressing. For the present account (see also Sections 15–16 below) may seem to fit most naturally with a relatively early date for the *Timaeus* (i.e., close to the *Republic*, and earlier than the *Parmenides, Sophist* and *Philebus*), as G. E. L. Owen had argued.[141] Indeed, Owen sees the *Timaeus* as standing at the end of Plato's middle period, and as forming the high point of his theory of Forms. But in the *Parmenides*, Plato came to see that the middle-period theory of Forms was fatally flawed. Thus in later works—beginning with the second part of the *Parmenides* itself—he either abandoned or extensively revised that theory. And what Plato is prepared to call Forms or genera in those dialogues turn out to be far less metaphysically extravagant entities than the middle-period Forms had been—roughly speaking, they are natural kinds—and so they prove more congenial to our own, more sober, philosophical sensibilities.

---

[139] See also K. Sayre, "The Role of the *Timaeus* in the Development of Plato's Late Ontology," *Ancient Philosophy* 18 (1998): 110 and n. 30; cf. p. 109 n. 28.

[140] Cf. ibid., p. 111 n. 32.

[141] "The Place of the *Timaeus* in Plato's Dialogues," *Classical Quarterly*, n.s. 3 (1953), reprinted in *LSD*. Owen is following Gilbert Ryle's view of the chronology of the dialogues. That chronology is implicit in "Plato's *Parmenides*," *Mind* 48 (1939), reprinted in *Studies in Plato's Metaphysics*, ed. R. E. Allen (London and New York, 1965). Ryle offers an explicit statement of his views of the order of Plato's dialogues in *Plato's Progress* (Cambridge, 1966), chap. 7, "The Timetable," pp. 216–300.

Owen's view has been philosophically attractive to many of his successors. Unfortunately, the best philological and stylometric evidence points towards a later date for the dialogue.[142] Thus the *Timaeus* belongs with works like the *Sophist* and *Philebus*, i.e., precisely those works where the new picture of Forms is presented—a picture that, according to Owen and many others, is incompatible with the earlier one in significant ways. (See also Section 16 below.)

First, granting that the *Timaeus* is in all likelihood late does not require taking it as merely recapitulating the metaphysical picture of, say, the *Republic* and *Phaedo*.[143] Consider only the prominent roles played by The Receptacle (which is wholly absent in the canonical middle-period dialogues), the Divine Craftsman, and the triangles: all suggest that the *Timaeus* picture is more likely a refinement or development of the earlier one, not a simple restatement of it. But now, as Kenneth Sayre suggests, a new possibility opens up. The *Timaeus* may have been Plato's *initial* response to the difficulties raised in the *first* part of the *Parmenides*. (This becomes possible, since the first and second parts of the *Parmenides* may very well have been written at different times.)[144]

Secondly, there is the fact that Leonard Brandwood and Gerard Ledger arrive at *different* sequences for these late dialogues.[145] Thus even if the *Timaeus* can be placed securely within the late *group* on the basis of stylistic or stylometric criteria, it may well not be possible to assign it a specific *place* within that group on the basis of such criteria.[146] This matters, because given the absence of a specific place within the late group, the sequence of dialogues favored by Sayre for philosophical reasons is not

---

[142] See L. Brandwood, *The Chronology of Plato's Dialogues* (Cambridge, 1990), and G. Ledger, *Re-counting Plato: A Computer Analysis of Plato's Style* (Oxford, 1989). C. Young's "Plato and Computer Dating," *Oxford Studies in Ancient Philosophy* 12 (1994) contains extremely useful summaries of these works and judicious criticisms of them, as well as a very sensible statement of the limitations of stylometry more generally. See also P. Keyser, "Stylometric Method and the Chronology of Plato's Works," *Bryn Mawr Classical Review* 3 (1992).

[143] See also Sayre, "The Role," pp. 93–95.

[144] See Ledger, *Re-counting Plato*, pp. 212–13, and Sayre, "The Role," pp. 122–23 and nn. 51 and 52.

[145] Brandwood: *Timaeus; Critias; Sophist; Statesman; Philebus; Laws* preceded by *Republic; Parmenides; Theaetetus* (see his *The Chronology of Plato's Dialogues*, pp. 250–51; cf. p. 206). Ledger: *Philebus; Clitophon; Epistles 7, 3, 8; Sophist; Statesman; Laws; Epinomis; Timaeus; Critias* also preceded by *Republic; Parmenides; Theaetetus* (see his *Re-counting Plato*, p. 208).

[146] See Young, "Computer Dating," pp. 242–47.

ruled out: *Parmenides* I; *Timaeus*; *Parmenides* II; *Philebus*.[147] I myself would want to insert the *Sophist* between *Parmenides* II and the *Philebus*.

Furthermore, even if the *Timaeus* should turn out to be later than that sequence suggests, this might not matter as much as has often been supposed. For the whole question of dating the dialogues is complicated by the fact that commentators assume (i) that Plato did not extensively revise his writings;[148] (ii) that with the possible exception of the *Laws*, a given dialogue was begun only after the 'previous' one was finished, i.e., that they were all composed at one sitting (as it were); and (iii) that Plato would not have pursued two different (and perhaps ultimately incompatible) paths of inquiry simultaneously. None of these assumptions should be taken for granted.

For our present purposes what matters is this: while the exposition that I adopt may suggest a certain relative date for the *Timaeus*, that is an artifact of the exposition. Even an extremely late date (as proposed, e.g., by Ledger) is, I believe, compatible with the sort of picture I am advocating. Showing exactly *how* it is compatible would, however, require developing an account that rejects assumption (iii) (see the previous paragraph) in favor of a *specific* suggestion for the two differing paths of inquiry, as well as offering a fully detailed analysis of virtually the whole *Timaeus*. Needless to say, both of these tasks would involve going far beyond the confines of the present inquiry.

But let us now turn to some details from the *Timaeus*. There we are told that we ought not to say "what became *is* what became, what becomes now *is* now becoming, and also what will become *is* what will become" (38b1–2).[149] Again one wonders: why not? The worry seems to be that

---

[147] Sayre, "The Role," p. 122. In accepting Sayre's account of the order of the dialogues, I do not mean thereby also to endorse his account of the philosophical content of the *Philebus*.

[148] Young ("Computer Dating," p. 227 n. 4) argues correctly that the remarks in Dionysius of Halicarnassus (*De Compositione Verborum* 25.210–12)—if they are to be believed at all— suggest only that Plato made some later stylistic revisions to his dialogues, not substantive ones. But if we know that Plato did carefully go over his works again, that to my mind makes it at least possible that he also made some substantive revisions. More subtly, it is possible that he wants us to reread earlier works with the lessons learned from later ones firmly in mind. (On this last point, see Wieland, *Platon und die Formen des Wissens*, pp. 83–94, esp. p. 90 ff.)

[149] There will presumably be, as it were, a metalinguistic use of 'is', according to which these all ought to be acceptable. Thus even in 27d6, the (omitted) verb that is required seems to be 'is', i.e.: "on the one hand, there <sc. is> what always is, . . . on the other hand, there <sc. is> what always becomes. . . ."

unless we take precautions and observe these restrictions, we run the risk of attributing being to the items in the realm of becoming, after all. But if Plato were merely committed to the view that all physical things are constantly changing, in all sorts of ways, it would be difficult to see why he should insist on these rather peculiar-sounding restrictions. For one is inclined to think that what becomes *is* a thing that becomes. Indeed it seems that a thing that becomes *really* is a thing that becomes (viz., τὸ γιγνόμενον γιγνόμενον ὄντως ἐστί), and so we ought to be able to say just that. In fact, Plato himself seems to allow for something like this at 48a5–7: "So if someone were to say how it [sc. the world] *really* came to be in this way . . ." (εἴ τις οὖν ᾗ γέγονεν κατὰ ταῦτα ὄντως ἐρεῖ . . .). Why then does Plato emphatically insist, at 38b1–2, that these kinds of claims must be ruled out? The traditional interpretation, I submit, has no good answer to this question.

However, given the picture of becoming advocated here, it is easy to see why Plato should have Timaeus saying the things he says. The claim that what becomes *is* becoming, suggests that the becoming (sc. thing; i.e., τὸ γιγνόμενον) satisfies Eleatic constraints on being and has a *nature* of a certain sort, namely, a *nature* to be wholly unstable, completely changeable, and always changing. But what is characteristic of the becomings is that they fail to satisfy those constraints and thus do *not* have *any* nature. As already suggested, it is because they lack natures that they are subject to change, always and in every way. It is not that they have the nature: to be subject to change, always and in every way. This will no longer look like a merely terminological difference as soon as one realizes that natures are principles of structure, order, systematicity, intelligibility, etc. It is part of the very notion of a nature in this strong sense, that it imposes constraints on what will be possible.[150]

---

[150] This is not meant as a claim about the word φύσις, or even about all the uses of word φύσις in Plato (on which, see D. Mannsperger, *Physis bei Platon* [Berlin, 1969]); it is rather meant as a claim about the notion of a nature as a metaphysical principle. Consider this passage from the *Phaedrus*: "But since a self-mover turned out to be immortal, one should not be ashamed about declaring that this is the *ousia* and the λόγος of soul; for every body that is moved from outside is without soul (ἄψυχον), while a body that is moved from within, from itself, is ensouled (ἔμψυχον, viz., alive), that being the nature of soul (ὡς ταύτης οὔσης φύσεως ψυχῆς)" (245e2–6). Hence a φύσις can be a principle of change (rather, of life), but of orderly, patterned, and therefore intelligible changes. Consider next a passage from the *Theaetetus*: "But in that other sphere I was speaking of—in the case of what's just or unjust, in conformity with religion or not—they're prepared to insist that none of them has by nature a being of its own (ὡς οὐκ ἔστι φύσει αὐτῶν οὐδὲν οὐσίαν ἑαυτοῦ ἔχον)" (172b2–5; tr. McDowell). This is said by Socrates, who obviously does not

If this is so, and if this notion of nature is imported by the use of 'is', then it is readily apparent why, strictly speaking, demonstrative pronouns like 'this' or 'that' should also not be applied to becomings. For if one speaks of a becoming as this rather than that, it will be all too easy to slip into thinking that is this rather than that, in other words, that its nature is to be this. But it has no nature, and so also not that nature.

Of course this special notion of becoming is very closely tied to the notions of change and generation. Indeed, we find Plato switching back and forth between the two uses within one and the same context. Now since being (οὐσία), in the strict sense of being, is not subject to change and hence does not change at all (much less come into, or pass out of being), the fact that an item is changing, or coming to be in the ordinary sense of coming to be, will be a *sign* or *symptom* of the fact that it is also a becoming (a γιγνόμενον) in Plato's specialized sense. Moreover, becoming in that sense will be a necessary condition for becoming in the ordinary sense; but since it is not also a sufficient condition, the beings (ὄντα), the things that can be said to be (in the ordinary sense of being), can also be becomings (γιγνόμενα) in Plato's sense. In the light of all this, it is not surprising that throughout the *Timaeus*, Plato moves rather freely between the two notions of becoming.

. . . . .

Let us return to the *Theaetetus*. Now in fact the items described in the Secret Doctrine *are always changing*, in every way; moreover, they are doing so for every perceiver. (This presumably accounts, in no small measure, for why the traditional interpretation of 'becoming' seems attractive to so many commentators.) But here too we need to recognize that the fact that they are becomings in the ordinary sense (i.e., things that are changing), is one only made possible by the metaphysically more basic fact that they are becomings, in the special sense (i.e., items subject to change in every way).

Given the characterization of the Secret Doctrine thus far, we might expect to find something that corresponds to the view that particulars are nothing but mixtures. At 154a8, it is suggested that a person "will never

share the view he reports. He thinks justice and holiness *do* have a being of their own by nature, i.e., by their own nature: and this being simply is their nature. Thus Plato at times uses 'The *X*', 'The being (*ousia*) of *X*' and 'The nature of *X*' interchangeably. (Cf. also the uses of φύσις in the *Sophist*.) Thus, at a minimum, if it is appropriate to speak of the Form, or the real being (*ousia*), it will also be appropriate to speak of the nature, and vice

be in the same condition with respect to himself"; and 154b1–8 suggests that because of the changes one undergoes, one will literally never be the same person. Socrates returns to this thought at 159b3–5, when he asks Theaetetus "if the healthy Socrates and the ill Socrates are like or unlike each other." Theaetetus responds that if he is asking about the *wholes*, the ill Socrates and the healthy Socrates, then these *wholes* are unlike. And after considering a few more examples, they agree that, strictly speaking, the ill Socrates is not the same thing as the healthy one (159d7–8). This hardly is a thought someone committed to a distinction between accidental and essential properties for sensible particulars would accept without further comment.

The agreement Theaetetus and Socrates reach thus shows that Theaetetus is a *mereological essentialist*, for he (apparently) just accepts the view that an item is not constituted out of its ingredients, but simply *is* its ingredients. And on such a view, there is indeed no way of characterizing the item (the whole mixture) other than by specifying exactly the ingredients of which it consists, the ingredients (the parts) which constitute it.[151] Thus if there is any change in the ingredients, we have what is a new item, strictly speaking. But this also means that any and all changes will, to use Aristotle's terminology, be substantial changes rather than alterations. Thus in the case of a human being, we are *not* in a position to insist on a (metaphyscially significant) difference between kinds of change in, say, the change from illness to health and in the one from living to dead.

The status, within the *Theaetetus*, of mereological essentialism and the view of becoming that leads to it, however, gives rise to a troubling question. There is widespread agreement that a later version of this view (or these views)—the so-called extreme Heracleitean position, or radical flux thesis—is presented in order to be *refuted* (see 181a–183c). Indeed, the radical thesis is shown to be *self-refuting*. Yet if the (earlier) picture of becoming—and hence of the participants—entails that later view, and thus if the earlier one is presented so that *it*, too, can be refuted (as Burnyeat argues), one might well doubt that such a view should be attributed to Plato as his own.[152] The problematic picture rather turns out to be one

---

versa. This suggests that if it is inappropriate to speak of real being (*ousia*), then it will also be inappropriate to speak of the nature, and vice versa.

[151] If one availed oneself of a notion of absolute space, it might be possible to identify the mixtures with their locations, rather than with just their ingredients. But this is an option that is not even raised.

[152] See Burnyeat, "Introduction," pp. 9–10; 46–47; 52–61.

to which Theaetetus proves committed, in virtue of having adopted the thesis that knowledge is perception. For the sake of argument, let us set aside a whole range of difficult issues of interpretation and simply grant that Plato does indeed seek to call into question the picture of the participants I have urged is his. Does this not wholly undermine my claim?[153] The matter is not as straightforward as it may appear. For even if Plato comes to criticize this picture of the participants, that does not show that he did not at one time hold it (or something relevantly similar). More importantly, even if Plato comes to repudiate this picture of the participants, *nothing* follows about what he proposes to put in its place. And we cannot simply assume that he had an 'ordinary' or 'commonsensical' (i.e., Aristotelian) understanding of sensible particulars as being objects with properties.

The following is one reason for rejecting any such assumption. In 184a–186e, Socrates offers another argument against the thesis that knowledge is perception, only now his argument is a direct one, not a reductio, as the earlier one had been.[154] The new argument depends on one crucial idea. (Let us again set aside a large number of difficult questions, ones that any full account of the dialogue would need to address.) That idea can be summarized as follows: perception is not simply a matter of the various senses (e.g., sight or hearing), or bodily organs (e.g., the eyes or ears), sensing their appropriate proper sensibles (e.g., colors or sounds); rather, we have to suppose that a *soul* or *mind* is involved (cf. 185d1–e2). More precisely, we need to suppose that a mind is involved, if we, as sensate beings, are to be able to distinguish sounds from colors, and to indicate when, say, one color is the same as another (185a8–b5); and in general, we need a mind—and a trained and educated one at that—in order to engage in "calculations regarding their being and advantageousness" (tr. Levett/Burnyeat; 186b11–c5). (And here, what these calculations are concerned with are either simple sensations, or simple judgements of sensation, like 'this is red', or 'there is red here'.)[155] However the various subtle and difficult questions about the entire passage are to be resolved,

[153] Several readers of earlier versions of this material raised this sort of objection in one form or another.

[154] See Burnyeat, "Introduction," pp. 52–65; cf. McDowell, *Plato: Theaetetus*, pp. 185–93.

[155] In addition to the works cited in the previous note, see J. M. Cooper, "Plato on Sense Perception and Knowledge: *Theaetetus* 184 to 186," *Phronesis* 15 (1970), and M. F. Burnyeat, "Plato on the Grammar of Perceiving," *Classical Quarterly*, n.s. 26 (1976).

it seems clear that Plato conceives of the soul/mind as being something *unified*, over and above, and distinct from, sensation (or the faculties of sensation). Moreover, it seems that it is precisely the mind's unity as a distinct item that first *gives unity* to the sensations (or simple judgments of sensation).

At this point, let us ask the following question: is there anything on the side of the *sensibles* that corresponds to the mind's unity, i.e., something over and above, and distinct from, the various sensible items (like colors and sounds)? Those who see in the Plato of the *Theaetetus* a precursor of idealism will, perhaps, be happy to answer 'no'. But if the answer should be 'yes', then it seems that there ought to be something like an *object* (in Aristotle's sense) that can serve as the bearer and 'unifier' of the various sensible items, i.e., the sensible *qualities*. If Plato were *both* targeting the view that sensible particulars are quasi-mixtures (or bundles of Form-Instances) *and* seeking to replace that view with a more 'commonsensical' one, then we could surely expect him to say something about the matter, especially at a moment in the dialogue where it would be very natural for him to offer a view of this sort.[156] But what is conspicuous about *Theaetetus* 184b–186e is that Plato says absolutely *nothing* about what the sensible particulars are supposed to be. (And saying that they are, e.g., individual human beings, like Theaetetus, does not yet address the question of what kind of item, say, an individual human being is supposed to be.) The conclusion to draw, I would urge, is that even if Plato is seeking to show the untenability of the quasi-Anaxagorean view of the participants, it is not clear what alternative he has in mind; indeed, it is not clear that he has any specific alternative in mind at all. As so often, he leaves a difficult philosophical task for his readers.

But in that case, it seems to me that we should see the picture of becoming—and of the participants—stated at 152d–e and 157a–b as being either a picture that Plato had at one time (e.g., in the *Republic*)

---

[156] To put matters very schematically. Plato does offer something like a transcendental argument for the unity of consciousness—for only the unity of consciousness accounts for our being able to perceive things (or formulate simple judgments about what we perceive) in the way in which we actually do perceive things (and actually do formulate perceptual judgments). One could argue (or so I am suggesting) that, in an analogous way, only something like the unity of objects can account for there being actual things, about which we can formulate perceptual judgments that can (then) be either true or false. Obviously, considerable discussion and argument would be needed to fill out this suggestion. In particular, one would need to establish whether the argument for the unity of consciousness might

been committed to, and which (possibly in a substantially modified form) he remains committed to; or a picture that Plato had at one time adopted (or considered adopting), but which he now (in the *Theaetetus*) sees as seriously flawed, and in need of massive revision or downright replacement. However, saying that the picture needs to be revised, is not yet to say *how* it should be revised; saying that it needs to be replaced, is not yet to say *what* it should be replaced with.

There is also another part of the *Theaetetus* that bears on the matters with which we are concerned, the so-called Dream Theory and the subsequent discussion of it (201d ff.). This section of the dialogue as well raises many issues, and the question of the provenance of the Dream Theory has never been adequately settled. Are these the views of some specific historical figure, e.g., Antisthenes, or some member of the Academy; or alternatively is it a view that arises out of confrontation with such a figure, say, again, Antisthenes?[157] However these questions are to be answered, there are certain striking similarities between the Dream Theory and Plato's own (earlier) views of Forms and participants.

To begin with, we find a fundamental distinction between simple elements on the one hand, and complex items on the other. Each element is itself by itself, and no account (in some sense of account) can be given of them; indeed, strictly speaking, they can only be named or labeled.[158] The complexes, on the other hand, are what they are in virtue of the elements in them, and so can be accounted for in terms of those elements.

Now in the course of exploring and criticizing the Dream Theory, the elements are described as *incomposite* (ἀσύνθετον), *uniform* (μονοειδές) and *without parts* (ἀμέριστον); the other items, the complexes, are compounded (σύγκειται) out of these elements (see 205c4 ff.). The echoes from the *Phaedo* and the *Republic* (and the *Symposium*) are clear. Here, however, the complexes are explicitly identified with their elements. Theaetetus says the syllable 'SO' (the first syllable of Socrates' name) simply is 'S' and 'O' (203a6–9). And the discussion in 204a7–205a10 makes

---

not, after all, bring with it some (suitable) version of the unity of objects. My claim is not that this cannot be so, but only that it is not *obviously* so.

[157] For criticism and review of earlier discussions, see M. F. Burnyeat, "The Material and Sources of Plato's Dream," *Phronesis* 15 (1970).

[158] 203b1–5 makes clear that if the elements have accounts they will have to be accounts of a different sort than those given of the complexes. Yet since Theaetetus in these very lines seems to be giving some sort of account of the elements under consideration (viz., letters/ phonemes), why does he go on (b5–8) to say the elements do not have accounts? Surely

clear that a whole is to be all its parts. Given such an identification, it would again be obvious that, say, the healthy Socrates and the ill Socrates are different items, just as the living Socrates and the corpse are.

Of course the Dream Theory is not accepted in toto, and by explicitly raising this point, we might think that Plato means to call attention to it as problematic.[159] Since neither the Dream Theory nor the Secret Doctrine of Protagoras are presented as Socrates' own view, and since the dialogue as a whole is aporetic, we will hesitate to see these passages as expressing Plato's own views at the time he wrote the *Theaetetus*. Yet this does not stand in the way of seeing these texts as being, at least *inter alia*, reflections on his own views in the earlier dialogues; and in light of the linguistic and doctrinal parallels, it seems quite reasonable in fact to read them in that way.

The *Timaeus* reinforces the suggestion that the notions of part, whole, and mixture are crucial for Plato's distinction between participants and Forms. For it is quite clear that Plato here too thinks of the participants as being mixtures, and of Forms as being wholes which have parts. Thus at 42e8–43a6, where the creation of human beings is discussed, we hear:

> They [i.e., the created Gods] borrowed portions (μόρια) of fire and earth, water and air from the world, . . . and bonded together what they took, . . . making each [sc. human] body a unity of all the portions.

And at 30c5–d1, Timaeus speaks of the created world as an animal, "of which the other animals, individually and in accord with their genera, are parts (μόρια)," resembling another (intelligible) item, The Animal Itself, which contains within it "all the intelligible animals."[160] (We may wonder how the two passages should fit together.)

---

different notions of what an account is must be involved. If this is so, saying that the elements have no accounts need not conflict with the view, found in the middle dialogues, that (what are treated there as) the primary elements, namely, the Forms, are definable entities. On 203b1–5, see also McDowell, *Plato: Theaetetus*, pp. 240–41, and Burnyeat, "Introduction," pp. 189–90.

[159] Burnyeat, "Introduction," pp. 134–218, esp. pp. 191–205, provides extensive commentary on the Dream Theory and its subsequent discussion. However, again, even if he is correct in thinking that Plato shows the view that a whole *is* (to be identified with) its parts to be untenable, it is not clear what, if anything, Plato is proposing as an alternative (cf. *Theaetetus* 205e). So it is also not clear *how* Plato supposes we can make sense of ordinary things—if, indeed, he supposes that we can.

[160] *Theaetetus* 157b8–c2 (the continuation of the passage quoted on p. 158 above) *may* also contain the suggestion that individuals are parts of species: "And one ought to speak the same way both of the *part* (κατὰ μέρος) and about the many *collected together*—collections

Now one might think that the first passage shows that human beings really are something, namely, fire and earth, and air and water. But it turns out that to think of these elements as genuinely elementary (i.e., as entities that cannot be divided or analyzed further) is a mistake: not only are they not like the syllables that make up words, they are not even like the letters that make up the syllables (48b5–c2). That is to say, fire and earth, and air and water, turn out to be complexes as well. And once the analysis is carried out as far as it can be, we are left with something that is indeterminate and featureless in its own right, namely, The Receptacle (see 50b–51b).[161] Thus it too, in an important sense, cannot be said to *be* anything in its own right (see 50d7, 50e4–5 and 51a7). This means that if we push the analysis far enough, there is not anything that a human being—or any sensible thing—can be said to be.[162]

The claim that there is not anything that a sensible thing is could easily lead one to suppose that sensible things simply are not, in other words, that they (somehow) are nothing. But sensible things in fact aren't absolutely nothing (τὸ μὴ ὄν). At the beginning of his exposition, Timaeus says:

---

to which <the name of> man or rock, or each animal or kind (εἶδος) is applied." If 'part' is taken to refer to (what we would normally think of as) individual human beings, rocks and animals (and if 'the many collected together' and εἶδος are taken to refer to kinds or species), then the point of 157a7–b8 would be being *extended* to cover kinds as well: 'this' and 'that' cannot be applied to them either; and species too only become whatever they 'are'. (To some extent, Plato would thus be anticipating a central part of the discussion of the Dream at 201c ff.—there is a kind of parity between parts and wholes, although that parity ultimately leads to trouble.) On the other hand, if, as is perhaps more usual (see, e.g., the translation of Levett/Burnyeat), 'part' is taken to refer to the quality-instances (and if 'the many collected together', and 'man', 'rock', etc. are taken to refer to the aggregates of quality-instances, i.e., *individual* humans, rocks, etc.), then 157b8–c2 would be reiterating the earlier point, not extending it. I would prefer to construe the sentence in the first way, but certainly cannot rule out the second way.

[161] It may seem to be an embarassment for the account that I am advocating that Plato, in this passage, repeatedly refers to the *nature* of The Receptacle. I am inclined to say that he is not employing 'nature' in its full, quasi-honorific sense here. The Receptacle, however, is an ultimate constituent or, better, principle of the material universe—even if it is characterless in its own right. Referring to it and its nature thus is a way of signaling that fundamental status. The fact that The Receptacle can only be apprehended "by a kind of bastard reasoning" (λογισμῷ τινι νόθῳ; 52b2) also suggests that the word 'nature' is here being used catachrestically, not in its normal sense. For a genuine *nature* (we would think) is precisely what is apprehendend by true reason. See also Plotinus *Ennead* II.4.10.

[162] A full account of the ontology of the *Timaeus* would need to say something about how the triangles figure in that ontology; for they (as it were) mediate between the intelligible world and the perceptible one.

170

Now, in my opinion, we need first to distinguish these: that which always is and has no becoming, and that which always becomes, but never is. The one can be grasped by thought together with reason, being always the same; the other, the opinable, is the object of belief together with irrational perception, becoming and passing away, but never really being. (27d5–28a4)

The traditional interpretation sees here a division into changeless eternal entities, and ones that are always changing. And the second occurrence of 'becoming' (28a2), where becoming is spoken of together with passing away, clearly refers to coming to be in some ordinary sense, that is, the generation of a thing, or the generation of some aspect of a thing (i.e., a change).[163]

Nevertheless the first occurrence of 'becoming' should be taken in the way suggested earlier. For if it is understood in that way, we can see Plato again announcing here the metaphysical distinction between things that have natures and those that do not. The very terms of that distinction make clear why the 'things' lacking natures need to be understood (to whatever extent they can be understood) in terms of the things that have natures, better, in terms of the natures. This also means that the contrast is not between a realm that contains things that are constantly changing, and a realm consisting of things that are always the same. It is rather because the one realm contains things that are (or have) natures, that it is always the same; and it is because the other realm consists of items lacking natures, that it is not always the same. In short, the distinction between metaphysically or ontologically primitive becoming and physical becoming (i.e., coming to be, ceasing to be, and change more generally) is brought out precisely in this passage, if read in the way suggested (cf. *Tim.* 29c3). It is thus also very natural for Plato, having presented that distinction, to proceed *immediately* to discussing ordinary, physical change and generation, for these are the hallmarks of the world of becoming.[164] But again, ordinary changes (and generation and destruction) are symptoms of ontologically primitive becoming, they are not what that kind of becoming is.

---

[163] We see something analogous in *Republic* VII. At 521d3–4, Socrates asks about "that study that will draw the soul from becoming to being"—clearly the reference is to the realm of participants on the one hand, and the realm of Forms on the other. But when he shortly thereafter speaks of "coming to be and dying" (521e3–5), he is referring to coming to be *within* the realm of becoming, as opposed to contrasting becoming with being.

[164] Again, note the parallel progression in *Republic* VII, 521d-e.

Thus, as Michael Frede observes, Plato's postulation of a realm of becoming "is by no means the innocuous, vague assumption that the ordinary objects of experience are subject to all kinds of change."[165] Nor is the claim that the participants are *composite* entities (things that have parts) the statement of the obvious and fairly trivial truth that ordinary, everyday things can be cut up or divided in various physical and spatial ways. We would hardly expect Plato to offer us such vapid generalities. He is instead presenting striking and radical metaphysical claims. In order to assess them, we would need to work out their full implications; and, indeed, reflecting on those implications might lead one to a new understanding, perhaps a rethinking of the original claims. (Such reflection presumably led Plato himself to do that, in the second half of the *Parmenides*, the *Sophist,* and the *Philebus*.)

Aristotle, of course, rejects this picture of ordinary things. Indeed, he thinks it is (ultimately) incoherent. Before returning to him in Part III, we should, however, briefly consider the view of the so-called Late-Learners from the *Sophist*. For they seem to have a picture of ordinary things that is strikingly different from Plato's, but that is, as we will see, strangely related to his picture.

15. THE LATE-LEARNERS: REAL BEING FOR ORDINARY THINGS

In the *Sophist*, the view of the Late-Learners comes to be discussed in connection with the question of how one and the same thing can be referred to by many names, or alternatively, of how a variety of predicates can properly be predicated of one and the same subject (251a). The Late-Learners, it seems, deny that this is possible. They hold that while it may be legitimate to say of (a) man that he is (a) man, or of (a) good that it is good (leave aside, for the moment, what this second claim is supposed to mean), it is not acceptable to say of (a) man that he is good.[166]

Let us examine this curious-sounding view more closely. On the basis of 251a–252b it seems that the Late-Learners allow for statements of the following form:

---

[165] Frede, "Being and Becoming," p. 52.

[166] Once again, the inelegant device of enclosing the indefinite article in parentheses is meant to remind us of the fact that Greek lacks an indefinite article. The relevance of this in the present context will emerge shortly.

This is a man
(A) man is (a) man
Socrates is (a) man

This is good
(A) good is good

This is white
(A) white is white

(Call these LL sentences.) Now superficially, some of these LL sentences look like Plato's own SP sentences. But it is important to realize that the Late-Learners are speaking about sensible items, not Forms. This becomes clear in 251b6–c1; for there colors, shape, size, and virtues and vices are attributed to the man referred to; and clearly it will only be an ordinary human being who has these sorts of features, not the Form or species, Man. And since there are no indications that the good referred to in that same sentence is to be thought of differently, the most reasonable assumption would seem to be that it, too, is an everyday item, not a Form. (Again, leave open for the moment, what sort of an item this might be.) The obvious question is, why should anyone want to insist on such an odd restriction on allowable statements about everyday things?

In the literature, we encounter the suggestion that the Late-Learners' position is the result of their failing to distinguish between a predicative use of the verb 'is' on the one hand, and an identifying use on the other, and then proceeding to insist that all occurrences of 'is' are to be treated as the 'is' of identity.[167] This suggestion is unattractive. As Michael Frede rightly asks in his book on the *Sophist*: "Why should the failure to distinguish the predicative use from the identifying use lead anyone to assimilate all occurrences of 'is' to the identifying 'is'—especially in light of the fact that, in the vast majority of cases, 'is' is obviously not being used to assert identity?"[168] Though more could (and should) be said on this point, I would like to turn to a different and rather more promising interpretation of the Late-Learners' view, namely, that of Frede himself.[169]

Consider again natural kinds and the objects falling under them. If we say of something that it is a horse, we cannot then go on to say of it— that very thing—that it is a cat. Similarly, if we say of something that it

---

[167] See, for example, J. L. Ackrill, "Plato and the Copula: *Sophist* 251–259," *Journal of Hellenic Studies* 77 (1957): 2–3.

[168] See Frede, *Prädikation und Existenzaussage,* p. 61.

[169] See ibid., chap. 5, § 3: "das '. . . ist . . .' der Spätlerner," pp. 61–67.

is an animal, we cannot say of that very thing that it also is a plant. Quite simply, being a horse is incompatible with being a cat, and vice versa; being an animal is incompatible with being a plant, and vice versa. One way of generalizing this observation is to note that the terms 'horse' and 'cat' are mutually exclusive *sortal* terms; so too the terms 'animal' and 'plant'.

Let us suppose, as a first approximation, that the Late-Learners treat *all* predicates as if they were competing, mutually exclusive sortal terms. Thus if something is (a) man, it is not also (a) good; and if something is (a) good, it is not also something else—for example, (a) man. The intuition, if we may call it that, which underlies the Late-Learners' restriction could be expressed like this: it does not make sense to say of something that it is something that it is not. But what (a) human being is, is (a) human being, and not, for example, (a) good. Similarly what (a) good is, is good, not anything else.

Now before proceeding any further, we need to remind ourselves of another feature of the Greek language which is of relevance. First, one way in which the difference between sortal terms and other predicate adjectives manifests itself in languages like English or German is through the presence or absence of the appropriate form of the indefinite article. Thus while we say:

> This is *a* man
> This is *a* cat
> This is *an* artifact

we also say:

> This is good
> This is beautiful
> This is white

Secondly, in the case of the first set of sentences, and ones like them, we can go on to formulate subject-expressions of the form 'this *X*' for further sentences like 'This man is good', 'This cat is beautiful', and so on. Moreover, and this is what is important here, these subject-expressions refer to the same items to which the pronoun 'this' referred in the original sentences.

However, in the case of the second set of sentences, and those like them, we cannot in general formulate such subject-expressions. Sentences like *'This good is . . .', or, *'This beautiful is . . .', are grammatically unacceptable (hence the asterisk). Color terms, at least in English and German, seem to constitute an exception; for we *can* construct sentences like 'This white is dingy', or 'This pink is shocking'. But notice that in such cases, the subject-expressions 'this white' and 'this pink' refer to the colors (or, as we might say, the *individual* colors), not to the item referred to by the word 'this' in the original sentence. Thus in these languages, there are very clear ways of distinguishing between sortal terms and predicate adjectives.

In Greek, however, matters are different. To begin with, as we have noted before, Greek lacks the indefinite article. Thus the counterparts of the first set of sentences would be:

This is man
This is cat
This is artifact

That is to say, sentences of the first and second type will be on a par morphologically and syntactically; there will be no obvious signal (like the indefinite article) to indicate whether the predicate-expression is a sortal term or a predicate adjective. Now we might think that this fact shows precisely that sortal terms are to be assimilated to predicate adjectives rather than the other way around. Here a second and more important feature of the language becomes relevant. If, in Greek, we have a sentence of the form 'This is X', it is possible to construct new sentences of the form 'This X is Y', where the subject expression 'this X' picks out the very same item as the word 'this' picked out in the original sentence, regardless of whether the predicate-expression in that original sentence was a noun or an adjective.[170] This second feature shows that predicate nouns and predicate adjectives are both, in a crucial respect, treated as if they were sortal terms.

Let us return to the Late-Learners. We can see why someone might want to say that a human being (say, Socrates) is a human being, and is not something else. For it is not the case that (first) there is something else which, however, is modified or qualified in a certain way so as (then) to be human. The object in question—if there is an object here at all—is already of a certain sort, namely, human; it is not as if there is some other object present which then (as it were) happens to be human. However, if we do not draw the distinction between objects and properties, or better,

---

[170] I owe this way of formulating the similarity between sortal terms and predicate adjectives in Greek to Michael Frede; cf. ibid., pp. 63–64.

if on account of those features of the Greek language adverted to above, we are not led to draw that distinction, we will be *able* to treat being good in the same way as being man, rather, in the same way as being *a* man. Thus let us suppose, with the Late-Learners, that we can point to something and say, '*This* is good and is not something else'. Here it is not the case that we have something of some sort which then happens to be good; rather, what we have is *already* of a certain sort, namely, good. In short, justs, goods, and beautifuls, and reds, whites, and blues, etc., are all treated as objects (or quasi-objects) wholly on a par with artifacts, plants, cats, horses, and humans. Thus we can also see why saying of a man that he is good, would be a matter of making two things into one, or looked at in another way, a matter of making one thing into two; and that is precisely what the Late-Learners object to (251b6–7).

Notice that the Late-Learners' view could be expressed using Butler's essentialist dictum: Every *thing* is what it is, and not another *thing*. I trust that by now we can see how this innocuous, even empty-sounding claim can come to seem deeply problematic.

. . . . .

The suggestion was that it is only a first approximation of the Late-Learners' view to say that it treats *all* predicates as if they were competing sortal terms. The reason for this qualification is that there is an obvious way in which the Late-Learners' view can be extended. Consider natural kinds, and think of them as arranged on Linnaean trees. Now if something is a horse, it is not a cat, and vice versa; and if something is an oak-tree, it is not a human, and vice versa; and of course, if something is a plant, it is not an animal, and vice versa. However, if something is a cat, it is an animal; if something is an oak tree, it is a plant. That is because being (an) animal is part of what it is to be (a) cat; and being (a) plant is part of what it is to be (an) oak. The reason the Late-Learners could allow their view to be extended in this way is that they could allow that if being *y* is *part* of what being *x* is, then being *y* is *not* something else—not something different from—being *x*. If the Late-Learners' view were extended in this way, then in addition to the sentences they already allow, sentences like

This is (a) man
Socrates is (a) man

they would allow *extended* LL sentences like

Socrates is (a) vertebrate
Socrates is (an) animal, etc.

The same strategy ought to carry over to the other sorts of sentences, i.e., in addition to

This is (a) maroon

they would allow

This maroon is (a) red
This is (a) red
This red is (a) color[171]

This extended view goes beyond the text of the *Sophist*. But if we adopt it, we can see how each thing might be thought to have a proper, proprietary account, that is, an account peculiar to it. For each *x*, such an account would, say, be a matter of specifying items that are higher on the tree on which *x* has a place. (Of course, each *x* is to occur on only one tree.) Now the thought that each thing—or at any rate, each thing of a certain sort—has a proprietary account (οἰκεῖος λόγος), is a view that we find in Socrates' Dream in the *Theaetetus* (201d ff.), and which is associated with Antisthenes.[172] And Antisthenes is often thought (somehow) to lurk behind both the view of the Late-Learners as well as the Dream. However, interpreters of these two dialogues have been singularly unsuccessful at spelling out what, exactly, the relevant Antisthenean view comes to; and given the state of the evidence concerning Antisthenes, that is hardly surprising.[173] It seems

---

[171] Of course, in this last set of sentences, we must regard the subject-expression in each sentence as referring to a quasi-object, not to the property.

[172] See Aristotle *Metaphysics* V, 29, 1024^{b}26–34: "A false λόγος is a λόγος about things that are not, insofar as it is false; thus every λόγος is false of something other than that of which it is true, for example, the λόγος of the circle is false of the triangle. Of each thing, there is, in a way, *one* λόγος, the one which states the essence; in another way, there are many λόγοι, since the thing itself and the thing affected are somehow (πως) the same thing, for example, Socrates and the educated Socrates. (And the false λόγος is not the λόγος of anything in an unqualified way.) Hence Antisthenes foolishly thought that no thing could be rendered (λέγεσθαι), except by its own, *proprietary logos* (πλὴν τῷ οἰκείῳ λόγῳ)—one λόγος for one thing—from which it followed that contradiction (ἀντιλέγειν) was impossible, and that speaking falsely (ψεύδεσθαι) was virtually impossible. Yet it *is* possible to render each thing not only by its own λόγος (τῷ αὐτοῦ λόγῳ), but also by the λόγος of something else (τῷ ἑτέρου)—now while this may yield something altogether false, it can also yield some truths [paraphrasing: ψευδῶς μὲν καὶ παντελῶς, ἔστι δ᾽ ὡς καὶ ἀληθῶς]." See also the works cited in the following note.

[173] Many interpreters question whether we should look for an Antisthenean view here at all; see, e.g., W. Hicken, "The Character and Provenance of Socrates' 'Dream' in the *Theaetetus*," *Phronesis* 3 (1958); G. Prauss, *Platon und der logische Eleatismus* (Berlin, 1966), pp. 161–74, esp. pp. 173–74; or Burnyeat, "The Materials and Sources of Plato's Dream." In his more recent "Introduction," Burnyeat suggests the following, more complicated possibility (with

to me that what really makes the extended view of interest is the fact that it is a richer, more complicated view—one which might seem attractive in a way that the simple, nonextended view does not. We could even introduce the notion of a *maximal* proprietary account. This would be an account which included *all* the things that can be included; if such an account were specifying an item's place within a genus-species hierarchy, it would refer to *all* the nodes higher on the tree than the item being specified. While it might still seem odd to suppose that the only possible *sentence* concerning a thing should be a proprietary account, we can perhaps see how, in a way, a maximal proprietary account would express everything the thing *is*, in some suitably strong sense of 'is'.

Notice how the self-predication sentences can be extended in an analogous way. Let us call any claim of the form 'X is Y' an *extended* SP sentence, if being y is part of what being x. Thus,

(A) Cat is (an) Animal
The Cat is (a) Vertebrate
The Siamese is (a kind of) Cat

will all count as extended SP claims. So too will

Justice is (a kind of) Virtue
White is (a) Color
Dancing moves (or, Dancing is Motion)

The familiar SP sentences thus will be limit cases of extended SP claims. (If we once again think of natural kinds arranged on Linnaean trees, then, to say of something which is higher on the tree that it belongs to something lower on the tree will be to make a *true* extended SP claim.[174] In the case

respect to Socrates' Dream): "that Socrates in the *Theaetetus* is not restating Antisthenes but making creative use of some Antisthenean materials" (p. 166). This suggestion is attractive, since it gives Plato a real target but frees us from the task of reconstructing Antisthenes's own view in all its detail. Burnyeat's suggestion of course still requires that we determine what the view Plato presents actually comes to. A further question, which cannot be pursued here, is whether it is appropriate, at the end of the day, to treat the Dream from the *Theaetetus* and the Late-Learners from the *Sophist* together. While I gesture in that direction, I by no means regard this question as settled.

[174] Linnaean trees are used to explicate (what I am here calling) extended SP sentences by C. Meinwald in her analysis of the distinction between πρὸς ἑαυτό and πρὸς τὰ ἄλλα predication in the *Parmenides*. See her *Plato's Parmenides*. I also owe the example 'Dancing moves' to Meinwald (ibid., p. 68).

of Linnaean trees, a *false* extended SP claim will be one that asserts such a relationship—between something higher and lower—which, however, does not in fact obtain.)

The real interest of such extended SP claims, of course, is that the predicates which they provide promise to take us beyond the place-holders (mentioned in Section 8) of the simple, nonextended SP sentences. There are obvious parallels between SP and LL sentences (and hence between extended SP and extended LL ones as well). It would thus not be at all surprising if there were parallels between the difficulties facing both, notably the restrictions on possible predications suggested by both accounts:

A Form can be only what is said of it in an (extended) SP sentence.

An ordinary thing can be only what is said of it in an (extended) LL sentence.

We are now in a position also to contrast the Late-Learners' view of ordinary things with Plato's view. While Plato, in the middle dialogues, had denied that ordinary things were, strictly speaking, anything at all—particulars turned out to be, as it were, nothing over and above bundles or clusters of Forms or Form-Instances, none of which is privileged—the Late-Learners do attribute being to ordinary things, but each ordinary thing is to be only what it is and nothing else. That is, for any *x*, *x* is only what *x* is qua *x*. The contrast could also be put like this: in the middle dialogues, Plato allows ordinary things to have many names, that is, a variety of predicates can be predicated of sensible particulars. But there is a high price to pay. No participant, it turns out, *is* any of the things it is said to be. At best, it *becomes* some of them. Ordinary things thus only have *ersatz* being, namely, becoming. And so while in a way they are many things (and so can have many predicates predicated of them), in another way they are not anything, because there is nothing which they are, strictly speaking.

The Late-Learners, on the other hand, do ascribe (what they call) being to ordinary things. (Leave aside that, according to Plato, this is ultimately part of the incoherence of their view.) So, on the Late-Learners' view, there is something each ordinary thing is, indeed, something it *really* is. However, by being only what it is, any ordinary thing cannot have a variety of predicates predicated of it; it certainly cannot have anything predicated of it which is not part of what it is. Thus ordinary attributions of features to things become impossible. And so, when the Late-Learners deny that a thing can be called by the name of another thing, in virtue of participating

179

in an affection which is (from) that other thing (*Sophist* 252b8–10), what they are denying is (to use Aristotle's terminology) that things can be called what they are called homonymously or paronymously after something else. But they can be called—indeed can only be called—(what they are called) synonymously after what they are. (Unless we allow extended LL sentences there will be no nontrivial cases of synonymy.) Thus a man cannot be called good, after goodness or the good; a man cannot be called white after the color white. But a man can be called man after man; a white can be called white after the color; a good can be called good after goodness. And perhaps Socrates can be called animal after animal; and perhaps a good can be called virtuous after virtue.[175] Plato, on the other hand, held—as we have seen—that everyday things are only called what they are called homonymously after something else.

16. DOES PLATO MODIFY HIS PICTURE IN SOME LATE DIALOGUES?

Before returning to Aristotle, some final observations about Plato. There is good reason to believe that Plato comes to have the resources to deal with some of the problems his view seems to give rise to, at least by the time he writes the second half of *Parmenides* and the *Sophist* (and the *Philebus*). Put most briefly, what Plato does is explicitly distinguish between two predicative uses of 'is'; better, he reinterprets the relation between 'is' in the sense of schema (I) and 'is' in the sense of schema (II) in Section 2.[176] This enables him to maintain that the self-predicational use of 'is' (involved, for example, in predicating genera of species, and higher species of lower ones)—in essence, the 'is' of schema (I)—and the everyday predi-

---

[175] Since there is no reason to suppose that the Late-Learners are endorsing a theory of Forms, we should not assume that the man, the white, the good, etc., after which things are called (what they are called) are Forms.

[176] See above, pp. 77–82. For more on the two uses of 'is', see Frede, *Prädikation und Existenzaussage,* and Meinwald, *Plato's Parmenides;* see also M. Frede, "Plato's *Sophist* on False Statements," and C. Meinwald, "Good-bye to the Third Man," both in the *Cambridge Companion to Plato,* ed. R. Kraut (Cambridge, 1992). C. Kahn describes this first use of 'is' as "the definitional copula, or 'is' of whatness"; see "Some Philosophical Uses of 'To Be' in Plato," *Phronesis* 26 (1981): 111. Kahn also usefully discusses the ὅ ἐστι *x* construction, which Plato often uses in contexts where what *x* is, is under discussion, pp. 127–29. A fuller treatment would also need to take into account Plato's use of ὅπερ ἐστί *x* (just what *x* is); cf. Deichgräber apud Frede, *Prädikation und Existenzaussage,* p. 12 n. 1.

cative use of 'is' are *not*, after all, competing or mutually exclusive uses. Thus in these dialogues he is even willing to say things like:

Motion is (in) motion
Motion is (at) rest![177]

The Many is many
The Many is one!

Not-being is not-being
Not-being is being![178]

Being is being
Being is not-being!

What we need to realize is that in each of these pairs of sentences, the first sentence should be understood as saying something about what the nature of the relevant Form is, while the second is saying something true of the Form, but is not specifying its nature.

And quite generally, for any statement of the form 'X is Y', we need to be clear about the way in which 'is' is being used. Now in certain cases, like

The One is one

the sentence will be true for both uses of 'is', but each statement says something quite different. On the one hand, this sentence could be used to specify the nature of The One; on the other, it could be used to say that The One has the attribute of being one, e.g., by being one Form. Yet in most cases, the statements will not only say something different, but will differ in truth value. Thus

The Same is different

will be false, if the 'is' is taken to specify the nature of The Same, but it will be true if it is taken to attribute difference to The Same, because The Same is different, for example, from The Different. We are now also able to see something extremely important about SP sentences:

---

[177] *Sophist* 256b6–7 (Burnet) in the *textus receptus*, which I am inclined to accept. Cornford adopts a proposal of Heindorf's, and interpolates lines that have the Eleatic Stranger rejecting the suggestion that Motion, in a way (πῃ), participates in Rest. This rejection depends, it seems to me, on failing to appreciate the force of the in-a-way qualification. For a correct rendition of this passage, see N. White's translation: Plato, *Sophist* (Indianapolis, 1993).

[178] On this pair, see *Sophist* 256e–257b.

The self-predicational use of 'is' is not the identifying use of 'is'.

This can be seen most readily, if we consider Forms, or species, which are not themselves highest on the tree on which they occur. Thus,

Justice is (a) Virtue

or

Dancing moves

would both be true self-predicational claims. For any full and proper account of what Justice is, will need to make clear that it is (a kind of) Virtue; and any full and proper account of what Dancing is, will need to show how it involves moving (sc. Motion). But in neither of these cases is there even any temptation to suppose that the claims being made are identity claims. The trivial looking SP sentences (of the form 'The X is X' or 'X-ness is X') thus will correspondingly be signaling that X (or X-ness) can be specified, in other words, that the item x is a definable entity. (The analogous point is true of the LL sentences.)[179]

Moreover, at least as far as Forms are concerned, Plato does seem to draw a distinction something like the one Aristotle draws between having a predicate predicated synonymously and having it predicated homonymously or paronymously. Thus when we say of Justice that it is (a) Virtue, the expression, 'virtue', is used synonymously of Justice and of Virtue; for in both cases, the account of what it is to be a virtue will be the same. On the other hand, when we say that The Just is different (e.g., from Beauty), the expression 'different' is being used differently than when we say 'The Different is different' (with 'is' being used in the first, not in the second way!). Why? In the case of Justice, we are saying something about what Justice is like, while in the case of Difference, we are saying something about its nature. Thus there is a way in which The Different and The Just are called 'different' homonymously.[180] Once again, while there obviously is much more to be said, we cannot pursue the issue of Forms or kinds further here.

---

[179] LL sentences classify or categorize items. If we allow nontrivial LL sentences, like 'Socrates is (an) animal', it is again obvious that these cannot be identity claims. Thus we should also not take the trivial LL sentences to be identity claims.

[180] In the preceding sentences, I have deliberately switched back and forth between the abstract nouns and the article + adjective construction, to remind us of the fact that for Plato there is no metaphysically significant difference between them.

Yet what of sensible participants? Given that Plato is prepared to say that Motion really both is and is not; that Not-Being is, or is (a) being; and that Being is not, or is (a) not-being, it is clear that the rolling about between being and not-being can no longer serve as the hallmark of the defective world of ordinary things. It was also part of the argument against the Late-Learners that we must be allowed to say a man is a being, and a good is a being; indeed, for any x and y, if y is truly predicated of x, x and y must both be beings.

Thus the revisions to the picture of Forms Plato arrives at in the second half of the *Parmenides* and in the *Sophist* do have implications for the status of ordinary, sensible things. However, there is one crucial issue which is still not resolved. An ordinary thing can now be, not merely become, many things; it can have many predicates predicated of it; and this fact does not, of itself, show that this thing is somehow deficient or imperfect. However, an ordinary thing will still not be anything *in and of itself*; it will still be whatever it is by *participation in something else*. One consequence of this is that, if we pick out an item (say, Socrates) which, let us suppose, is (a) man, is pale, and is good, it is not clear that any of the following three claims is privileged (because it is not clear *how* one would be privileged over the others):

What this is, is a man, who also is pale and good.

What this is, is a pale (thing), which also is (a) man and good.

What this is, is a good (thing), which also is (a) man and pale.

Here we need to add an important qualification. In saying that it is not clear whether any of the three claims is privileged, because it is not clear how one would be privileged over the others, I do not mean to claim that an ordinary speaker would not, in fact, prefer the first of these sentences (or rather, its counterpart in ancient Greek). The point rather is that Plato, absent some further argument or theoretical apparatus, is not in a position to insist that the first sentence should be privileged. For it is unclear how he can say that something in or about the cluster of 'things' which an everyday thing is, is privileged. But we might well have the intuition that the first of these sentences should clearly be privileged over and against the second and third. Of course, *we* may have this intuition as a result of the influence of Aristotle, rather than as a result of something like naive, prephilosophical common sense. With that thought in mind, let us return to him.

The *Categories* Picture Once More: An Alternative to Platonism and Late-Learnerism

> Let us then say how we call one and the same thing by
> several different names.
> (*Plato*, Sophist 251a5–6)

1. Aristotle's Introduction of Paronymy

In the *Topics*, Aristotle sets out to analyze dialectical arguments. Such arguments include, but are not limited to the kinds of arguments we find Socrates using in the early dialogues of Plato. And in those dialogues, one of the crucial things Socrates does—indeed, his doing this often is what gives rise to the subsequent discussion—is to ask, with respect to a variety of things, what those things are. This of course is his famous 'What is *X*?' question. As we know, Socrates often finds that his interlocutors answer the question unsatisfactorily. There are a variety of ways in which their answers can be unsatisfactory, but one way—to which Socrates repeatedly calls attention—involves saying of *x*, what it is *like* rather than saying what it *is*. This in turn suggests that Socrates believes a sentence of the form '*X* is *Y*' can be used in at least two ways: either to say what *x* is, or to say what *x* is like. (There might of course be further possibilities.) Thus if one wishes to argue with Socrates, or more generally, if one wishes to argue in a Socratic manner (whether as the questioner or the respondent), one will need to be clear about the difference(s) between these two types of claims. One will also want to know more about what each type of claim asserts. Part of Aristotle's project in the *Topics*—most clearly in Book VIII, but also throughout the rest of the treatise—is to provide guidance for those who would participate in question-and-answer exchanges, and quite generally, in dialectical discussions. And it is in turn as a part of this guidance, that Aristotle believes that he needs to delineate more carefully the different uses of a statement of the form '*X* is *Y*', which Socrates had relied on.

As we saw in Part I, one assumption Aristotle makes is that in a sentence of the form 'X is Y', the subject- and predicate-expressions, X and Y, respectively, introduce two items x and y, and that if such a sentence is true, then y is in fact predicated of x. (Strictly speaking, this is only true of some such sentences, those I labeled 'revelatory'; for present purposes, we can restrict ourselves to only these sentences, and ignore the complications posed by the nonrevelatory ones.) This way of proceeding leads Aristotle to conceive of predication as τὶ κατά τινος predication, his favored formulation for expressing that something is predicated of something (the words literally mean: 'something of something'). A full discussion of Aristotle's picture of predication would need to take account of various reservations one might have about this way of proceeding.[1] However, in the present contetxt, those reservations can be set aside, since Plato implicitly relied on a conception of predication that is (in the relevant respects) the same. It is, however, again worth recalling that even sentences which are not initially in the form 'S is P' can be reformulated to conform to the canonical schema (for example, a sentence of the form 'S φ's' can be recast as 'S is φ-ing').

One of the first questions we could ask in trying to become clear about the differences between the different uses of simple assertoric sentences, is whether it is different sorts of *items* (introduced by the expressions X and Y) which make for the two different sorts of claims. Thus we might think that all items of one type can be used to say what something is, while items of another type are to be used to say of something what it is like; or we might think that only certain sorts of items are even candidates about which the 'What is X?' question can meaningfully be asked. On the other hand, we might think that it is not so much something about the items x and y that makes for the difference between saying what x is and saying what x is like, as it is something about the *expressions* X and Y

---

[1] The Stoics, for example, think that this sort of formulation makes it all too tempting, in certain cases, to hypostasize predicates. Their treatment of predicates as incomplete λέκτα ('sayables' is the usual rendering) is meant to reflect (what they take to be) the fact that certain truths about a thing (viz., a real being) do not require the presence of some *other* thing, but can be accounted for by a state, condition, or disposition (a πῶς ἔχον, in their terminology) of the one and only thing that is there. (Thus if a hand is made into a fist, such that the sentence 'This hand is a fist' is true, there aren't two things, the hand and the fist, or the hand and fistness; there is just the hand, disposed or arranged a certain way.) The Aristotelian way of representing predication (as expressed in a simple assertoric sentence) will encourage us to look for at least two items—a third one might be whatever it is that is picked out by the copula.

themselves. Finally we might think that it is neither the items nor the expressions which *directly* make for the difference, but rather something about the ways in which 'is' is being used, in sentences of the form 'X is Y'.

Consider the following pair of inferences, which suggests that Aristotle is pursuing the last strategy:

This is white	This is white
White is (a) color	White is (a) color
*Hence this is (a) color	Hence this is (a) color

Here we have a startling result: according to Aristotle, the inference on the left does not go through (indicated by the star before the conclusion), the one on the right does! Why? Aristotle evidently holds that there is both a (logically, not grammatically) transitive use of 'is', and a nontransitive one. Indeed, as we saw in Part I, the converse of the transitive use corresponds to what he calls the SAID OF relation in the *Categories*, while the converse of the nontransitive use corresponds to what he calls the being IN relation. Notice that the transitive use is one which specifies *what something is*—it does so by, for example, assigning the item introduced by the subject-expression to a place within a genus-species hierarchy. It thus corresponds to the 'is' of schema (I), which we considered in connection with Plato in Part II, Section 2. The nontransitive use seems to be involved in specifying what something is like, rather than saying what it is. But from this observation about the different uses of 'is', we can, according to Aristotle, also discover something about the actual (nonlinguistic) items being talked about in the two cases. In the left-hand inference, the subject-expression 'this' refers to *a white thing*; in the right-hand one, it refers to *the white of a white thing*. What this difference comes to, would obviously need to be explored further.

As part of that exploration, we should ask: what is the item of which we are being told what it is? It would appear to be: the color or quality, white, which is being assigned (part of) a place within its appropriate genus-species hierarchy. Recall also that, for Aristotle, there are several such hierarchies which, in a way, are mutually irreducible.[2] Thus, six feet is (a) length, length is (a kind of) size, hence six feet (long) is (an individual) size. Or, cauterizing is (a) surgical procedure, surgical procedures are (kinds of) activity, hence cauterizing is (a kind of) activity. And so on.

---

[2] There is some question whether Aristotle is really committed to their mutual irreducibility. On this issue, see D. Morrison, "The Taxonomical Interpretation of Aristotle's *Categories*: A Criticism," *Essays in Ancient Philosophy*, vol. 5 (Albany, N.Y., 1992).

Thus when 'is' is being used transitively, it is being used to say of something, what it is (see, e.g., *Topics* I, 9, 103ᵇ27–37).[3] In addition, according to Aristotle, the things concerning which we are being told what they are, are of distinct types: for example, a quality is not a size, nor a size a quality; and so on. But so far, this all involves only one of the two uses of 'is'. What role does the nontransitive one play?

We can perhaps best approach this question by asking a slightly different one: what are the connections between the two uses of 'is'? Consider two other pairs of inferences, first:

This is (a) man	This is white
Man is Rational Animal	White is (a) color
Hence this is (a) rational animal	*Hence this is (a) color[4]

Let us stipulate that the subject-expression 'this' in fact refers to the same item in both of the above cases. Notice that when it does refer to the same item, **that item must be (a) man and cannot be the color.** For if it were the color, the first premise in the left-hand inference would be false. Thus there is a sort of asymmetry between the two inferences, because of an asymmetry between the first premise in each. Next consider:

This white (thing) is (a) man	This man is white
Man is Rational Animal	White is (a) color
Hence this white (thing) is (a) rational animal	*Hence this is a color

This third pair of inferences reveals a further asymmetry: it seems an inference conforming to the left-hand schema will go through, no matter which description of the item we use as the subject-expression in the first premise, so long as that first premise actually is true; however, it seems that any inference conforming to the right-hand schema will not go through, even if the first premise is true, unless the item referred to by

---

[3] A useful discussion of the relation between *Top.* I, 9 and the 'What is *X*?' question is provided by M. Frede, in his "Categories in Aristotle," in *Studies in Aristotle*, ed. D. J. O'Meara (Washington, D.C., 1981); reprinted in Frede, *Essays*. See also O. Apelt, "Die Kategorienlehre des Aristoteles," in his *Beiträge zur Geschichte der griechischen Philosophie* (Leipzig, 1891), esp. pp. 119–31.

[4] There may be contexts in which some sentences of this type can be understood as: 'Hence this *has* (a) color'. It seems to me that the more natural construal, however, is the one adopted in the text. Aristotle at any rate, relies on an idea that is (in the relevant respects) the same, that is to say, for Aristotle, the right-hand inference really does not go through.

the subject-expression in the first premise actually is the color or the quality. (In other words, *ousiai* can be referred to successfully by categorematic expressions derived from various nonsubstance categories, e.g., 'this white (one)', 'this six-foot-tall (one)', and so on, while nonsubstantial items cannot be referred to successfully by categorematic expressions derived from any category other than their own.)

What are we to make of these observations? Aristotle (in effect) claims that these facts about inferences reveal a fundamental fact of ontology. While it is true that there are a variety of mutually irreducible hierarchies structured by the SAID OF relation, all but one of these hierarchies are connected to the remaining one by means of the being IN relation in the following way:

> *All* the items in any one of (what we may now call) the *dependent hierarchies* are, ultimately, IN at least *one* thing from the *privileged hierarchy*; on the other hand, *none* of the things in the privileged hierarchy is IN *any* item from one of the dependent hierarchies.

Thus, to return to our examples, it is because white is IN man, but no man is IN white, that we have the differences between the two inferences in each pair.[5]

Here there are two major complications that might be thought to bear on the issue(s) at hand. First, in the *Categories*, Aristotle speaks of both an individual man (viz., a particular human being) and a nonindividual man (viz., the species), and he speaks of both individual nonsubstantial items and nonindividual ones. Since Aristotle actually speaks of individual and nonindividual *qualities* (consider the contrast between knowledge-of-grammar and knowledge in *Cat.* 2, 1ᵃ25–ᵇ3), discussion of the individual/nonindividual contrast in the case of the nonsubstantial categories quite generally has in practice usually been restricted to the category of quality.[6]

---

[5] O. Apelt has a conception, similar to the one presented here, of the relation between different kinds of inferences on the one hand, and the privileged and dependent hierarchies on the other. His useful observations are, however, undercut somewhat by introducing a distinction between "nur begriffliches Sein" (existing only as a concept), characteristic of the nonsubstantial items, and "wirkliches Sein (Dasein)" (actual existence), characteristic of the primary *ousiai*. (See "Die Kategorienlehre des Aristoteles," pp. 121–31.) I see no evidence for the suggestion that items in the nonsubstance categories exist only insofar as we think of them, or anything like that. They are indeed dependent beings, but what they depend on are the *ousiai*, not minds.

[6] That Aristotle thinks of knowledge as a quality—in his technical sense of quality—in the *Categories* is made clear by *Cat.* 8, 8ᵇ25–9ᵃ13.

And here commentators have frequently assumed that when Aristotle says that qualities are predicated of *ousiai* by being IN them, he means that (i) individual qualities are IN particular *ousiai*, and that (ii) nonindividual, i.e., general or generic qualities are IN general *ousiai*, i.e., the genera and species of the particular *ousiai*. Thus an individual white could be IN Socrates, but color would be IN bodies quite generally. However, we should consider the possibility that Aristotle allows for a more complicated picture, as represented in the diagram:

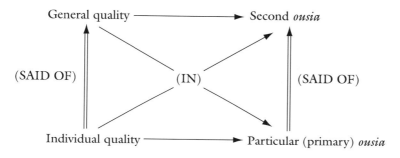

Therefore, in addition to (i) and (ii), we have that both (iii) an individual quality could be IN a second *ousia*, and (iv) a general quality could be IN a particular *ousia*.[7] It is perhaps worth noting that the view which allows for only (i) and (ii), i.e., for no 'diagonal' cases of being IN, must have it that there will be exactly as many intermediate species/genera of quality (and quantity, activity, place, etc.) as there are intermediate species/genera of *ousia*. This seems like a very strong and (even in the context of the Academy) highly implausible assumption. Moreover, it surely introduces needless complexity of its own.

Secondly, there is also the by now well-known further controversy regarding what individual nonsubstances are. (i) On what has come to be known as the traditional view, they are property-instances, individuated by their bearers, i.e., the individual (viz., primary) *ousiai*. Thus in the case of quality, Socrates' pallor and Plato's pallor would both be individual qualities, the first in virtue of being *Socrates'*, the second in virtue of being *Plato's*. The other major view (ii) holds that they are (somehow) individuals in their own right, e.g., by being *infimae species* of nonsubstances, no longer further divisible by further differentiae. Thus if color is a quality,

---

[7] On this issue, see M. Frede who favors the possibility of 'diagonal' being IN ("Individuen bei Aristoteles," *Antike und Abendland* 24 [1978]: 17 ff.), and K. Oehler who rejects it as needlessly complicated (*Aristoteles Kategorien* [Berlin, 1984], pp. 183–84).

this green and *that* green could be individual qualities if they can no longer be subdivided in terms of (say) hue, saturation and brightness. The most dramatic difference between (i) and (ii), as noted in the introduction, is that according to (ii), individual nonsubstantial items can be shared by more than one *ousia*, while according to (i) that is impossible by definition.[8] It seems to me that (ii) is clearly preferable, but that this emerges most strikingly only if—unlike most of the literature—one considers and focuses on nonsubstantial categories besides quality. (Consider even only the questions of how the categories, *where* and *when*, are to be individuated by primary *ousiai*.)

I do not propose to settle either of these questions here, but would like to point out that however these difficult and important matters are to be resolved, it is clear that the fundamental asymmetry referred to above will remain. Hence these complications turn out not to matter for the issue(s) at hand.

So let us return to those issues. It would be tempting to suppose that Aristotle's being IN relation corresponds to the 'is 'of schema (II) from Part II (see pp. 77 and 82 above), the 'is' we had identified as the 'is' of participation.[9] Giving in to that temptation is unproblematic, up to a point. Thus Socrates will be white, because he participates in white (so Plato); or because white is IN Socrates (so Aristotle). Similarly, Socrates will be just, because he participates in justice (the Platonic account), or because justice is IN Socrates (the Aristotelian one). But matters are not so simple, because while Plato or the Platonists would also want to say that Socrates is a man, since he participates in the Form or species, Man, Aristotle denies that Man is IN Socrates.

The reasons why Aristotle denies this look fairly simple. First, the expression 'this man' is not ambiguous in the way 'this white' is; for it cannot be used to refer, on the one hand, to a man (a thing), and on the other, to something distinct from the man (say a quality), which the man, however, has. Thus while there can be the white of the white thing, or the justice of the just thing, there cannot be the man of the man, nor the human of the human (thing). (This point, on its own, simply begs the

---

[8] There has been considerable discussion of this matter; see the the literature referred to in the introduction, p. 10 n. 11 above.

[9] N.B.: This will not correspond to Aristotle's own use of the notion of participation in the *Topics*; see Part II, n. 5 above. The present claim is that the 'is' expressed by the being IN relation can be used to *reconstruct* Plato's notion of participation, or at any rate, a central part of it.

question. At the very least, Aristotle would need to say considerably more than he does in the *Categories*.) Secondly, Aristotle holds that whatever can properly be called a man can also have the definition (of Man) predicated of it; recall *Topics* VI, 1: "the definition (ὁρισμός) of man ought be true of every man" (139ᵃ26–27). Thus, if being a rational animal is what it is to be a man (or is part of what it is to be a man) then rational animal can also be predicated of a particular man; for example, we can say of Socrates that he is a rational animal. But this means, given the account of the SAID OF relation, that rational animal is SAID OF Socrates, the individual. And given the relation between synonymy and the SAID OF relation, it also means that Socrates and the species, Man, are called 'man' synonymously. Moreover, Aristotle believes he is able to force the Platonists to agree on this last point. Let them give whatever account of being human they wish to give: that account will also apply to ordinary human beings; and if it does not, that only shows that it is not an account of being human after all. (The Platonists may be able to reply that the account does apply both to individuals and to the Form, but in different ways. So once again, Aristotle's claim by no means settles the matter.)

We can formulate the Aristotelian position of the *Categories* and the *Topics* in terms of the by now familiar essentialist dictum: everything is what it is, and not another thing. But by restricting the notion of a *thing* to objects (viz., the primary *ousiai*), Aristotle is able to say that objects, in addition to being the objects they *are*, also are qualified, quantified, located, affected, active, related to other objects, and so on, in various ways. But it is only these further nonsubstantial 'things' which a given object 'is', rather than what it *is*, that can properly be IN that object.

The Platonists' mistake thus is simply the failure to recognize that certain things are SAID OF (what Aristotle conceives of as) ordinary objects; alternatively, it is the failure to recognize that *not everything* can be IN the participants.

The Late-Learners' mistake is an exact counterpart to the Platonists' mistake: they are committed to the idea that any (genuine) predicate is only SAID OF its subject; alternatively, they are committed to the claim that *nothing* is IN anything.

Aristotle's position in the *Categories* and *Topics* is that we only arrive at an acceptable metaphysical picture of ordinary objects—or at least, of the most important kind of objects, the particular *ousiai*—if we realize that only *some* of what is predicated of them is IN them; for it is also the case that *some* of what is predicated of them must be SAID OF them.

Equally, only *some* of what is predicated of them is SAID OF them; for it is also the case that *some* of what is predicated of them must be IN them.

But Aristotle also and crucially believes that there is a simple linguistic test, which will reveal to us what kind of item we are dealing with, in any case of τὶ κατά τινος predication. Suppose *y* is predicated of *x* (but we do not yet know whether *y* is SAID OF or is IN *x*), and suppose (again) this fact is expressed by a sentence of the form '*S* is *P*', where *S* introduces *x* into discourse, and *P*, *y*. Now suppose someone wishes to make *y* the subject of some other, further sentence.

The first question to ask is: can *y* be referred to by an *abstract noun*, or not? (We shortly will consider the interesting and problematic case 'humanity' poses.) If it can be (that is, if we can use the term '*Y*-ness'), then we know that *y* is IN *x*, in other words, *y* is not (part of) what it is to be *x*. And this is the case of paronymy. Thus Aristotle gives an answer to the problem from the *Sophist* which we considered in connection with the Late-Learners—how can we call a thing by a name other than its own, when it participates in some affection from something else, i.e., how can we apply the name of this other thing to the first thing (252b8–10; cf. 251a5–6)? Example: Suppose a thing (say Helen of Troy, or the Zeus of Pheidias) is beautiful. 'Beauty' is the name of something through which, or on account of which, the thing—in our case, the person or the statue—can be affected in a certain way, namely, so as to be beautiful, and so come to deserve to be called 'beautiful'.

If we approach the issue in this way, we can see that being called *P* homonymously after *y* is a degenerate case of paronymy. It is degenerate, because there is *no* difference, at the lexical level, between *the name* of the affection—what we thought of as its *proper name* in Part I—and the *common name* of the things affected. Thus we need a second part to our test, we need to ask: can the *definition* of *y* be applied to *x*? If not, *y* is again IN *x*. Thus 'white' is the name of something which is IN Socrates, if he is white, because although the common name (i.e., the predicate-expression 'white') and the proper name of the item introduced by that expression (i.e., 'white' again) are the same, the definition of what it is to be white cannot be predicated of Socrates (for it is not the case that Socrates is a color of such-and-such a sort). It is only if the predicate-expression passes *both* tests—that is, if the item *y* introduced by the predicate-expression *P* cannot be referred to by an abstract noun, *and* if *P* can be replaced by the appropriate definition—that *y* will be SAID OF *x*.

If we consider the test (from *Cat.* 1ᵇ10–15, 2ᵃ19–34) in this way, we can also see that the primary contrast with which Aristotle is working is not, *pace* Owen (cf. Part I, n. 7 above), the one between homonymy and synonymy, but rather the one between paronymy and synonymy. Once we recognize the clear difference between paronymy and synonymy, we will be in a position to see that homonymy is to be assimilated to paronymy. Now this test looks as if it is meant to be purely (or almost purely) linguistic, insofar as it seems that we need not have any *antecedent* metaphysical views or commitments. But the real significance of the '-onymies' is that they allow Aristotle to exploit one feature of the Greek language Plato had ignored (viz., the distinction between abstract nouns and the neuter adjective + definite article construction) and another he had (according to Aristotle) failed fully to appreciate (namely, the distinction between transitive and nontransitive uses of 'is'). Aristotle takes these features both to reveal and, in a way, to underwrite a deep, hierarchically conceived, *ontological* distinction between objects and their properties.

2. SOME DIFFICULTIES

There are, however, at least three problems for the thought that a purely linguistic test is sufficient for Aristotle's purposes. First, while Aristotle does not explicitly say so, it seems he means to rule out nonsubstances of nonsubstances (in other words, a nonsubstantial item can only be IN an *ousia*, not IN some other nonsubstantial item). This is most easily illustrated by considering the case of what one might call qualities of qualities.[10] Thus if something, say, an azalea, is bright red, it is the azalea which has the quality, bright red, not the red of the azalea which has the quality, brightness. While we may in the end wish to agree with Aristotle, he surely would need to say more about why the first alternative is preferable to the second. Secondly, in order for the test to be reliable, we need to be able to rule out that there are, or could be, abstract nouns which name the genera and species of natural kinds; otherwise, a natural substance could be named paronymously after its kind, which would undermine the whole set of distinctions. Thus we must be able to rule out that the predicate-expression, 'man' or 'human', introduces an item which can properly be referred to by some appropriate abstract noun. Consider now

---

[10] Matters are in fact more complicated; for certain passages suggest that Aristotle does allow for things like qualities of qualities. See also Morrison, "The Taxonomical Interpretation of Aristotle's *Categories*: A Criticism."

the terms 'manhood' or 'manliness' on the one hand, and 'humanity' or 'humaneness' on the other. While we may have some reservations about this, it does seem that these terms all refer to something else—certain qualities—not to the natural kind itself.[11] But we would need to know if this sort of thing is true across the board. Aristotle certainly does nothing to show that all such abstract nouns *must* always refer to some other quality, and not to the natural kind itself (nor to the being of the natural kind).

The third and most significant difficulty is posed by the differentiae. According to the sort of view Aristotle is articulating, differentiae serve in part to constitute the species and genera which they differentiate. Thus, for example, suppose that rational is the differentia of human being. In that case, a human being does not merely happen to be rational; being rational rather is part of what it is to be a human being. Yet this means that the expression 'rational' should not introduce a quality—in Aristotle's technical sense of quality. The reason this must be so is that the item to which the adjective 'rational' refers, is not something that is IN humans; rather it is SAID OF them.[12] Thus we should also not be able to use an abstract noun like 'rationality' to refer to this item; for if we could use such a noun, then humans would be called 'rational' paronymously after the quality, rationality. On the other hand, it seems both that we can unproblematically form at least *some* such abstract nouns, and more importantly, that such nouns do refer to the very item that is predicated of whatever the differentia is predicated. To return to our example, we *can* form the noun 'rationality', and it seems to refer to the same item as the adjective 'rational' does, when we say of humans that they are rational. In short, it seems that there is after all a quality, rationality. This tension in Aristotle's treatment of the differentiae of *ousiai* surfaces in the *Categories* and *Topics*. For some of what he says clearly assimilates these differentiae to the genera and species of *ousiai*; other things he says assimilate them to qualities.

In a nutshell, the problem is as follows. Suppose that everything is either an *ousia* or a nonsubstantial item (certainly *Categories* 1–4 would suggest this); and that every *ousia* is either an individual, or a species or genus of individual *ousiai*. The second part of this supposition implies that the differentiae of *ousiai* cannot be *ousiai*. Given the examples Aristotle actually

---

[11] See also G. E. L. Owen, "The Platonism of Aristotle," in *LSD*, p. 210. Of course this does not mean that none of these abstract nouns could ever, in our ordinary discourse, be used to refer to the natural kind. The suggestion is only that Aristotle's denial that they are so used has some prima facie plausibility.

[12] See *Cat.* 5, 3ª21–28.

produces (e.g., footed, two-footed, winged, or aquatic at 1ᵇ18), it is most natural to assimilate them to qualities (cf. also *Topics* IV, 122ᵇ12–24; 128ᵃ26–7; VI, 144ᵃ9–19, esp. 18–19; 144ᵇ31–145ᵃ2). However, given 3ᵃ21–28 and the synonymy principle presented in 3ᵃ33 ff.—primary *ousiai* (and non-highest genera) are called (what they are called) synonymously after their differentiating differentiae—differentiae of *ousiai* cannot be qualities or any other nonsubstantial items that are IN *ousiai* rather than SAID OF them. Hence, given the initial dichotomy, it seems most natural to assimilate differentiae to *ousiai* after all. (See *Topics* I, 101ᵇ18–19, where differentiae are associated with the genera, i.e., in the case of *ousiai*, with secondary *ousiai*; cf. also *Topics* VII, 153ᵃ15–22 and 154ᵃ24–28, which would most naturally be read as implying that the differentiae of *ousiai* are *ousiai*.) It is presumably this difficulty that leads Porphyry (*In Cat.*, 95, 17–33) to speak of the differentia as a ποιότης οὐσιώδης (i.e., a substantial quality) which is to say, as an item that is both an *ousia* and a quality. In effect, Porphyry repudiates the initial dichotomy. (There will be related difficulties for the differentiae of the various kinds of nonsubstantial items.)

I do not believe that this problem can be resolved in a wholly satisfactory way.[13] But even if it could be, an appropriate resolution would hardly be the result of a simple inspection of the lexical inventory of Greek and the surface grammar of the language. Thus the grammatical tests Aristotle proposes are not *by themselves* sufficient to sustain the metaphysical distinctions he wishes to draw—the qualification is important, because it raises the question of whether this metaphysical picture could be sustained in other ways. Be that as it may, it should be clear, at least in outline, what that picture is.

3. The "Antepraedicamenta" as an Introduction to the "Praedicamenta": The Project of the *Categories* Reconsidered

We have already seen (in Part I) how the distinctions of the first two chapters of the *Categories* go hand in hand, and we have seen (in Part II) how various things we find in Plato's work might serve to motivate those

---

[13] For a useful discussion of many of the problems the notion of differentiae in the *Categories* and *Topics* gives rise to, see D. Morrison, "Le statut catégoriel des différences dans l' 'Organon,' " *Revue philosophique* (1993); he provides a considerably more nuanced

distinctions. In particular, examining Plato has allowed us to see why Aristotle should attribute such importance to paronymy and synonymy as opposed to mere undifferentiated eponymy. But there is at least one very important question about the "Antepraedicamenta" remaining. How do cc. 1–3 function as an introduction to cc. 5–10?

The *Categories* is a work that can seem strikingly free of argument in favor of the terminology, distinctions, and so on, it presents.[14] Thus if the treatise were concerned merely to present the doctrine of the genera of being, i.e., the claim that there are *ousiai*, primary and secondary, and that there are a variety of nonsubstantial items, dependent on the *ousiai*, it seems entirely possible that one could have a work, beginning with c. 4, which simply announced what the various kinds of beings are. The "Antepraedicamenta" alter the character of the actual treatise from the work imagined in two ways. First of all, the connection with Platonic theorizing is brought out. Admittedly, there are no direct references to Plato. But we have been able to see how Aristotle's distinction between the various '-onymies' grows out of reflection on, and disagreement with, Plato's account of eponymy as the relation between a participant being called (what it is called) from or after the relevant Form or Forms. Thus at a minimum, the "Antepraedicamenta" serve to locate the project within the context of Academic ontology.[15] Secondly, as we saw in Part I and noted again in Section 1 of Part III, the "Antepraedicamenta" contain linguistic tests on the basis of which the ontological classification is supposed to proceed.[16] However, given the reservations expressed about those tests, this fact may seem like an enormous liability. Thus we should briefly reconsider the kind of project these tests reflect.

One way of understanding the Late-Learners' view is as the claim that there are no accidental properties, that no thing has any accidental prop-

---

discussion of the passages (about differentiae) mentioned, but even he concedes that the tension or inconsistency adverted to is not wholly eliminable (p. 158).

[14] This is in fact most true of the first several chapters; from c. 5 on, Aristotle seems to proceed somewhat more dialectically, considering objections, modifying proposals, and so on. His discussions also make clear that the *context* for the entire set of distinctions is Academic dialectic. This is confirmed by *Topics* I, 1–15, which should in any event be read together with the *Categories*. See also S. Menn, "Metaphysics, Dialectic and the *Categories*," *Revue de Métaphysique et de Morale* 100 (1995).

[15] For the relevance of a different part of Academic ontology for understanding the *Categories*, see Philipp Merlan, "Beiträge zur Geschichte des antiken Platonismus: I. Zur Erklärung der dem Aristoteles zugeschriebenen Kategorienschrift," *Philologus* 89 (1934).

[16] This emerges especially clearly if the lines from c. 5 are transposed into c. 2, as suggested in Appendix 1 to Part I.

erty. If this is right, at least roughly, then it seems that change is impossible; more precisely, it seems that there is no way of distinguishing between *change* and *replacement*. (Let us assume without argument that in a case of genuine change there is something which persists through the change, even though there are ways in which what was there before the change is different from what is there after the change; in other words, there is a way in which there is only *one* thing throughout the change. And let us assume that in a case of replacement, there is first one thing, before the replacement, and then another, afterwards; in other words, there is a way in which there is *more* than one thing here.) Thus in order to distinguish between change and replacement, it will be necessary, at a minimum, to decide amongst cases where we in fact have (only) one thing, and those where we have more than one. Consider now a restriction characteristic of the Late-Learners, their refusal to allow 'a man is pale' as a meaningful statement. Clearly they are not in a position to give an account of someone becoming tan after having been pale, or becoming healthy after having been ill. We need to note the following: it is not only because they refuse to countenance claims like 'Socrates is pale', 'Socrates is tan', and so on, that they cannot speak of these changes. For if they redescribe matters and speak of the pale thing, they cannot say that *it* becomes tan. Why not? Something tan is obviously a tan thing, and equally obviously, a tan thing is not a pale thing. Thus the description of an ordinary change seems to involve "making one thing into two" (cf. *Sophist* 251b6–7). At best we could have two things, first a pale thing, then a tan thing. Consider next the claim that Socrates is a man. (This is something we have been assuming the Late-Learners would allow.) When Socrates perishes, there no longer is any man who Socrates could be. So we should also not say that Socrates becomes a corpse, or that a man becomes a corpse. For a man is not a corpse. Again, it seems we have two things, first a man (Socrates), then a corpse. (Of course, in this second case, the 'two things' assumption may seem less troubling; Aristotle, for example, endorses a version of it in the *De Anima* and in the *Metaphysics*.)

The problem here is not only that the two cases will be assimilated to one another, but that there is no clear way of distinguishing cases (such as those we have been looking at) where there is some 'connection' between the earlier and the later object, and cases where there simply are two objects, one earlier, one later, with no relevant connection between them at all. The conclusion to draw thus also is not merely that all instances of change (i.e., cases we would so describe) are treated as instances of replacement, but that both notions become problematic together, and,

197

in effect, drop out together. Perhaps we can—waiving Plato's worries that the Late-Learners could do so only on pain of incoherence—continue to speak of sameness and difference (i.e., an object can be the same at two different times; or there can be different objects at different times), but since we cannot *metaphysically* distinguish instances of difference where there is some connection between earlier and later, from those where there is none, this still will provide no footing for ever speaking of change rather than replacement, or vice versa. (I emphasize 'metaphysically', because the problem is not an epistemological one at all: it is not the result of some epistemic deficiencies the Late-Learners believe we have; this rather is how, according to them, things are.)

On the other hand, the Platonic view characteristic of the middle dialogues could be understood as the claim that ordinary things have only accidental properties. We have seen (in Part II, p. 165 above) how this leads Plato—explicitly in the *Theaetetus*—to treat the transition from being healthy to being ill as on a par with the transition from being alive to being a corpse. Here too, though, matters are much more problematic. In this case it again looks as if we cannot draw a distinction between change and replacement. But is replacement being assimilated to change, or change to replacement? The rough and ready way in which I have characterized these two notions, in effect, associates change with accidental properties. But what exactly is it, on the Platonic picture, that persists through the change? If an item is simply to be identified with the cluster of things it 'is' (which is to say, the things it *becomes*, in Plato's technical sense of becoming), then it seems that any time any element or ingredient in the cluster is different, we have a different item. Thus it seems that no such cluster can, strictly speaking, persist through the 'change' of one of its constituents. Hence it also seems that such clusters, regarded as wholes, cannot, strictly speaking, change; they can only come-to-be, or cease-to-be, all at once.

Are we then again dealing with cases of replacement? At first, of course, it seems that this is exactly what must be going on: replacing one of the elements in a cluster (for example, substituting a share of The Healthy for a share of The Ill) results in a new and different cluster; in effect, the first cluster has been replaced by the second one. Yet there will once more be a problem with demarcating such cases—those where there is a real connection between the earlier and the later clusters—from those where we simply have two different clusters. It is tempting to think that various sorts of constraints can be used for distinguishing between the two kinds of cases: one might hold, for example, that not all the elements in a cluster can be replaced simultaneously; or one might require that we not only consider the clusters at the initial time and the final time but also at all times in between, and then urge that there be sufficient 'overlap' between 'stages' to give us (at least something like) persistence. No doubt such strategies can be pursued—think of various versions of 'temporal-slice metaphysics'. But it is worth noting that one can fairly readily construct examples which push in a certain direction: namely, pushing us to identify and isolate something in the cluster at the earlier time, such that if *it* is still present at the later time, we will have the desired sort of connection between the earlier cluster and the later one. But this now suggests that there is, after all, something essential in the cluster, over and above its simply being the aggregate of the constituents it is (with the constituents present in it in just the 'proportions' in which they are present). But the thought had been that *nothing* in or about the thing is essential, because everything is accidental. Thus it seems that we will not be able to distinguish replacement (of the sort that allows for at least something like persistence) from cases where there simply are two or more things, wholly and utterly unconnected.[17] Moreover, it looks as if the claim that everything in or about a thing is accidental is itself in trouble. We have just seen that any time a constituent is changed, we have something that is, strictly speaking, a *new* cluster. Thus far from having only accidental properties, it seems that everything about a cluster is essential, inasmuch as if anything is changed, we have a different cluster! Of course, what this really shows is that, described in the way it has been described, the claim that everything about a *thing* is accidental makes no more sense than the claim that everything about a *thing* is essential.

Aristotle does not *expressis verbis* offer any of these considerations in the *Categories*; indeed, one striking feature of this treatise is the fact that

---

[17] A serious engagement with temporal-slice metaphysics and other (relevantly similar) projects for 'constructing' objects out of allegedly simpler and ontologically less suspect items is obviously beyond the scope of the present discussion. But the general worry is this. If the slices are really to be ontologically fundamental, it seems that we need a way of (metaphysically) identifying each slice that does not rely on its being a-slice-of-this-object versus being a-slice-of-that-object (otherwise it seems that the objects will be fundamental after all). But now, how can we identify the *right* slices and the *right* operations of mereological fusion (or whatever) so as to give us what we prephilosophically thought of as the objects (as opposed to various gerrymandered or kooky 'objects')? See also P. Simon, *Parts: A Study in Ontology* (Oxford, 1987), esp. pt. 2, "Mereology of Continuants," pp. 173–251. Temporal-slice metaphysicians tend to be ingenious, and thus have ways of meeting this kind of objection. And indeed, my contention is not that such projects will not work, but that intuitive pressures in favor of some kind of essentialism will remain.

he does not seem to be concerned with, much less address, issues involving change, persistence, and replacement at all. Nevertheless, it seems to me that one of the key insights of the work is that, when speaking about things, it only makes sense to regard some things about a thing as essential, if we also treat something else in or about it as accidental; likewise, it only makes sense to regard some thing in or about a thing as accidental, if we treat something about it as essential. (In the previous sentence, I am obviously—and deliberately—using the term 'thing' in as wide a way a possible.) And the most fundamental part of this insight is Aristotle's discovery of *things*, that is, the realization that certain items in our ontology need to be bona fide things, need to be genuine objects; for as genuine objects they can thus be the subjects—the underlying things—for everything else in the ontology. (In the preceeding sentence, I am using the term 'thing' in its narrow sense.)

At this point, however, one might raise the following objection. It is certainly true that Aristotle sets out to solve problems about identity and persistence by relying on a notion of essence, and thus also on a contrast between what an object is essentially, and what it (merely) happens to be. But isn't all of this simply to beg the question against Plato—and others? After all, why suppose that identity does depend on essence? On the one hand, it is clearly not the case that people are either debarred from re-identifying objects (over time), or unjustified in doing so, absent any theory about these issues. On the other hand, as mentioned, there are sophisticated philosophical theories that seek to show that we do not need to be essentialists of any sort. (Indeed, anti-essentialism, in various guises, may well be the dominant current metaphysical outlook.)

In fact, I believe that there are powerful considerations in favor of linking identity with essence. (Kripke's arguments about identity and necessity, for example, seem like they could be extended to apply to Aristotle's notion of essence in a fairly natural way.) Yet let us set all such considerations aside. It seems to me that Plato is still not in a very good position vis-à-vis Aristotle on this matter. To begin with, he does not have available the sophisticated devices—like 'temporal slices'—contemporary philosophers use. But Plato cannot fall back on ordinary discourse and observe that we do, after all, use sentences in subject-predicate form; that we do, after all, succeed in re-identifying things over time; and so on. The reason he cannot avail himself of these simple facts is that, given his own discussions, and the problems and paradoxes they seek to address (as well as the problems and paradoxes they in turn give rise to), Plato is *committed* to providing a theoretical account of these issues.

Moreover, once Aristotle's picture of ordinary things is firmly in place,[18] Plato's thoughts about the participants must seem either highly problematic or like a vague anticipation of Aristotle's picture. One thing they cannot be is expressions of an 'innocent' view of the world. For Plato has already traveled so far down the path of philosophy—of revisionist metaphysics—that falling back into an allegedly pretheoretical way of seeing things must appear question-begging. But he has not traveled far enough to reach the Aristotelian position. This is not to say that Aristotle's views cannot be rejected. Of course they can be. But these views (now) need to be worked through and overcome, not simply denied.

To put the point another way: *we* can no longer embrace the metaphysical pictures of the Presocratics. This is not because they are false; it is not even to say that they are false. Rather, given the subsequent history of metaphysics, we either simply *project* some later view onto the Presocratics (and then say that they dimly anticipated it), or we need to *recover* what they were trying to do. For given that history, much of what they say is no longer straightforwardly available as philosophically coherent. It seems to me that *our* situation vis-à-vis Plato's view (or views) of the participants is exactly the same. Once again, this is not because it is false; it is not even to say that Plato's view is false. Rather, given the subsequent history of metaphysics, we tend to project a later view—Aristotle's—onto Plato (and then find that he did not formulate it as well as Aristotle did). If we resist the temptation of projecting Aristotle back onto Plato we will find that Plato is far stranger—more of a Presocratic (so to speak)—than we might have thought. So the task will also be to recover Plato's views. I believe all of this remains true, even if we accept that Plato came to see serious difficulties with his Anaxagorean view of the participants and sought to abandon it. For once we give up on trying to interpret Plato in Aristotelian terms, it will be far more difficult to attribute to Plato a simple, quasi-Aristotelian view of the participants, as objects with properties, differing from Aristotle only on the question of whether or not those objects have essences. In fact, it may turn out that Plato did not arrive a new view of the participants that was satisfactory even by his own lights. (Clearly, an

---

[18] The question when Aristotle's picture comes to be firmly in place is a difficult one. It is certainly not the case that it comes to be common sense immediately.

extensive investigation of the late dialogues would be needed for addressing this matter.)

To return to Aristotle: although he does not introduce considerations about change in urging his distinctions, certain claims in *Categories* 5 bear out that he is concerned with it. For there we are told that it is distinctive of *ousiai* that they admit contraries (4ª10 ff.). The claim is obviously not that an *ousia*, e.g., Socrates, is both healthy and ill, or both pale and tan, at one and the same time. The claim rather is that an *ousia* can have one feature at one time, and an opposed feature at another, while remaining one and the same *ousia*. But that just is to say that *ousiai* can change whilst remaining the same; in other words, *ousiai* can really be *subjects* for change (and can thus be called 'substances'), *because* they can change their features.

If these considerations are at all along the right lines, then the "Anteprae-dicamenta" serve not merely to locate Aristotle's *Categories* within the larger context of Academic debates. Rather by insisting that objects both have some things SAID OF them, and have some things IN them, Aristotle is (as we have seen) implicitly pointing out the deficiencies of the alterna-tives given by the Late-Learners and by Plato. To put the point another way, the related contrasts between synonymy and paronymy/homonymy on the one hand, and between something being SAID OF something and something being IN something on the other, grow out of Aristotle's reflecting on and coming to terms with those deficiencies, and these con-trasts are the (highly compressed) formulation of his preferred alternative, his middle way if you will. Thus if the "Antepraedicamenta" were absent from the treatise, it would be still more difficult to see the reasons Aristotle finds Platonism and Late-Learnerism (as he understands them) unaccept-able. The presence of the "Antepraedicamenta" makes it possible to un-cover a line of criticism, reflection, and reformulation that clearly links the *Categories* to Plato's concerns whilst also showing the enormous dis-tance he has traveled from Plato.

Moreover, if this picture of the role of Chapters 1–3 is along the right lines, then we can also perhaps come to see the linguistic tests in a more favorable light than suggested before, in Section 2. Since antiquity, one of the standard questions about the *Categories* has been whether Aristotle is there trying to classify expressions (λεγόμενα), or entities (ὄντα), or expressions on the basis of entities, or entities on the basis of expressions. (Still other possibilities have been considered, but they do not matter for our purposes.) This question, or these questions, arise in the first instance in connection with the talk of entities and expressions in c. 2. I have in effect been claiming that Aristotle wished to use expressions as a basis for classifying entities. And the problem this suggestion encountered was that the inventory of expressions and the 'grammar' governing their use seemed insufficiently restrictive to serve as the basis for the desired schema of ontological classification.

Suppose, however, we weaken the claim only slightly. Aristotle sets out to use facts about language and its use, *not* to ground metaphysical claims *directly*, but for *heuristic purposes*: to a certain extent, usage reveals ontological facts; once we have become clear about those facts, they will inform our response to further linguistic data. In other words, the ontology does not stand or fall with the linguistic tests, they rather provide a route into the ontology; and once we are sufficiently clear about that ontology, we can dismiss recalcitrant linguistic data as irrelevant. This skeletal suggestion can be fleshed out a bit. There clearly are transitive versus intransitive uses of 'is', and there clearly are cases where predicate-expressions can be replaced by accounts or definitions, and cases where they cannot be so replaced. Focusing on an ontology of things and their features, and grafting it onto Plato's basic distinction between what is general and what is particular, allows Aristotle to preserve (what he takes to be) Plato's insights while avoiding many of the difficulties both Plato's view and the strangely related view of the Late-Learners give rise to. Of course, once the thing versus feature contrast is viewed from *within* the particular versus general contrast, two further moves will seem extremely natural. First, it will be almost irresistible to understand the latter contrast as one of particulars versus their species and genera—especially since Plato and the Academy had already paved the way here (say in the use of the so-called method of collection and division to establish genus/species hierarchies). Secondly, one will wish to find a role for differentiae roughly along the lines Aristotle actually sketches—this especially in light of the fact that his (essentially Platonic) view of definition (see, e.g., *Top.* I, 4–5) requires differentiae as that which allows for the differentiation of a genus into its species, and of species into their subspecies. (It would also be natural *for us* to take a further, third step and construe the primary contrast as one of particular things versus general features. Yet here the fact that Aristotle countenances general objects [viz., genera and species of *ousiai*] and individual features shows that he has not fully replaced the ontology of the Platonists.)[19]

---

[19] On this point, cf. Frede, "Individuen bei Aristoteles," p. 31.

But it will hardly be surprising if the linguistic tests fail to converge perfectly with the requirements of the theoretical picture. Thus the difficulty about the differentiae of *ousiai* could be solved by terminological legislation, the stipulation that we not recognize abstract nouns corresponding to differentiae, or, if faced with such nouns as unavoidable linguistic data, not recognize that they have anything like the ontological import abstract nouns corresponding to qualities have. Considered on its own, such a move cannot help but appear ad hoc and unmotivated, not to say bizarre. But in the context of Aristotle's overall project, we can see it as a final step that needs to be taken in order to make the linguistic investigations and the ontological reflections converge. Viewed this way, the ultimately unsatisfying account of paronymy with respect to the differentiae of *ousiai* may have seemed a small price to pay for what is otherwise a systematic and attractive picture.

Epilogue

SOME FINAL observations. If the mark of success for a philosophical distinction, view, or theory is that it comes to be so widely accepted that the distinction, view, or theory no longer seems to be distinctively philosophical, but seems simply to be part of ordinary discourse or common sense, then Aristotle's distinction between objects and their properties in the *Categories* should be counted as a virtually unparalleled success. His claim that every genuine thing is what it is, but also is qualified, quantified, located, related to other things, affected, and so on, seems so natural and obvious, that we have enormous difficulty seeing that Plato (and various Presocratics) not only did not accept it, but had views incompatible (better: only very problematically compatible) with the central distinction on which Aristotle relies.

This difficulty leads to others. In general it has not been adequately recognized that (what in effect amounts to) presupposing the ontology of the *Categories* actually stands in the way of understanding Plato's project, especially in the middle dialogues.[1] The failure to recognize this leads to a second failure. Aristotle's criticisms of Plato are not meant merely to replace one conception of *form* with another—indeed, in the *Categories*, the Platonic conception of Forms seems not to be Aristotle's primary target at all—rather his aim is also to articulate a wholly *new* picture of the items that Plato had taken to be the *participants*, that is, ordinary things. Keeping this in mind, and keeping in mind that the various distinctions between part and whole are no less important for metaphysics than the more frequently discussed distinctions between what is particular and what is general, and between objects and their properties, should help us not only in trying to understand more clearly Plato's own ontological picture (from both the middle and the late period), but also in working through and understanding Aristotle's criticisms of, and alterations to, Plato's metaphysical project.

It is a further and highly ironic mark of the *Categories'* success, that for a long time, commentators had failed fully to appreciate that in the central books of the *Metaphysics*, Aristotle largely abandons his earlier picture.

---

[1] Gerold Prauss is one commentator and interpreter who explicitly does recognize this. See "Ding und Eigenschaft bei Platon und Aristoteles," *Kant-Studien* 59 (1968) and *Plato und der logische Eleatismus* (Berlin, 1966).

For Aristotle comes to think that ordinary things cannot, after all, be fundamental items. In particular, in order for them to be the kind of ordinary things we ordinarily take them to be, they must exhibit a certain metaphysical structure—a structure which Aristotle seeks to delineate with his distinctively theoretical notions of form and matter, and their equally theoretical correlatives, actuality and potentiality. To explain how and why he comes to be dissatisfied with the *Categories'* picture, and what he seeks to replace it with, would, however, be the subject for another, even longer story.

Select Bibliography

ANCIENT AUTHORS: TEXTS, TRANSLATIONS, AND COMMENTARIES

Works by Aristotle and Plato

Aristotle. *Aristotelis Opera*. Ed. I. Bekker. 4 vols. Berlin, 1831–36.
———. *The Complete Works of Aristotle*. Ed. J. Barnes. 2 vols. Princeton, N.J., 1984.
———. *Aristotelis Categoriae et Topica cum Porphyrii Isagoge*. Ed. I. Bekker. Berlin, 1843.
———. *Categoriae et Liber De Interpretatione*. Ed. L. Minio-Paluello. Oxford, 1949; repr. 1956.
———. *Aristotle's Categories and De Interpretatione*. Tr. by J. L. Ackrill. Oxford, 1963.
———. *Kategorien*. Tr. K. Oehler. Berlin, 1984.
———. *De Caelo*. Ed. D. J. Allan. Oxford, 1955.
———. *De Ideis*. Ed. D. Harlfinger. In *Il "De Ideis" di Aristotele e la teoria platonica delle Idee*. Ed. W. Leszl, pp. 21–39. Florence, 1975.
———. *Ethica Nicomachea*. Ed. I. Bywater. Oxford, 1894.
———. *De Generatione Animalium*. Ed. H. J. Drossaart Lulofs. Oxford, 1965.
———. *Aristotle on Coming-to-be and Passing-away.* [= *De Generatione et Corruptione*]. Ed. H. H. Joachim. Oxford, 1922.
———. *De Generatione et Corruptione*. Tr. C. J. F. Williams. Oxford, 1982.
———. *Metaphysica*. Ed. W. Jaeger. Oxford, 1957.
———. *Aristoteles 'Metaphysik Z': Text, Übersetzung und Kommentar*. Ed. M. Frede and G. Patzig. 2 vols. Munich, 1988.
———. *Physica*. Ed. W. D. Ross. Oxford, 1956.
———. *Aristotle's Physics, I–II*. Tr. W. C. Charlton. Oxford, 1970.
———. *Topica et Sophistici Elenchi*. Ed. W. D. Ross. Oxford, 1958; repr. 1970.
Plato. *Platonis Dialogi Selecti*. Ed. L. Heindorf. 5 vols. Berlin, 1802–10.
———. *Platonis Opera*. Ed. J. Burnet. 5 vols. Oxford, 1900–1906.
———. *Plato Complete Works*. Ed. J. Cooper. Indianapolis, 1997.
———. *The Collected Dialogues of Plato*. Ed. E. Hamilton and H. Cairns. Princeton, N.J., 1961.
———. *Parmenides*. Tr. M. L. Gill and P. Ryan. Indianapolis, 1996.
———. *Phaedo*. Ed. I. Bekker. London, 1825.
———. *Plato: Phaedo*. Tr. D. Gallop. Oxford, 1975.
———. *Protagoras and Meno*. Tr. W. K. C. Guthrie. Harmondsworth, 1956.
———. *Republic*. Tr. G. M. Grube, rev. C. D. C. Reeve. Indianapolis, 1992.

Plato. *Sophist.* Tr. N. White. Indianapolis, 1993.

———. *Plato: Thaeaetetus.* Tr. J. McDowell. Oxford, 1973.

———. *Theaetetus.* Tr. M. J. Levett, rev. M. F. Burnyeat. Indianapolis, 1990.

Works by Other Authors

Alexander of Aphrodisias. *In Aristolelis Metaphysica Commentaria.* Ed. M. Hayduck. *Commentaria in Aristotelem Graeca* (*CAG*), vol. 1. Berlin, 1891.

———. *On Aristotle's Metaphysics 1.* Tr. W. E. Dooley, S.J. Ithaca, N.Y., 1989.

Ammonius. *In Aristotelis Categorias Commentarius.* Ed. A. Busse. *CAG*, vol. 4, part 4. Berlin, 1895.

———. *On Aristotle's Catgeories.* Tr. S. M. Cohen and G. B. Matthews. Ithaca, N.Y., 1991.

Boethius. *In Categorias Aristotelis Libri Quattuor.* Ed. J.-P. Migne. *Patrologia Latina*, vol. 64., Paris, 1847.

Euripides. *Hippolytus.* Ed. W. S. Barrett. Oxford, 1964.

Herodotus. *Historiae.* Ed. C. Hude. 2 vols. 3d ed. Oxford, 1927.

———. *The Histories.* Tr. A. De Sélincourt, rev. J. Marincola. London, 1996.

Hippocrates. *Ancient Medicine.* In *Hippocrates* I, tr. W. H. S. Jones. Loeb Classical Library. London, 1923.

———. *Hippocratis De Diaeta.* (*Corpus Medicorum Graecorum* I 2, 4.) Ed. and tr. R. Joly. Berlin, 1984.

———. *Regimen.* In *Hippocrates* IV, tr. W. H. S. Jones. Loeb Classical Library. London, 1931.

———. *Hippocratis De Natura Hominis.* (*Corpus Medicorum Graecorum* I 1, 3.) Ed. and trans. J. Jouanna. Berlin, 1975.

———. *The Nature of Man.* In *Hippocrates* IV, tr. W. H. S. Jones. Loeb Classical Library. London, 1931.

Lysias. *Orationes.* Ed. C. Hude. Oxford, 1912.

———. *Lysias.* Tr. W. R. M. Lamb. Loeb Classical Library. London, 1930.

Olympiodorus. *Prolegomena et in Categorias Commentarium.* Ed. A. Busse. *CAG*, vol. 12, part 1. Berlin, 1902.

Porphyry. *Isagoge et In Aristotelis Categorias Commentarium.* Ed. A. Busse. *CAG*, vol. 4, part 1. Berlin, 1887.

———. *On Aristotle's Categories.* Tr. S. K. Strange. Ithaca, N.Y., 1992.

Simplicius. *In Aristotelis Categorias Commentarius.* Ed. K. Kalbfleisch. *CAG*, vol. 8. Berlin, 1907.

———. *In Aristotelis Physicorum Libros Quattuor Prius Commentaria.* Ed. H. Diels. *CAG*, vol. 9. Berlin, 1882.

Speusippus. P. Lang. *De Speusippi Academici Scriptis, Accedunt Fragmenta.* Bonn, 1911.

———. L. Tarán. *Speusippus of Athens*: *A Critical Study with a Collection of the Related Texts and Commentary* (= Philosophia Antiqua, vol. 39). Leiden, 1981.

Thucydides. *Historiae.* Ed. H. S. Jones. 2 vols. Oxford, 1900–1902; reprinted 1963.

———. *Thucydides.* Tr. C. Foster Smith. Loeb Classical Library. 4 vols. London, 1928–52.

Xenocrates. R. Heinze. *Xenokrates: Darstellung der Lehre und Sammlung der Fragmente.* Leipzig, 1892.

Xenophon. *Expeditio Cyri.* Ed. C. Hude, rev. J. Peters. Leipzig, 1972.

———. *Anabasis.* Tr. C. L. Brownson. Loeb Classical Library. 2 vols. London, 1922.

Collections of Various Authors

Diels, H. *Die Fragmente der Vorsokratiker.* 6th ed., rev. W. Kranz. 3 vols. Berlin, 1951.

Edmonds, J. M. *Elegy and Iambus.* Loeb Classical Library. 2 vols. London, 1931.

Page, D. L. *Poetae Melici Graeci.* Oxford, 1962.

Wellman, M. *Fragmente der sikelischen Ärzte.* Berlin, 1902.

West, M. L. *Iambi et Elegi Graeci.* 2 vols. Oxford, 1971–72.

REFERENCE WORKS

Brandwood, L. *A Word Index to Plato.* Leeds, 1976.

Duhoux, Y. *Le verbe grec ancien: Éléments de morphologie et de syntaxe historiques.* Louvain-La-Neuve, 1992.

Liddell, H. G., and R. Scott. *A Greek-English Lexicon.* Rev. H. S. Jones. Oxford, 1940; reprinted 1968.

Schwyzer, E. *Griechische Grammatik.* 4 vols. Munich, 1950–71.

Smyth, H. W. *Greek Grammar*, rev. G. Messing. Cambridge, Mass., 1956.

MODERN AUTHORS: ARTICLES, BOOKS AND COLLECTIONS

Ackrill, J. L. "Plato and the Copula: *Sophist* 251–259." *Journal of Hellenic Studies* 77 (1957): 1–6. Reprinted in *Studies in Plato's Metaphysics.* Ed. R. E. Allen, 207–18. London, 1965.

Annas, J. *An Introduction to Plato's Republic.* Oxford, 1981.

Apelt, O. "Die Kategorienlehre des Aristoteles." In his *Beiträge zur Geschichte der griechischen Philosophie*, pp. 101–216. Leipzig, 1891.

Arpe, C. "Substantia." *Philologus* 94 (1941): 65–78.

Austin, J. L. "ἀγαθόν and εὐδαιμονία in the *Ethics* of Aristotle." In his *Philosophical Papers*, 2d ed., ed. J. O. Urmson and G. J. Warnock, pp. 1–31. Oxford, 1970.

Baldry, H. C. "Plato's 'Technical Terms.'" *Classical Quarterly* 31 (1937): 141–50.

Barnes, J. "Aristotle and the Methods of Ethics." *Revue internationale de la philosophie* 34 (1981): 490–511.

Barnes, J. "Homonymy in Aristotle and Speusippus." *Classical Quarterly*, n.s. 21 (1971): 65–80.

———. *The Presocratic Philosophers.* 2 vols. London, 1979.

———. "Roman Aristotle." In *Philosophia Togata*, vol. 2, ed. J. Barnes and M. Griffin, pp. 1–69. Oxford, 1997.

Bealer, G. "Predication and Matter." *Synthese* 31, nos. 3/4 (1975): 493–508.

Bestor, T. W. "Common Properties and Eponymy in Plato." *Philosophical Quarterly* 28 (1978): 189–207.

———. "Plato's Semantics and Plato's *Parmenides.*" *Phronesis* 25 (1980): 38–75.

Bogaard, P. "Heaps or Wholes: Aristotle's Explanation of Compound Bodies." *Isis* 70 (1979): 11–29.

Bolton, R. "Plato's Distinction between Being and Becoming." *Review of Metaphysics* 29 (1975–76): 66–95.

Brandwood, L. *The Chronology of Plato's Dialogues.* Cambridge, 1990.

Brentlinger, J. "Incomplete Predicates and the Two-World Theory of the *Phaedo.*" *Phronesis* 17 (1972): 61–79.

———. "Particulars in Plato's Middle Dialogues." *Archiv für Geschichte der Philosophie* 54 (1972): 116–52.

Brinton, L. *The Development of English Aspectual Systems.* Cambridge Studies in Linguistics, vol. 49. Cambridge, 1988.

Brown, L. "Being in the *Sophist*: A Syntactical Inquiry." *Oxford Studies in Ancient Philosophy* 4 (1986): 49–70.

Burnet, J. *Greek Philosophy*: *Thales to Plato.* London, 1914; reprinted 1950.

Burnyeat, M. F. "The Material and Sources of Plato's Dream." *Phronesis* 15 (1970): 101–22.

———. "Plato on the Grammar of Perceiving." *Classical Quarterly*, n.s. 26 (1976): 29–51.

Cherniss, H. *Aristotle's Criticism of Plato and the Academy.* Baltimore, 1944.

———. *Aristotle's Criticism of Presocratic Philosophy.* Baltimore, 1935.

Classen, C. J. "The Study of Language amongst Socrates' Contemporaries." *Proceedings of the African Classical Associations* 2 (1959): 33–49. Reprinted in *Sophistik.* Ed. Classen, 215–47. Darmstadt, 1976.

Code, A. "Aristotle: Essence and Accident." In *Philosophical Grounds of Rationality*, ed. R. Grandy and R. Warner, 411–39. Oxford, 1986.

———. "Aristotle's Response to Quine's Objections to Modal Logic." *Journal of Philosophical Logic* 5 (1976): 159–86.

———. "On the Origin of Some Aristotelian Theses about Predication." In *How Things Are,* ed. J. Bogen and J. McGuire, 101–31. Dordrecht, 1985.

———. "Reply to Michael Frede's 'Being and Becoming in Plato.' " *Oxford Studies in Ancient Philosophy*, suppl. vol. (1988): 53–60.

Comrie, B. *Aspect.* Cambridge, 1976.

Cooper, J. M. "Plato on Sense Perception and Knowledge: *Theaetetus* 184 to 186." *Phronesis* 15 (1970): 123–46.

Cresswell, M. J. Review of F. C. White, *Plato's Theory of Particulars. Australasian Journal of Philosophy* 61 (1983): 323–26.

Dancy, R. "On Some of Aristotle's First Thoughts about Substances." *Philosophical Review* 94 (1975): 338–73.

———. *Two Studies in the Early Academy.* Albany, N.Y., 1991.

Denkel, A. *Object and Property.* Cambridge, 1996.

Denyer, N. "Plato's Theory of Stuffs." *Philosophy* 58 (1983): 315–27.

Diller, H. "Hippokratische Medizin und attische Philosophie." *Hermes* 80 (1952): 385–409.

Dörrie, H. Ὑπόστασις: *Wort- und Bedeutungsgeschichte.* Nachrichten der Akademie der Wissenschaften in Göttingen, phil.-hist. Kl., no. 3. Göttingen, 1955.

Ebert, T. "Gattungen der Prädikate und Gattungen des Seienden bei Aristoteles." *Archiv für Geschichte der Philosophie* 67 (1985): 113–38.

Edelstein, L. "The Role of Erixymachus in Plato's *Symposium.*" *Transactions of the American Philological Association* 76 (1945): 85–103.

Fine, G. "Critical Notice: R. M. Dancy, *Two Studies in the Early Academy.*" *Canadian Journal of Philosophy* 22 (1992): 393–409.

———. "Immanence." *Oxford Studies in Ancient Philosophy* 4 (1986): 71–97.

———. *On Ideas: Aristotle's Criticism of Plato's Theory of Forms.* Oxford, 1993.

Frede, D. "The Impossibility of Perfection: Socrates' Criticism of Simonides' Poem in the *Protagoras.*" *Review of Metaphysics* 39 (1985–86): 729–53.

Frede, M. *Essays in Ancient Philosophy* (collected papers). Minneapolis, 1987.

———. "Being and Becoming in Plato." *Oxford Studies in Ancient Philosophy*, suppl. vol. (1988): 37–52.

———. "Categories in Aristotle." In *Studies in Aristotle.* Ed. D. J. O'Meara (= Studies in Philosophy and the History of Philosophy, vol. 9), pp. 1–24. Washington, D.C., 1981. Reprinted in Frede, *Essays*, pp. 29–48.

———. "Die Frage nach dem Seienden: *Sophistes.*" In *Platon: Seine Dialoge in der Sicht neuer Forschungen.* Ed. T. Kobusch and B. Mojsisch, pp. 181–199. Darmstadt, 1996.

———. "Individuen bei Aristoteles." *Antike und Abendland* 24 (1978): 16–39. Reprinted as "Individuals in Aristotle," in Frede, *Essays*, pp. 49–71.

———. "Plato's *Sophist* on False Statements." In *The Cambridge Companion to Plato.* Ed. R. Kraut, pp. 397–424. Cambridge, 1992.

———. *Prädikation und Existenzaussage: Der Gebrauch von '. . . ist . . .' und '. . . ist nicht . . .' in Platons Sophistes.* Hypomnemata, vol. 18. Göttingen, 1967.

———. "Titel, Einheit und Echtheit der aristotelischen Kategorienschrift." In *Zweifelhaftes im Corpus Aristotelicum.* Ed. P. Moraux and J. Wiesner. Berlin, 1983. Reprinted as "The Title, Unity, and Authenticity of the Aristotelian *Categories*," in Frede, *Essays*, pp. 11–28.

Fujisawa, N. "Ἔχειν, Μετέχειν and Idioms of 'Paradeigmatism' in Plato's Theory of Forms." *Phronesis* 19 (1974): 30–58.

Furley, D. "Anaxagoras in Response to Parmenides." *Canadian Journal of Philosophy*, suppl. vol. 2 (1976): 61–85. Reprinted in Furley, *Cosmic Problems*, pp. 47–65. Cambridge, 1989.

Furth, M. "Elements of Eleatic Ontology." *Journal of the History of Philosophy* 6 (1968): 111–32. Reprinted in *The Presocratics*. Ed. A. P. Mourelatos, pp. 241–70. Garden City, N.Y., 1974.

———. *Substance, Form and Psyche*. Cambridge, 1989.

Gaiser, K. *Protreptik und Paränese bei Platon*. Stuttgart, 1959.

Gerlach, J. ΑΝΗΡ ΑΓΑΘΟΣ. Munich, 1932.

Gosling, J. "*Republic* Book V: τὰ πολλὰ καλά etc." *Phronesis* 5 (1960): 116–28

Griswold, C. L. "Commentary on Sayre." *Proceedings of the Boston Area Colloquium in Ancient Philosophy* 9 (1993): 200–211.

Hacker, P. M. S. "Substance: The Constitution of Reality." *Midwest Studies in Philosophy* 4 (1979): 239–61.

Hambruch, E. *Logische Regeln der Platonischen Schule in der Aristotelischen Topik*. Wissenschaftliche Beilage zum Jahresbericht des Askanischen Gymnasiums zu Berlin. Berlin, 1904.

Haslanger, S. "Parts, Compounds, and Substantial Unity." In *Unity, Identity and Explanation*. Ed. T. Scaltsas, D. Charles, and M. L. Gill, pp. 129–70. Oxford, 1994.

Heidegger, M. "Die Frage nach der Technik." In Heidegger, *Vorträge und Aufsätze*, pp. 9–40. Pfullingen, 1954.

———. "Logos (Heraklit, Fragment 50)." In *Vorträge und Aufsätze*, pp. 199–221.

———. "Moira (Parmenides, Fragment VIII, 34–41)." In *Vorträge und Aufsätze*, pp. 223–48.

———. "Der Spruch des Anaximander." In Heidegger, *Holzwege*, pp. 296–343. Frankfurt, 1950.

———. "Der Ursprung des Kunstwerks." In *Holzwege*, pp. 7–68.

Heinaman, R. "Non-substantial Individuals in the *Categories*." *Phronesis* 26 (1981): 295–307.

———. Review of F. C. White, *Plato's Theory of Particulars*. *Journal of Hellenic Studies* 103 (1983): 172–73.

———. "Self-Predication in Plato's Middle Dialogues." *Phronesis* 34 (1989): 56–79.

Heitsch, E. *Die Entdeckung der Homonymie*. Abhandlungen der Geistes- und Sozialwissenschaflichen Klasse der Akademie der Wissenschaften und Literatur. Mainz, 1972.

Hicken, W. "The Character and Provenance of Socrates' 'Dream' in the *Theaetetus*." *Phronesis* 3 (1958): 126–145.

Husik, I. "On the *Categories* of Aristotle." *Philosophical Review* 13 (1904): 514–28. Reprinted, together with his "The Authenticity of Aristotle's *Categories*," (*Journal of Philosophy* 36 [1939]: 427–31), as "The Categories of Aristotle," in I. Husik, *Philosophical Essays: Ancient, Mediaeval and Modern.* Ed. M. C. Nahm and L. Strauss, pp. 96–112. Oxford, 1952.

Irwin, T. H. *Aristotle's First Principles.* Oxford, 1988.

———. "Plato's Heracleiteanism." *Philosophical Quarterly* 27 (1977): 1–13.

Jaeger, W. W. "Diocles of Carystus: A New Pupil of Aristotle." *Philosophical Review* 49 (1940): 393–414. Reprinted in his *Scripta Minora*, vol. 2 [= Storia e Litteratura, vol. 81], pp. 243–65. Rome, 1960.

———. *Diokles von Karystos: Die griechische Medizin und die Schule des Aristoteles.* Berlin, 1938.

———. "Diokles von Karystos und Aristoxenos von Tarent über die Prinzipien." *Festschrift Otto Regenbogen*, pp. 94–103. Heidelberg, 1952. Reprinted in his *Scripta Minora*, 2:441–453.

———. "Tyrtaios über die wahre ἀρετή." *Sitzungsberichte der Preußischen Akademie der Wissenschaften*, phil.-hist. Kl. (1932): 537–68. Reprinted in his *Scripta Minora*, 2:75–114.

Jespersen, O. *The Philosophy of Grammar.* London, 1924.

Johnston, M. "Constitution Is Not Identity." *Mind* 102 (1992): 89–105.

Kahn, C. "Some Philosophical Uses of 'To Be' in Plato." *Phronesis* 26 (1981): 105–34.

———. *The Verb 'Be' in Ancient Greek.* Foundations of Language, suppl. ser., vol. 16. Dordrecht, 1973.

Kapp, E. "Die Kategorienlehre in der aristotelischen Topik" (1920). First published in his *Ausgewählte Schriften*, pp. 215–53. Berlin, 1968.

Karpp, H. *Untersuchungen zur Philosophie des Eudoxos von Knidos.* Würzburg-Aumühle, 1933.

Keyser, P. "Review of G. Ledger *Re-counting Plato: A Computer Analysis of Plato's Style*." *Bryn Mawr Classical Review* 2 (1991): 422–27.

———. "Stylometric Method and the Chronology of Plato's Works: Review of L. Brandwood, *The Chronology of Plato's Dialogues*." *Bryn Mawr Classical Review* 3 (1992): 58–73.

Konstan, D. "Erixymachus' Speech in the *Symposium*." *Apeiron* 16 (1982): 40–46.

Kraut, R., ed. *The Cambridge Companion to Plato. Cambridge*, 1992.

Kripke, S. "Identity and Necessity." In *Identity and Individuation.* Ed. M. Munitz, pp. 135–64. New York, 1971.

———. *Naming and Necessity.* Cambridge, Mass., 1980.

Kuehn, J.-H. *System und Methodenprobleme im Corpus Hippocraticum.* Hermes Einzelschriften, vol. 11. Wiesbaden, 1956.

Kurke, L. "Crisis and Decorum in Sixth-Century Lesbos: Reading Alkaios Otherwise." *Quaderni urbinati di cultura classica*, n.s. 47 (1994): 67–92.

Ledger, G. *Re-counting Plato: A Computer Analysis of Plato's Style.* Oxford, 1989.

Lewis, F. *Substance and Predication in Aristotle.* Cambridge, 1991.

Lloyd, G. E. R. "Who Is Attacked in *On Ancient Medicine?*" *Phronesis* 8 (1963): 108–26.

Loraux, N. "La 'Belle Mort' spartiate." *Ktema* 2 (1977): 105–20.

———. *The Invention of Athens.* Tr. A. Sheridan. Cambridge, Mass., 1986.

McCabe, M. M. *Plato's Individuals.* Princeton, N.J., 1994.

McDowell, J. "Falsehood and Not-Being in Plato's *Sophist.*" In *Language and Logos.* Ed. M Schofield and M. Nussbaum, pp. 115–34. Cambridge, 1982.

Mair, A. W. "General Relative Clauses in Greek." *Classcial Review* 32 (1918): 168–70.

Malcolm, J. *Plato on the Self-Predication of Forms: Early and Middle Dialogues.* Oxford, 1981.

———. "Semantics and Self-Predication in Plato." *Phronesis* 26 (1981): 286–94.

Mann, W.-R. "The Origins of the Modern Historiography of Ancient Philosophy." *History and Theory* 35 (1996): 165–95.

Mannsperger, D. *Physis bei Platon.* Berlin, 1969.

Matthews, G. B. "Accidental Unities." In *Language and Logos.* Ed. M. Schofield and M. Nussbaum, pp. 223–40. Cambridge, 1982.

———. "The Enigma of *Categories* 1a20 ff. and Why It Matters." *Apeiron* 22, no. 4 (1989): 91–104.

Meinwald, C. "Good-bye to the Third Man." In *The Cambridge Companion to Plato.* Ed. R. Kraut, pp. 365–96. Cambridge, 1992.

———. *Plato's Parmenides.* Oxford, 1991.

———. Review of M. M. McCabe, *Plato's Individuals. Archiv für Geschichte der Philosophie* 78 (1996): 65–68.

Menn, S. "Metaphysics, Dialectic and the *Categories.*" *Revue de métaphysique et de morale* 100 (1995): 311–37.

Merlan, P. "Beiträge zur Geschichte des antiken Platonismus: I. Zur Erklärung der dem Aristoteles zugeschriebenen Kategorienschrift." *Philologus* 89 (1934): 35–53.

Mills, K. W. "Some Aspects of Plato's Theory of Forms: *Timaeus* 49c ff." *Phronesis* 13 (1968): 145–70.

Moraux, P. *Der Aristotelismus bei den Griechen.* 2 vols. Berlin, 1973–84.

Morrison, D. "Le statut catégoriel des différences dans l' 'Organon.' " *Revue philosophique* 183 (1993): 147–78.

———. "The Taxonomical Interpretation of Aristotle's *Categories*: A Criticism." In *Essays in Ancient Philosophy,* 5:19–46. Albany, N.Y., 1992.

Mourelatos, A. "Heraclitus, Parmenides, and the Naive Metaphysics of Things." In *Exegesis and Argument.* Ed. E. N. Lee, A. P. D. Mourelatos, and R. Rorty, pp. 16–48. Assen, 1973.

Nehamas, A. "Plato on the Imperfection of the Sensible World." *American Philosophical Quarterly* 12 (1975): 105–17.

214

———. "Predication and Forms of Opposites in the *Phaedo.*" *Review of Metaphysics* 26 (1972–73): 461–91.

———. "Self-Predication and Plato's Theory of Forms." *American Philosophical Quarterly* 16 (1979): 93–103.

Oliver, A. "The Metaphysics of Properties." *Mind* 105 (1996): 1–80.

Owen, G. E. L. *Logic, Science and Dialectic* (collected papers), (*LSD*). Ed. M. Nussbaum. Ithaca, N.Y., 1986.

———. "Aristotle on the Snares of Ontology." In *New Essays on Plato and Aristotle.* Ed. R. Bambrough, pp. 69–75. London, 1965. Reprinted in *LSD*, pp. 259–78.

———. "Eleatic Questions." *Classical Quarterly*, n.s. 10 (1960): 84–102. Reprinted in *Studies in Presocratic Philosophy*, vol. 2, ed. R. E. Allen and D. J. Furley, pp. 48–81. London, 1975. Also in *LSD*, pp. 3–26.

———. "Inherence." *Phronesis* 19 (1965): 97–105. Reprinted in *LSD*, pp. 252–58.

———. "Logic and Metaphysics in Some Earlier Works of Aristotle." In *Aristotle and Plato in the Mid-Fourth Century*, ed. I. Düring and G. E. L. Owen, pp. 163–90. Göteborg, 1960. Reprinted in *LSD*, pp. 180–99.

———. "Plato on the Undepictable." In *Exegesis and Argument.* Ed. E. N. Lee, A. P. D. Mourelatos, and R. Rorty, 349–61. Assen and New York, 1973. Reprinted in *LSD*, pp. 138–47.

———. "The Place of the *Timaeus* in Plato's Dialogues." *Classical Quarterly*, n.s. 3 (1953): 79–95. Reprinted in *Studies in Plato's Metaphysics.* Ed. R. E. Allen, pp. 313–38. London, 1965. Also in *LSD*, pp. 65–84.

———. "The Platonism of Aristotle." *Proceedings of the British Academy* 51 (1966): 125–50. Reprinted in *LSD*, pp. 200–220.

———. "A Proof in the *Peri Ideōn.*" *Journal of Hellenic Studies* 77 (1957): 103–11. Reprinted in *Studies in Plato's Metaphysics.* Ed. R. E. Allen, pp. 293–312. London, 1965. Also in *LSD*, pp. 165–79.

Parsons, T. "An Analysis of Mass Terms and Amount Terms." *Foundations of Language* 6 (1970): 362–88.

Patterson, R. *Image and Reality in Plato's Metaphysics.* Indianapolis, 1985.

Patzig, G. "Bemerkungen zu den Kategorien des Aristoteles." In *Einheit und Vielheit.* Ed. E. Scheibe and E. Süßmann, pp. 60–76. Göttingen, 1973.

Peck, A. L. "Anaxagoras: Predication as a Problem in Physics." *Classical Quarterly* 25 (1931): 27–37, 112–20.

Pouilloux, J. *Recherches sur l'histoire et les cultes de Thasos*, vol. 1. Etudes Thasiennes, vol. 3. Paris, 1954.

Praechter, K. "Nikostratos der Platoniker." *Hermes* 57 (1922): 481–517. Reprinted in his *Kleine Schriften.* Ed. H. Dörrie (= Collectanea, vol. 7), pp. 101–37. Hildesheim, 1973.

Prauss, G. "Ding und Eigenschaft bei Platon und Aristoteles." *Kant-Studien* 59 (1968): 98–117.

Prauss, G. *Platon und der logische Eleatismus.* Berlin, 1966.

Reeve, C. D. C. "Motion, Rest and Dialectic in the *Sophist.*" *Archiv für Geschichte der Philosophie* 69 (1985): 47–64.

Reinhardt, K. *Parmenides und die Geschichte der Philosophie.* Bonn, 1916.

Ross, W. D. *Plato's Theory of Ideas.* Oxford, 1951.

Rusten, J. "Structure, Style and Sense in Interpreting Thucydides: The Soldier's Choice (Thuc. 2.42.4)." *Harvard Studies in Classical Philology* 90 (1986): 49–76.

Ryle, G. "Letters and Syllables in Plato." *Philosophical Review* 59 (1960): 431–51.

———. "Logical Atomism in Plato's *Theaetetus*" (1952). First published in *Phronesis* 35 (1990): 21–46.

———. "Plato's *Parmenides.*" *Mind* 48 (1939): 129–51, 302–25. Reprinted in *Studies in Plato's Metaphysics.* Ed. R. E. Allen, pp. 97–147. London and New York, 1965.

———. *Plato's Progress.* Cambridge, 1966.

Sayre, K. M. "The Role of the *Timaeus* in the Development of Plato's Late Ontology." *Ancient Philosophy* 18 (1998): 93–124.

———. "Why Plato Never Had a Theory of Forms." *Proceedings of the Boston Area Colloquium in Ancient Philosophy* 9 (1993): 167–99.

Schofield, M. *An Essay on Anaxagoras.* Cambridge, 1981.

Schwartz, E. *Ethik der Griechen.* Stuttgart, 1952.

———. *Das Geschichtswerk des Thukydides.* Bonn, 1925.

Shiel, J. "Boethius and Andronicus of Rhodes." *Vigiliae Christianae* 11 (1957): 179–85.

Simons, P. *Parts: A Study in Ontology.* Oxford, 1987.

Smith, J. A. "General Relative Clauses in Greek." *Classical Review* 31(1917): 69–71.

Sonnenschein, E. A. "The Indicative in Relative Clauses." *Classical Review* 32 (1918): 68–69.

Strang, C. "The Physical Theory of Anaxagoras." *Archiv für Geschichte der Philosophie* 45 (1963): 101–18. Reprinted in *Studies in Presocratic Philosophy*, vol. 2, ed. R. E. Allen and D. J. Furley, pp. 361–80. London, 1975.

Strange, S. "Plotinus, Porphyry, and the Neoplatonic Interpretation of the 'Categories.' " *Aufstieg und Niedergang der Römischen Welt* II.36, 2: 955–97.

Szlezak, T. A. *Platon und die Schriftlichkeit der Philosophie.* Berlin, 1985.

Tarán, L. "Speusippus and Aristotle on Homonymy and Synonymy." *Hermes* 106 (1978): 73–99.

Van Cleve, J. "Three Versions of the Bundle Theory." *Philosophical Studies* 47 (1985): 95–107.

Vlastos, G. Review of F. M. Cornford, *Principium Sapientiae. Gnomon* 27 (1955): 65–76. Reprinted in *Studies in Presocratic Philosophy*, vol. 1, ed. D. J. Furley and R. E. Allen, pp. 42–55. London, 1970.

———. "The Third Man Argument in the *Parmenides.*" Reprinted with an addendum in *Studies in Plato's Metaphysics.* Ed. R. E. Allen, pp. 231–263. London and New York, 1965.

Wallace, J. "Positive, Comparative, Superlative." *Journal of Philosophy* 49 (1972): 773–82.

Wedin, M. "Nonsubstantial Individuals." *Phronesis* 38 (1993): 137–65.

———. "The Strategy of Aristotle's *Categories.*" *Archiv für Geschichte der Philosophie* 79 (1997): 1–26.

Wheeler, S. C. "Attributives and Their Modifiers." *Nous* 6 (1972): 310–34.

Whitaker, C. W. A. *Aristotle's De Interpretatione: Contradiction and Dialectic.* Oxford, 1996.

White, F. C. "The Compresence of Opposites in *Phaedo* 102." *Classical Quarterly,* n.s. 27 (1977): 303–11.

———. "Particulars in *Phaedo,* 95e–107a." *Canadian Journal of Philosophy,* suppl. vol. 2 (1976): 129–47.

———. "The *Phaedo* and *Republic* V on Essences." *Journal of Hellenic Studies* 98 (1978): 142–56.

———. "Plato's Middle Dialogues and the Independence of Particulars." *Philosophical Quarterly* 27 (1977): 193–213.

———. *Plato's Theory of Individuals.* New York, 1981.

White, N. P. "Forms and Sensibles: *Phaedo* 74B–C." *Philosophical Topics* 15 (1987): 197–214.

———. "Perceptual and Objective Properties in Plato." *Apeiron* 22 (1989): 45–65.

———. Review of M. M. McCabe, *Plato's Individuals. Ancient Philosophy* 17 (1997): 525–29.

Wieland, W. *Platon und die Formen des Wissens.* Göttingen, 1982.

Wilamowitz-Moellendorf, U. von. "Das Skolion des Simonides an Skopas." *Nachrichten der Königlichen Gesellschaft der Wissenschaften zu Göttingen,* phil.-hist. Kl. (1898): 204–36. Reprinted in his *Sappho und Simonides.* Berlin, 1913.

Wilson, J. C. "Aristotelian Studies, I." *Göttingsche Gelehrte Anzeigen* (1880): 449–74.

Woodruff, P. Review of F. C. White, *Plato's Theory of Particulars. Ancient Philosophy* 5 (1985): 91–95.

Young, C. M. "Plato and Computer Dating." *Oxford Studies in Ancient Philosophy* 12 (1994): 227–50.

Index Locorum

[Aristotle's works are listed in their traditional order; all other works are listed in alphabetical order. Page numbers in **boldface** indicate that the passage in question is quoted in full, or almost in full, on that page.]

Index Rerum

Abstract Nouns: 16, 26, 47 and n.25, 55–56 and n.46, 120, 182n.180, 192–93. *See also* Article + Adjective Construction

Academy, The: 42, 43n.15, 46, 62n.8, 74, 168, 189

Accounts (and Definitions): 26, 41n.9, 43 and n.15, 44–45, 47, 53–54 and n.43, 88, 129n.89, 168 and n.158, 191, 192, 203; proprietary, 177–78; —, Antisthenes' view of, 177 and n.173; —, maximal, 178

Anaxagoras: 29–30, 32, 108–117, 123, 124, 149–50, 152; and Anaxagoreanism: 29–30, 32, 34, 117–118, 148, 150, 151, 152, 155, 201

Aristotle's Criticisms: of Anaxagoras, 32 and n.45, 157; of the Late-Learners, 34–35, 191, 202–203; of Plato, 21, 30, 34, 152, 153–54, 157, 191, 202–203, 205; —, problems for: 200–202

Article + Adjective Construction: 15–16, 26n.42, 47 and n.25, 78–79, 120, 182n.180, 193. *See also* Abstract Nouns

Aspect, verbal: 42–43, 104n.44, 105–106 and nn.47–48

'Becomes', the verb: in Greek, 89–90; —, compatible with 'is', 89, 98–100; —, contrasted with 'is', 100–101, 101–103; —, 'funerary' use of, 98, 103, 104 and nn. 44–45, 105 and n.46; —, ordinary use of, 84–85; —, refers to change, 90–91, 93–95; as used in the *Protagoras*, 91–98; —, by Hesiod and Prodicus, 93–94; —, by Simonides, 92–93; —, by Socrates, 94–98; as used in the *Theaetetus*: 158–59; as used in the *Timaeus*: 162–64, 171. *See also* Becoming; Being; 'Is'

Becoming: 84, 89–91; and Change, 19, 85, 93–95, 164, 171–72; Plato's metaphysical notion of, 19, 82, 84–87, 97, 124–25, 157, 162–64, 167–68, 171–72, 198; —, contrasted with Being, 19–20, 28–29, 82, 84, 97, 124–25, 157, 162–64, 171, 179, 183. *See also* 'Becomes'; Being; 'Is'

Being: 3n.3, 19–20, 76; accidental versus essential, 32, 83, 127, 183, 199–201; Anaxagoras's notion of, 29; Parmenides' notion of, 29; Plato's notion of, 12n.16, 13 and n.17, 19 and n.26, 77, 82, 157, 171–72, 179, 181–83; in virtue of itself, versus in virtue of something else, 77, 123, 124–25, 142–48, 183. *See also* 'Becomes'; Becoming; Beings; 'Is'

Beings: 3, 7–9, 11, 13, 26, 112, 183; Hermodorus's classification of, 144–45; Plato's classification of, 13 and n.17, 85–7, 107 and n.49, 108, 143–44. *See also* Entities

Bishop Butler's Essentialist Saying: 76, 79, 81, 176, 191

Bundles, of Form-Instances: 30, 125, 156, 179. *See also* Clusters; Mixtures

Categories, the: alternate opening sentences of, 58 and n.2, 59–60; chronology of, 4–5; and the *De Interpretatione*, 66–67; and dialectic, 4n.4, 196n.14; and Platonic ontology, 5–6; subject matter of, 58–60, 202–203; unity of, 39–41

Causes: 78–79, 121. *See also* Elements; Ingredients; Platonic Forms

Cave Analogy: 129–30

Change: 33–34, 85, 113, 171–72; and Anaxagoras, 113, 115, 116–117, 124–25; and the *Categories*, 202; Late-Learners' rejection of, 197–98; *ousiai* as subjects for, 202; Parmenides' rejection of, 90–91; Plato's view of, 125–26, 164, 165, 171; substantial versus accidental, 33–34, 83, 116–117, 124–25, 165, 197–200; versus being subject to